On the threshold of the twenty-first century, Mexico has become more active on the world scene as a result of globalization, while striving to reaffirm the traditional values that have shaped its cultural identity. Today modern-day Mexico proudly presents the world with its splendid collection of deeply rooted traditions and customs, prominently featuring its folklore, and its varied and tantalizing culinary arts, which have already conquered the palates of many countries throughout the world.

The astounding variety of its dishes, the robust character of its sharp flavors, the brilliant color of its ingredients, the magical texture of its mixtures, have helped to place Mexican gastronomy at the highest levels of universal cuisine.

Mexico, because of its tradition and history, is a land of joyful songs, a symphony of color, magical fantasy, and full and penetrating flavor that extends the wings of creative genius to all directions of the universe. It is a world beyond time where refuge is taken in the human warmth of the sun of its ancestors, with a gaze fixed on a horizon of optimism and happiness.

Sebastián Verti

ACKNOWLEDGMENTS

The author wishes to express his gratitude to the individuals in **Grupo Editorial Diana** who participated in the preparation of this book:

José Luis Ramírez Cota
Executive President

José Luis Ramírez Magnani
Editor

I wish to thank to the editorial team in **Grupo Editorial Diana**.

With love and deep respect to the Royal Family of Spain, King Juan Carlos and Queen Sofía, Felipe prince of Asturias, and the infantas Cristina and Elena, for their affection for Mexico.

The author also wishes to thank Manuel Ríos Herrera, President and General Director of the Centro Artesanal Buenavista (Buenavista Handicraft Center), the largest in America, for his generous efforts in the promotion of folk art appreciation in Mexico.

To José Luis Loredo Martínez, distinguished guardian of the Mexican Cuisine, my gratitude for his constant support in the dissemination of Mexican traditions.

Distribution
(Sales and orders)
GRUPO EDITORIAL DIANA
Corporate Headquarters
Roberto Gayol 1219
Col. del Valle
C.P. 03100, México, D.F.
Tel. 575-07-11 • 559-27-00
Fax 575-32-11 • 575-1818
Telex 01777618 DIMEME

Dear Friends,

This book, which has been well received in Mexico, was written with one fundamental purpose: to share with the Mexican public the essence of the values, traditions, and customs that distinguish the culture of this country. Sebastián Verti, its author, has dedicated his life to researching and disseminating these roots of Mexican identity.

It is with a similar purpose that we decided to translate this work into other languages, to make it available to a larger public. This will allow others to share in the appreciation of the marvelous expressions of Mexican culture, which occupies a special place among the greatest civilizations of the world.

The Editor

CLUB DE MUJERES PROFESIONISTAS Y DE NEGOCIOS

SOR JUANA INÉS DE LA CRUZ

Afiliado a la Federación Internacional, Nacional y del Distrito Federal

OTORGA EL NOMBRAMIENTO
al libro

TRADICIONES MEXICANAS

 **GRUPO EDITORIAL DIANA**

DE

SEBASTIÁN VERTI

como

EL LIBRO DEL AÑO
*POR SU EXTRAORDINARIO CONTENIDO EDITORIAL
EN FORTALECER LAS RAÍCES
DE NUESTRA CULTURA NACIONAL*

ÁFRICA DEL SUR, ALEMANIA, ARGENTINA, ARUBA, AUSTRALIA, BAHAMAS, BANGLADESH, BARBADOS, BÉLGICA, BELICE, BERMUDAS, BOLIVIA, BOTSWANA, BRASIL, CANADÁ, COLOMBIA, COSTA RICA, COREA, ECUADOR, EL SALVADOR, ESPAÑA, ESTADOS UNIDOS, FINLANDIA, FILIPINAS, FRANCIA, GRANADA, GRECIA, GUATEMALA, GUYANA, HAITÍ, HONG KONG, HOLANDA, INDIA, INDONESIA, IRÁN, ISRAEL, ITALIA, JAMAICA, JAPÓN, JORDÁN, KENYA, LÍBANO, LESOTHO, INGLATERRA, MÉXICO, MOROCCO, NUEVA ZELANDA, NICARAGUA, NIGERIA, NORUEGA, PAKISTÁN, PARAGUAY, PANAMÁ, PERÚ, ST. KITIA, SANTA LUCÍA, SINGAPUR, SUDESTE AFRICANO, SUIZA, SUECIA, THAILANDIA, TRINIDAD, REINO UNIDO, ZAMBIA.

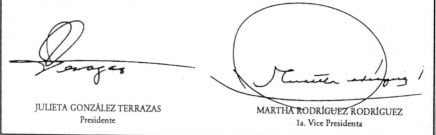

JULIETA GONZÁLEZ TERRAZAS
Presidente

MARTHA RODRÍGUEZ RODRÍGUEZ
1a. Vice Presidenta

"Book of the year" nomination given by the Career and Business Women's Club *SOR JUANA INÉS DE LA CRUZ* to *TRADICIONES MEXICANAS* by Sebastián Verti.

Sebastián Verti

Mexican Traditions

EDITORIAL DIANA
MEXICO

First edition, June, 1993

Cover design: Carlos Valdés
Typeset and design by: DOBLE ELE ll Servicios Editoriales

Translation: Bertha Díaz de León de Valverde
Photography: Javier Cabrera, Juan Daniel Torres Polo, Enrique Salazar Hijar y Haro, y Andrés Zavala.

ISBN 968-13-2490-0

Ever since the early years of my life I learned to love Mexico and to love our highest values, at the geographical frontier of our country.

Both my father and my mother engraved in my mind THE LOVE FOR OUR VERY OWN THINGS. To them, with all my love, the pride of my words.

Your whistle breaks the silence of the air with the
melody you whistle.
And thus it remains, forever,
in my childhood's heart.

Now that you are far away, in infinity...
so far...
When your memory rips my nostalgia.
I hear your whistled melody as I did in days gone by.

Whistle, whistle, whistler from the sky
at the silent rhythm of my tears.
Whistle, whistle, Father Whistler,
So my heart may bloom.

Mexico, Mexico where I was born and where I have lived, is a wonderful and imposing synthesis of Mesoamerican cultures, and of the Western culture in its Spanish source. Our cultural identity, our national pride, is found in this synthesis.

My sincere respect, together with my gratitude, to those who today are symbols of Mexico's and Spain's national traditions.

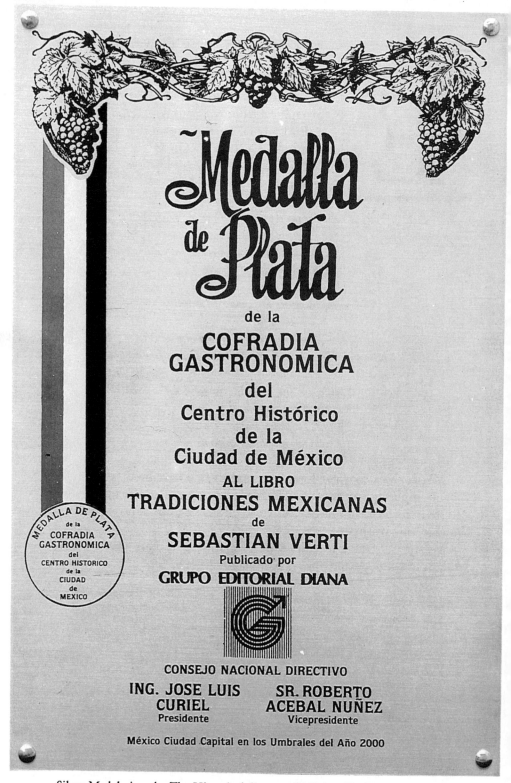

~Medalla de Plata

de la
COFRADIA GASTRONOMICA
del
Centro Histórico
de la
Ciudad de México
AL LIBRO
TRADICIONES MEXICANAS
de
SEBASTIAN VERTI
Publicado por
GRUPO EDITORIAL DIANA

CONSEJO NACIONAL DIRECTIVO

ING. JOSE LUIS CURIEL
Presidente

SR. ROBERTO ACEBAL NUÑEZ
Vicepresidente

México Ciudad Capital en los Umbrales del Año 2000

Silver Medal given by The Historical Center of México City's Gastronomical
Guild to the book *TRADICIONES MEXICANAS* by Sebastián Verti.

CONTENTS

THE LOVE FOR OUR VERY OWN THINGS

The book *Mexican Traditions* has a single origin and a single reason: love for our own.

This work is the result of various investigations and studies made in the classic sources of the nation's history, and of the direct knowledge of our traditions through the numberless travels undertaken during more than twenty years throughout the Mexican geography.

Since this book was written basically for those who love and revere national things, and yearn to make them known to future generations, the text is published in a summarized way, in clear language and with great care to conform to historical truth.

Tradition is transmitted in an everyday simple way, from parents to children, without pomp, with the naturalness of the customs which are lived from day to day. Therein lies their strength and purity, as a nation's cultural expression.

Mexico has a wealth of traditions and customs, which is why Ramón López Velarde perceived it as an intimate and unbreakable country.

The sharp pragmatism of our present society does not frighten me, as it sometimes leads to ingenuous admiration of foreign cultural expressions, which in turn adopts those "disconcerted and disconcerting" cultural archetypes that are born and die without leaving any trace, except the commercial short-lived fashions which encouraged its precarious existence.

I am more enthusiastic with the conviction that Mexico has its own culture, shaped and magnified during thirty centuries of history. Mexico's monumental and majestic cultural tradition originated on the American continent's soil. The colossus sculpted by the Olmec ancestors' brilliant and

13

magical hands was the awakening of Mexican historical times. The statues and columns in Tula and the pyramids and temples of the Mayas, the Toltecs and the Aztecs thus witness it. And, also, —why not say it?— the fertile branch of Occidental and Christian tradition, implanted in the native culture. The colonial cathedrals and palaces which are still majestic and monumental, proclaim this.

From the blending and mixture of these two wellsprings of spiritual energy, emerges the Mexican culture which identifies us in the universal scope.

This book has been written to encourage the noble and legitimate pride of being and feeling Mexican, and it could well be the threshold to awaken the interest in becoming acquainted with Mexico's cultural values and studying these more profusely.

Mexico has found the strength to impel its cultural dynamics in the whirlpool of the great historical crisis. The heroic deeds initiated by Vasconcelos when the Mexican Revolution of 1910 had not yet ended and they can vouch for this. There, in the epicenter of armed violence, the modern rebirth of Mexican culture made its way.

It is stimulating to me to believe that the strength and the courage to begin a cultural renovation could emerge from the present crisis, on which Mexico of the 21st century will be established.

So that this may be possible, it is necessary to reconsider the threads of our own tradition; we must reassess our historical legacy.

Only in this way will it be worthwhile to attempt to enrich culture historically with our own and new works.

When the national spirit rediscovers the values attached to traditions and customs, the cultural identity of the Mexicans will be strengthened, and will be in a position to continue the work of our ancestors.

When the life of a nation is impregnated, nurtured daily with its cultural tradition, the national spirit will be revitalized and will become fertile and creator of history.

With this optimism and enthusiasm which encourage my vocation to promote and divulge Mexican cultural values, I have written the pages of these books, pages which long to be merely the seed of restlessness to awaken the admiration and value of Mexican things.

I am aware that this is only the initial task of spiritual ecology —using a current similarity of our times— of a labor of cultural purification and recovery, so that the rhythm of our urban and technical society will not bury our historical memory.

POPULAR TRADITIONS IN MEXICO

Since tradition is the simplest and easiest way of communicating or transmitting cultural and artistic expressions throughout time it is also the simplest and most direct way of making history.

Since tradition is a living and communitary history, it has a human dimension, a social dimension, a geographic dimension and also a temporary dimension and, above all these qualities, it has the virtue of amalgamating present-day man with his past and with his native land. It is the thread that weaves the fabric of generations and provides sense, color, flavor, profile, cultural character and social appearance.

Hence, the impulse which encourages me to promote *The Traditionalist Popular Movement* in our country, and hence my enthusiasm to form a literary accumulation of popular traditions in Mexico.

The ancestral soul of our nation throbs and vibrates therein; the authentic face of our own things are reflected therein.

Let our traditions be those who speak for our enthusiasm.

CHRISTIAN
MEXICO

FEAST OF THE QUARTER OF THE CHILD JESUS IN COYOACÁN

On January 1st, the liturgical calendar celebrates the Circumcision of the Redeemer: the ritual that gave the Holy Child the name of Jesus. An old neighborhood in Coyoacán that has this name celebrates this festivity. The neighbors celebrate their patron, and children, dressed in white, just as their joy is pure, go to church to receive their First Holy Communion. Adults follow them, their faces transformed with nostalgia.

Later, all is joy: the music, the delicacies, the balloons that rise to the sky as a symbol of hope and good will. It is almost unbelievable that this neighborhood is a suburb of the great national city!

Feast of the Epiphany
Gold, incense and myrrh

Day of the Epiphany (The Three Magi) at the Alameda Central Park

January sixth at the Alameda Central Park. At the epicenter of the capital city, the children assemble, children who use and enjoy for the first time the toy which the Three Magi, coming from the East, left in their old shoe at dawn —the Three Wise Men who followed the star of Bethlehem, of the Christ Child.

Improvised actors representing the Magi, or Christmas sculptures, await among the festive fountains for the father or mother to place their children in readiness for the promised photograph. And the miracle occurs: the Alameda is transformed into a garden of balloons, dreams and illusions.

Worship of the Magi

At the time Jesus was born in Bethlehem of Judea, under the reign of Herod, three Wise Men coming from the East arrived in Jerusalem and asked, "Where can we find He who was born King of the Jews? We clearly saw His star from the East and we are here to worship Him."

As soon as this news reached King Herod, he was startled, and with him all of Jerusalem. He quickly summoned all the penmen in the town and the high priests so that they might inform him of the place where Jesus would be born.

And they answered: "In Bethlehem of Judea. Mikeas predicted this: 'And you, Bethlehem, land of Judea, you are not the least of Judeas' main clans. From your entrails will be born the Messiah who will instruct my country Israel.' "

Herod summoned the Magi, spoke to them alone and asked them to tell him about the events and the time when the star appeared. And he sent them to Bethlehem, saying: "Go to Bethlehem, inquire about the birth of the Child. When you have found Him, let me know so that I, too, can worship Him."

The Magi listened to the king and got on their way. As they began their journey, the star which they had seen in the East appeared again; it was in the sky before them. The star guided them until it arrived at the place of birth and it stopped where the Child was found.

Upon seeing that the star had stopped, the Wise Men's heart burst with joy. They entered the manger, found the Child with His mother, Mary and they knelt to worship Him. Then they opened their chests and offered Him their gifts: gold, incense, and myrrh.

Later, their dreams warned them that they should not return to Herod and they took another route and returned to their kingdoms.

This is Saint Matthew's simple account regarding the events that changed the face of the earth: Humanity had gained a Redeemer forever; history's first Epiphany had been celebrated.

As the Epiphany is an essential aspect of Catholic liturgy, the missionaries were careful to establish this festivity in the Mexicans' awareness. And, to make it more attractive, they made the believers participate —symbolically —in the gifts offered by the Magi to Jesus.

Thus began the custom of offering and receiving gifts, mainly in relation with children, who in time asked for the toy they most desired in a letter to their favorite King.

THE KING'S RING-SHAPED BREAD

The family supper reigns in the festivity of the Magi. As the Epiphany is one of the great feasts in Christian liturgy, communities and families celebrate it since old days with a supper wherein a large cake is cut. It should be mentioned that some historical sources mention that this was a Roman custom that the church combined into the celebration of the Epiphany.

One way or another, the fact is that during the Middle Ages the cake, or the ring-shaped bread, formed part of the Epiphany's supper.

This tradition came from Spain to Mexico during the early years of the viceregal reign. The Wise Men's supper was made traditional with its ring-shaped cake, accompanied with a delicious chocolate drink originating in this land of New Spain.

The ring-shaped bread is a fine cake carefully and delicately prepared. Although the term "ring-shaped bread" indicates that it must be round, the Mexican Wise Men's ring-shaped cake is oval.

This is because, as the number of guests to the supper increased, it was necessary to make it bigger and oval-shaped. To dress it finely, it is usually decorated with preserved fruit such as figs, quince, cherries, etcetera, which improve the flavor, beside embellishing it.

It is not easy to determine when the custom of hiding a porcelain Christ Child inside the cake's dough began, but according to chronicles it is known that the habit of placing a preserve or a lima bean in the cake was very old.

Whoever found the lima bean or the preserve was spiritually obliged to present the house's Christ Child in the manger at the nearest church on February 2 (in Mexico called the day of the Candlemas).

In Mexico's days of chivalry, this obligation was ritually fulfilled, and perhaps the substitution of the lima bean or preserve with the Child arose because sometimes the person who was eating consumed the piece of cake complete with lima bean in order to avoid the obligation.

Surely, one day, some clever lady who one year remained without the Festivity of Candlemas and without a godfather for her Christ Child, began to introduce a porcelain child which was difficult to eat —and more difficult to digest— although, to tell the truth, there are still some people who remain without their festivity because, somehow, the person who finds the child feigns ignorance or discretely hides the little figure. In other words, in order to avoid the obligation, he or she "se hace rosca."*

THIMBLES AND RINGS

The above can explain why in our times, various children are placed in the ring-shaped cake, either to share the obligation so that it may be less onerous, or because it is more difficult to have several persons hiding or eating the Child.

In some of Mexico's provinces, in order to increase the excitement of the supper and the expectation of the surprise, a ring is usually placed in the cake, which means a forthcoming wedding, as well as a thimble, which predicts an unmarried state for the year.

This was how relationships between godfathers and parents not only began at these suppers, and friendships with neighbors were strengthened, but also how romances began with the excuse of the thimbles and rings.

---

* *Hacerse rosca* (to become a ring-shaped cake) is an idiom meaning that a person feigns ignorance. (T.)

Certainly, in the past amusements were not greatly varied and thus ingenuity was necessary to have fun.

Nowadays, things seem to have changed. It seems that it is not necessary to use your imagination to establish courtships or engagements at gatherings where words exceed and crowds make things easier. But the custom of the ring-shaped cake survives, which encourages one to think that it is possible that Mexican families will once again get into the ancestral habit of having supper with the family and enjoy themselves with close friends.

It is necessary to take advantage of the round cake's commercial touch to encourage the rescue of a beautiful tradition that makes family ties become closer, as well as those of the community's neighbors. There is no doubt the Three King's Supper is very much our own.

GETTING READY FOR THE FEAST OF CANDLEMAS

The Christ Child dolls are dressed in La Merced

How the obligation originated of dressing the Christ Child arises, the baby dolls found in the Three Kings' Cake, and the big "tamale" party of the Child's parents and godparents.

From now on, please do not say, "The little doll in the round cake." It is far better to say, "the figure of Child Jesus Christ or "the Little Child," as this is a sweeter and more correct way of expressing it.

On the night of January 6th, the knife descends slowly and softly, breaking the crunchy decorated crust of the fluffy King's Round Cake covered with sugar and dry fruits. Suddenly, whack! The knife is obstructed and refuses to cut. It's useless to insist. The person who cut the slice, "hit upon" the Child, and there's no way out: he or she will be the Child's godfather or godmother on February 2, the Feast of Candlemas. The lucky person accepts with resigned laughter and the promise of fulfilling the obligation assumed.

First of all, the Child must be dressed. In those January days, there are many signs reading: "Christ Child dolls and Little Child figures are dressed here," mainly around the neighborhood of *La Merced*, a typical marketplace full of Mexico's great traditions, in the beautiful locality of Venustiano Carranza.

Dressing the child is an art cultivated by many people —due to religious

23

devotion or to earn a few extra pesos— carried out with so much care, that there are those who even show the client a kind of "catalogue of saints" in colored pictures so that the customer may choose the way in which he wants the Child to be dressed. The favorites clothes are: the Child of the Doves, all in white, with a little turtle dove in his hands; the Blessed Child of Atocha in red and green with a small staff; and Little Saint Francis, dressed in a brown vestment and holding a small animal in his arms.

If the godfather desires, he can have the recently purchased Christ Child dressed, or he may ask the host or hostess of the house where the Kings' Cake was cut, and where the Child has remained in his manger, to do so. When the Child has been dressed he is laid in a small basket decorated with flowers, and then he is taken to early mass on the morning of February 2, to be blessed. Immediately thereafter, the Child is given to the owner, who places the Child in a little chair inside a special niche where he will remain all year, with a lit candle to "enlighten him." On the other hand, the tiny figure of the Child in the King's Round Cake can be dressed and then given as a gift without further ceremony.

In any event, either way of presenting the gift is followed by a party that will gather anew the friends and perhaps a few last-minute guests, on February 2. Since expenses are covered by the Child's "godfather," it is understandable that someone may prefer to nearly choke and swallow the little figure with difficulty, instead of confessing that he or she found it, as well as someone who "manipulates" the Cake so that the Child is found "with certainty" by the boss or the mother-in-law.

BLESSING OF THE LITTLE ANIMALS
JANUARY 17

DAY OF ABBOT SAINT ANTHONY

The devout prayer of Saint Francis of Assisi is religiously fulfilled on the day of Abbot Saint Anthony. The Garden of San Fernando —located on one side of the oldest cementery in the capital— becomes a domestic zoo: a rooster crows here, a parrot talks there, a lap dog barks here and there, the cats growl, and a thousand birds sing, while a wise turtle watches impassively from its owner's shoulder the tender spectacle of the blessing of the little animals, those creatures who with their existence make men and women who live crowded in the big city, feel more human.

One of the most beautiful and oldest Christian traditions is, undoubtedly, that of the Blessing of the Little Animals, celebrated since long ago in Mexico on January 17, Day of the Abbot Saint Anthony.

This tradition, of enormous human content, reaffirms the coherence existing between man and the entire creation, where the natural order of things simply indicates that, although the human being is at the ontological peak, the remaining living creatures —animals, plants, and even lifeless things— should be treated with the respect that entails a deep feeling of harmony and universal unity; a simple link between man and nature, or as modern ecologists would say, an integration of the human being with his environment.

The tender ceremony of the blessing of the little animals represents and diffuses all this.

WHY THE DAY OF ABBOT SAINT ANTHONY?

This tradition, linked to the figure of Abbot Saint Anthony —one of the oldest and most venerated Catholic saints (252-356) —is one of the most universal, although each country imprints its own characteristics on the festivity.

Abbot Saint Anthony was one of the first ascetic founders of monastic life. He was born in Upper Egypt in 251 in Koman, a town near Memphis. From the age of 20, upon his parents' death, he embraced religious life, after dividing his fortune among the poor. Devoted to meditation, he founded several religious communities far from the cities. Thus, under severe discipline and constant exercise of prayer, he discovered in the immense book of nature, God's divine wisdom and love. This saint's biographers state that he had the habit of blessing the animals and the plants, making the sign of the cross over them while invoking the name of Christ; for this reason, his image is represented with a staff in the shape of a cross and a piglet with a little bell tied on its neck.

This also explains why, after his death —in 356— respected and revered by emperors, sages, and illustrious pagans, he was soon adopted as patron of farmers, cattle raisers —and the association of butchers themselves— who invoked him as protector of domestic animals.

INTRODUCTION OF THIS CUSTOM IN MEXICO

In our country, this custom of blessing domestic animals on the Day of Abbot Saint Anthony was introduced by Franciscan priests, owing to whom this tradition was deeply rooted and gained popularity throughout the country. The faithful approach the church, carrying a sample of the animal species which is more closely linked to their occupation, work, or affection, adorned with ribbons, flowers, beads or ornaments made especially for this ceremony, which is thus made more colorful.

RELIGIOUS BACKGROUND OF THE POPULAR FES-
TIVITIES

In Mexico, the feast of February 2 is linked to the traditional Round Cake of the Three Kings. Whoever got the Child should present Him in church on the Day of Candlemas. For this purpose, it is necessary to dress and adorn the Child, buying special clothes —luxuries made with the fantasy of Mexican seamstresses, and the thrones where the Child may sit.

After the celebration of the birth of Christ, and the Worship by the Magi, one of the most deeply rooted popular festivities is the "Day of Candlemas," because the image of the Child Jesus Christ is blessed during this celebration, as well as the candles that are carried with the Child. This custom originated with the liturgical feast of the purification and presentation of the Child Jesus.

The scenic image of the presentation of the Child in the Parish of Coyoacán —with the offering of doves— precedes the blessing of the various figures of the Child God, dressed in purple and silk; one can see black, white, copper-colored, and tanned figures, sitting on their thrones or lying on baskets full of flowers. The candles that will be lit when the year's tribulations arise are likewise blessed. The germinated sage seeds which will be placed at the Altar de Dolores (Altar of Sorrows) are also blessed.

The festivity ends with the godfathers' and parents' supper, where a meal of *tamales* will be served. The *tamales* can be stuffed with pork, chicken, sliced peppers, beans, *mole* (special dish made of various kinds of peppers, nuts and other delicacies), cheese, corn and even strawberries with raisins, accompanied with sauces, and *atoles* (beverages thickened with ground corn) of different flavors, and hot chocolate.

IN TIMES OF JESUS

The law of Moses prescribed in the Leviticus ceremony that every woman who gave birth to a child should be purified. If the baby born was a boy, he should be circumcised eight days after his birth and the mother should stay at home during thirty-three additional days purifying herself with meditation and prayer.

After observing this law, the mother, together with her husband, went to church to take the offering, consisting of a lamb and a dove or turtledove, which the needy could fulfill by offering two doves or turtledoves. However, devout people had the habit of also taking the baby, especially when it was a first-born male child, to consecrate him to Yahve.

According to Saint Luke, Mary and Joseph decided to obey this rule and they took the Child to Jerusalem. As they were poor, their offering consisted of two white doves. There, Simon, who was just and devout, and moved by the Holy Spirit, took Jesus in his arms when Mary and Joseph entered with the Child, and blessed Him with the following prayer: *Et nunc dimitte servum tuun* (Now Thou can take Thy Servant from the Earth).

Among his praises, he prophesied that the Child would be the light that would illuminate the gentiles, and that He would be the glory of Israel. This is the symbolism of the candles which represent the light of Jesus Christ in every home.

TLACOTALPAN, VERACRUZ AND THE FEAST OF CANDLEMAS

Tlacotalpan is located on the left border of the Papaloapan River, exactly on the lowest leeward region (opposite side of the wind). It is located merely 100 kilometers from the city of Veracruz, arriving in approximately one hour via the beautiful picturesque Veracruz-Alvarado highway; one can also arrive via the Cordoba highway to Tierra Blanca, Santa Cruz and Cosamaloapan.

The most remote notes that are known about Tlacotalpan date back to 1461, when Moctezuma Ilhuicamina travelled through the Papaloapan. Juan de Grijalba's expedition navigated through the Papaloapan in 1518, and it was at that time when Pedro de Alvarado imposed his own name on the town of Atlizintla (now Alvarado) and to the Papaloapan River (but the latter has maintained its native name throughout the centuries). Its ecclesiastic record dates back to 1699 and its civil files began in 1763.

Tlacotalpan was granted the title of "town" in 1699, and was elevated to the category of "village" in 1862. The title of "city" (even to State capital level) was granted on May 9, 1885 by General Alejandro García, governor and military commander of the state of Veracruz. In 1968, it was declared a "typical city" through a decree issued by the governor of the State.

CAVALCADE IN TLACOTALPAN

The Feast of Candlemas, dedicated to the virgin bearing the same name and the city's patron saint, is celebrated here. The commemoration is celebrated from January 31 to February 9. With the tourists' approval and for their enjoyment, the festivity begins with a cavalcade. A parade on horseback where the women display the splendor of their beauty, dressed in the classical *Jarocho* (term meaning pertaining to the state of Veracruz) costume. The next day, at the Esquina del Toro (the Bull's Corner), the first bull jumps out of the river and —together with five more bulls— wanders all over the city, to the delight of the townspeople and visitors. This festivity is similar to that of *San Fermín* in Pamplona, Spain. On February 2, the festivity begins with the classic *Mañanitas* (a Mexican serenade) in honor of the Virgin of Candlemas, and the procession with the image of the virgin through the Papaloapan River is carried out in the evening.

The Xochimilca *Niñopa*

Child Jesus who sings and plays

Xochimilco, land of ancestors, land of *trajineras* (colorful raft-like vessels) and flowers is also the land of legendary traditions.

The devotion to the *Niñopa* is one of these. The *Niñopa* is a Child Jesus Christ, similar to, and at the same different from the figures of the Child Jesus that we see in our homes, and which our devout grandmothers took to be blessed on Candlemas Day.

The *Niñopa* is one of these, but somewhat different, because his home is all of Xochimilco —ever since more than four hundred years ago.

A miraculous Child Jesus

This beautiful child who wanders around, dressed luxuriously with new clothes in every neighborhood having *chinampas* (floating gardens) is called *Niñopa* by his faithful friends, meaning "Patron Father Child" or "Patron Child," because almost from the beginning of the period of evangelization, the ancient Xochimilcas begged for favors and worshipped him.

The essence of this tradition is the love and devotion towards this Child Jesus, whom the Xochimilcas, today and evermore, have truly loved. They dress him, they take good care of him, they pamper him, they give him toys and, exceeding their limitations, they give him their love together with their offerings. But, not only do they go to him when they require favors, it is a custom and a tradition to visit him always.

They imagine him alive

A child surrounded by light, arises
from his cradle, seeking his toys in the darkness

They say that at night, he does what every other child does: he gets up to play and asks for his meal. They even say that one day he fell and hurt his forehead, "...but since he is Holy, he healed himself and made his wound disappear, although no one cured the scratch."

Therefore, since the child has life, the inhabitants in the neighborhoods

30

of Xochimilco speak of the *Niñopa* as though he were their very own, close to their heart, like someone who as a child gives them confidence and strength, and never abandons them.

That is why the *Niñopa* with his closet full of clothes, does not always live in the same house; he sleeps at the steward's house.

Neighbors can take him for a walk through the streets or canals in Xochimilco, but they must return him at night to his cradle in the steward's house, so that his caretaker can put on his little pajamas, and lull him to sleep: "Get in bed; it is time to sleep."

The *Niñopa* is happy, he enjoys the clothes, the toys, the robes and pajamas in his closet.

Devotion to the *Niñopa* has generated an entire organization in the neighborhood, through which, on February 2 each year, Candlemas Day, the stewardship changes —a turn established until the year 2020— and everybody competes for the honor of giving the Child shelter in their home, regardless of the fact that expenses incurred by the stewardship and by the innkeepers are usually high and the income is relatively limited. Nevertheless...it's worthwhile to have the privilege!

That is why the *Niñopa* celebrations are quite splendid.

This is how the stewards and innkeepers work twice or three times as hard so that the festivals they organize for their Patron Child will not lack food, music and joy.

Everybody agrees that the Child is very generous and repays them in abundance for the sacrifices and efforts made on his behalf.

This is how a collective morale has been created around this devotion. Far in advance, the neighbors ask the steward to allow them to take the Niñopa to their home, to accompany them in a celebration of a birthday, or a family event; everyone who lives in the house puts it in order, decorates, and extends it and works harder and with a great deal of effort to obtain more income and thus offer the best. But perhaps the most important thing is that from the very day in which the steward grants them permission, everyone tries to behave better in order to be worthy hosts of the Holy Child.

Thus, this is a popular religious custom, based upon sincere and enormous faith in God. Simple people who, with their humility raise their spirit to forget all their misery and the noise of the big city.

IN THE LAND OF *TRAJINERAS* ANY NIGHT WHATSOEVER, A CHILD CRIES SURROUNDED BY LIGHT

The devout are certain that the Niñopa cries when someone misbehaves, and upon hearing him weeping among the canals and *trajineras*, prayer and repentance spontaneously arise:

> *Perdónanos Niñito,*
> *perdona nuestros pecados.*
> *No llores más por nosotros.* *

And that is how the *Niñopa* laughs, sings, plays, walks down the streets...and his lovely little shoes are scratched. When he feels that someone isn't well, he is sad, pale and haggard and then it is time to repent and pamper him in Xochimilco. In short, the Miraculous Child of many centuries in the *chinampas* resides and lives in Xochimilco, the place of vegetables, flowers and *trajineras*.

DO YOU WISH TO SEE HIM?

Become a child, and ask in any of Xochimilco's neighborhoods, where the *Niñopa* is found; then go and leave at his feet some blue marbles or a pair of little red shoes, but among the games and laughter, also leave your love and tenderness.

One thing is certain: the *Niñopa*, the Child Jesus Christ of the *chinamperos*, the Child with the little white hands and rosy face who plays every day with his marbles, his clover, and his little wooden cars loaded with flowers, lives and resides among the Xochimilcas since more than four centuries ago, loving and protecting them.

And the men, women and children of the land of floating gardens, of canals illuminated by the sun, at the feet of the majestic volcanoes, in order to partly repay their *Niñopa* for all the favors received, take care of him, pamper him and worship him, day after day.

And this enormous faith, this boundless love blends with the ever beautiful landscape, with the ever open sky, in the loftiness of the infinite mystery of the eternal.

---

*Forgive us, little Child, forgive our sins. Stop crying for us.

When the day is beautiful and it is very hot, we take him to the canals and, in his special chalupa *(little boat decorated with flowers), he runs through all the* chinampas, *wearing his little straw hat to avoid the heat.*

If you could only see him dressed like the Pope! Our Child looks beautiful!

The Niñopa *is the only image which provides strength and unity to the inhabitants of Xochimilco.*

We work all year round for our Niñopa: *we want him to be happy, no food or music should be missing in his festivity.*

We usually knit or buy him a little gown to wear new when he visits each of our homes.

Our Child Jesus, our Patron Child is a lifeless being that has come to life in the imagination of those who love him blindly.

We owe him everything. Those who used to drink a lot now work twice as hard for the Niñopa *and they are doing better.*

The Niñopa *has entered the hearts and the minds of the inhabitants of Xochimilco and of many other people from other places who come to see him.*

The Xochimilcas work hard for him. The make their houses bigger, hoping that the Niñopa *will visit them and when his image arrives, the surround him with gifts, candles, and a large table full of sweets, meat, barbecued meat,* tamales *and* atole.

ASH WEDNESDAY

To receive ashes means that I undertake to declare that I wish:

1. To live in the love of others and to be at their service.
2. To value myself and others.
3. To live as the Lord Jesus lived.
4. To discover myself as the living image of God, and builder of the world.
5. To find a way, together with others, of building a better society in economic, political, and social terms.
6. To build Jesus' community, with other Christians.

Renouncing:

1. To living without love and with indifference towards others.
2. To underestimate myself and others.
3. To get carried away with publicity slogans.
4. To get carried away with bad habits and false values and principles.
5. Irresponsibility in the presence of social problems.
6. Individualism and seclusion.

Ashes are not:

1. A magic act so that things go well with us, or to prevent evil.
2. An obligation.

Ashes are a sign that I wish to die with Christ to be resurrected with Him.

Memento, homo, quia pulvis
es et in pulverem revertiris

The bells are still ringing and the notes of the joyous vernacular music can still be heard; there is still confetti and "romancing" and the sleepy crowd will come to church to pray to the Creator of the World: *Memento, homo, quia pulvis es et in pulverem reverteris*. This sacramental phrase has been repeated throughout the centuries, by the lips of Catholic priests, and the faithful kneel to receive the sign of the Cross on their foreheads.

34

At the Shrovetide carnival, the crowds, wearing multicolored and exotic disguises, deceive each other mutually with the question: "Do you know me, Little Mask?" which they ask each other and mingle in the happy bustling crowd seeking pleasure.

Concentrating on ourselves, and without the mask that we wear many times out of convenience, to hide our feelingss or the truth when facing life's realities, some people as faithful believers, others as imitators, await on their knees so that the priest may place the sign of Catholicism that has been accepted for that day.

The ashes are generally made with the dust of images which have been destroyed and with burned blessed palm leaves. The priest usually takes the ashes which have been blessed with consecrated water, and with his finger, makes this sign. However, in some cases, the sign of the Cross is made with cork, and this is called "Jesus Christ."

Often, the vanity of some ladies made them go to the churches where they received the "Jesus Christ," as they did not want to have an imperfect sign of the cross on their forehead. A few devout women would cover their foreheads with oil or grease to keep the sign of the cross there during all Lent.

In some Huichol towns in Jalisco and Nayarit, up to the middle of the century, they had the habit of celebrating this ceremony in a strange way. In Peyotlán, at dawn, the chief of the tribe would gather all the neighbors around him, distribute them according to their age and then give each his cross made of palm leaves; when everyone had a cross, they considered it an amulet which would protect them from any danger. In their language, they pronounced sacramental words and then abandoned themselves to ritual dances to the rhythm of the *chirimía* (a special wind instrument) all day. At nightfall, they returned home to put the crosses in a visible place. In several Otomí towns in the state of Hidalgo near Actopan, at the beginning of the last century, ceremonies similar to those described, also took place. The only difference was that black-corn *tamales* were made, which were cooked at night on huge pots and then they were distributed while the *cacique* (chief) also distributed a few blessings.

In towns on Lake Pátzcuaro —Janitzio and Pacanda— Father Mendoza declares that around 1880, he saw a strange ceremony taking place, consisting of the following: the *cacique* painted a cross on the nape of the devout persons and distributed gifts, then everyone abandoned themselves to dancing.

MEXICAN GASTRONOMIC TRADITION FOR LENT

Proper culinary heritage of the Mexicans

The early historians of our country who reported on how occidental culture encountered Mexican culture, testify to the profound religious spirit of the Indian peoples and how this spirit also included nutritional customs and habits; in other words, there was an entire gastronomical tradition linked to the religious beliefs and ceremonies.

Therefore, it is not strange that when the Catholic missionaries —who tried to take advantage of the Indian's deep religious feeling— carried out the spiritual conquest, changes were made in the nutritional habits characteristic of the religious festivities and adapted them to the uses and customs demanded by the rites of the new religion.

Thus, a 'Lenten cuisine as well as a Christmas cuisine originated in New Spain, since Christian liturgy revolves around these two cycles.

These traditions, which have lasted to our times, are essentially pre-Hispanic, since they are Indian dishes (as in the case of dishes such as *nopales* (prickly pears), squash flowers, *guauzontles* (a certain plant grown in Mexico), *verdolagas* (small-spinach-like plants), potatoes, *moles* with many spices, and *tamales*, to mention a few.

Thus, the Lenten dishes form an authentic Mexican gastronomical tradition which, it must be added, is enriched with the elements contributed by Spanish cuisine.

Regarding the culinary tradition for Lent, this seems to be dominated by two ritual elements which are essentially: fasting and abstinence.

Fasting compels a person to eat a single meal, which is the day's principal meal; as for abstinence, as the name indicates, the use of meat in all its varieties is forbidden, but not as far as vegetables and fish are concerned, and these may be eaten in all their infinite varieties.

Mexican gastronomy contributes to the world vegetables which are universally consumed, such as potatoes, squash, sweet potatoes, corn, chili, avocados, *nopales* and many others which are consumed during the so-called days of abstinence during Lent. Thus, an infinite number of dishes are carefully prepared with great spiritual devotion; this is why Mexican cuisine for Lent is a high-quality gastronomic tradition.

To confirm the above, suffice it to mention a few examples: the *nopales* in the almost infinite variety of preparations with eggs, with *mole*, in salads, etcetera; *romeritos* (rosemary leaves) in *mole*, with its classical cakes made of dry shrimp, the tiny dry fish (*charales*) from Pátzcuaro and Zirahuén, covered with beaten eggs; squash made in little cakes stuffed, chopped in green tomato sauce, etcetera; squash flower and *huitlacoche* (edible fungus in corn). All of these are enriched with the contributions of peas, green beans, lima bean soup —the prelude of any Lenten meal worth mentioning— until reaching the so-called poor-man's pie, and the Aztec pies made with squash flower, tender squash, cheese, cream and green peppers or other varieties of peppers. And, of course, the infallible *tamales*: made with shrimp, cheese, *nopales* or the simple *corundas* or *uchepos* (variety of *tamales*) with sliced green peppers. The regions by the sea contribute, with their variety of fish, typical dishes such as shrimp soup, *chilpachole* (soup prepared with various kinds of seafood and fish), and the typical Creole dishes such as *huachinango* (a type of red snapper) *a la Veracruzana* or *bacalao* (codfish) *a la Vizcaína*.

It should be mentioned that the Mexica cuisine was very adequate for the Lenten festivities, as there was no beef, pork or many other kinds of bovine meat in Mexico.

As for desserts, an entire variety of delicious pastries and desserts originated made with chocolate, glazed fruit and wheat flour. Thus, various typical desserts were born, such as *capirotadas*, *torrejas*, rice cakes, *migotes* and royal eggs, *tamales* and a thousand other treats capable of satisfying the most refined taste.

As for beverages, the famous flavored fruit drinks are the ideal complement of Lenten gastronomy from which *aguamieles* and *pulques* (fermented agave drinks) are not missing.

Thus, we would venture to affirm that Mexican Lenten gastronomy is one of the most delicious and varied in the world, and luckily for us, it is an ancestral and living tradition in Mexican cuisine.

THE TRADITION OF THE SAMARITAN'S FRESH WATER FRUIT-FLAVORED BEVERAGES

On the third Friday of Lent, the tradition of offering the Samaritan's fresh water beverages is celebrated.

The liturgy for the third Friday of Lent includes the passage from the Gospel where John tells about that beautiful episode when Jesus —after leaving Judea due to the intrigues of the Pharisees— travels to Samaria, and in the ancient city of Sicar he stops, close to a hot noon, by a well, belonging to the patriarch Jacob, to quench his thirst. The legendary Samaritan is standing at the mouth of the well and Jesus says to her:

"Give me water to drink."

The woman, surprised because a Jew speaks to a public sinner, asks Jesus:

"How can you, a Jew, ask me for drinking water, if I am Samaritan?"

Jesus takes advantage of this circumstance to declare Himself, for the first time, the Redeeming Messiah before a scorned people such as the Samaritan, and precisely before a woman who was living with her sixth lover. And this woman —after a profound dialogue with Jesus— runs to call her people to meet the Messiah, remarking that even though he had never seen her before, he knew all about her life.

"Could it be because he is Christ?" repeated the Samaritan over and over.

And John narrates how, because of the Samaritan, there were many from this people who believed in Jesus' doctrine, to the point where they made him remain among them two days.

To perpetuate this passage from the life of Jesus, as well as the conversion of the Samaritans, some Christian communities in Mexico established the tradition of offering fresh water around noon at the entrance of the churches, perhaps to make amends for the Samaritan's doubt when she did not give Jesus water immediately.

This custom, like many others, had been buried by the rhythm of modern life, but every third Friday of Lent, the Association of Pro-Bethlehem People of Mexico decided to revive it in the heart of Mexico City —at the ancient square of Santo Domingo, offering the traditional fresh water of the Samaritan at the end of the ceremony.

Traditions such as this promote harmony among neighbors and make urban coexistence more loving because they make the spirit of the Capital's residents more human and their spirits are elevated.

THE ALTAR OF OUR LADY OF SORROWS, PROFOUND MEXICAN TRADITION

Prelude to Holy Week

The preference which the Mexican people have always had for Mary, Mother of Jesus, in any of her appearances, has always been proverbial, and naturally, the most outstanding is the people's devotion towards the Virgin of Guadalupe in Mexico.

The devotion to the Virgin of Sorrows (The Sorrowful Mother), or the Virgin of Solitude, as Mary is known in her three appearances next to the Cross, is not surprising.

Indeed, this liturgical festivity was established to commemorate the Virgin Mary's Seven Sorrows. The tradition of the Altar to worship the Virgin of Sorrows is linked to the day of Candlemas (February 2), in memory of the child Jesus' presentation at the temple, the blessing of the candles, the Purification of the Virgin Mary, and her encounter with Simeon the prophet, who predicted and told the Virgin that her Son would be "a sign of contradiction" and that Mary's soul would be "pierced by a sword," a scene which is illustrated in many paintings and wood carvings, when placing a dagger in Mary's heart.

The name of our Lady of Sorrows comes from this. The name of the Sorrowful Mother proceeds from the hymn which is sung during Mass on that day.

Devotion to the Sorrowful Virgin is very old in Catholic liturgy, as witnessed in the hymn *Stabat Mater Dolorosa Iuxta Crucem Lacrimosa* recited in Mass on Passion Friday, or on the Day of the Seven Sorrows.

Therefore, ever since the beginning of Colonization, renowned Mexican painters, such as Baroque painters Juan Correa (second half of the 17th century and first half of the 18th, Cristóbal de Villalpando (17th century painter) and Miguel Cabrera (1695-1768, born in the state of Oaxaca) created beautiful paintings of the Sorrowful Mother which, like the crèches and the altars to the dead are not only placed in churches, but also in houses (this was how the custom of installing the Altar to the Sorrowful Mother in Mexican homes was extended).

Some Mexico City historians prefer to repeat that Sorrowful Friday in Mexico originated due to a petition made by Don Bernardo de Gálvez in 1786. In fact, what New Spain's forty-ninth viceroy did, was merely to revive the festival that had already been celebrated during the Poppy Flower Festival in the Santa Anita Drive, an old custom that originated the tradition of the people visiting the Altar to give the Virgin poppies and other flowers.

The reason that induced the Count of Gálvez to carry out this gesture, which the residents of the capital fervently followed, was that in 1785 there was a great *famine*, so it was consequently called "the Year of Hunger" and the following year, an evil plague fell upon the people, so it was therefore called "The Year of the Plague."

These misfortunes led to providing greater strength to the celebration of the offerings at the Altar to the Sorrowful Mother, and during more than a century the altar was established at the Old Drive at Santa Anita. Strangely enough this Passion Friday custom has always been very much alive in Santa Anita, and this tradition continues in that region and is also linked to the tradition of *La Flor más Bella del Ejido* (The Most Beautiful Flower in the Region), which is now held in Xochimilco, the Friday before Passion Friday.

The Altar of Sorrows was installed as a prelude to Holy Week, for the purpose of commemorating the Virgin Mary's sorrows due to her Son Jesus Christ's Passion.

As mentioned above, altars were set up, both in the churches and in the houses dedicated to worship the Virgin Mary in her appearance as the Sorrowful Mother, who is distinguished by her Suffering Face, bathed in tears. In the center, the image of Mary was placed, either in a sculpture or in a painting, always accompanied by a cross and different objects which, with different symbolism, completed the picture.

This event marked moments of spiritual meditation and, at the same time, of wholesome amusement, as it promoted sharing with friends and relatives, both while preparing the festival, and while visiting the different altars.

After choosing the proper place in the house, which was usually the most important and the prettiest, the faithful selected the images and the objects to assemble and decorate the altar; tables and stairs for the altar's different levels; white linen for the background, containers to hold *the multiflavored water which would commemorate the Virgin's tears*, and which would be consumed by visitors; flower pots with greenery and flowers; large candles decorated with crepe, oranges painted with gold and crowned with paper banners, and at the foot of the altar, rugs made of colored powders or seeds, with different tones and shapes, representing the Passion's various symbols with great imagination and ability.

In some places in Mexico it is also customary to decorate the altars with sprouted sage seeds, blessed on Candlemas Day, and in some towns, such as San Miguel de Allende, Guanajuato, people who visit the Altar are offered a delicious sweet made of *chilacayote* (bottle gourd) or heavenly angels' hair (like spun sugar).

Religious traditions instituted since the viceregal period are part of our cultural background.

PALM SUNDAY

The Gospel says that before His Passion, Jesus entered Jerusalem trium-
phantly, riding a small donkey; on his way, an improvised carpet of palm
leaves covered the road.

Mexican tradition remembers this, and devoted hands of anonymous
artists weave and mingle palm leaves and wheat hay to worship the Redeemer with different figures.

At the entrance of the Metropolitan Cathedral, hundreds of people
assemble, who with their palm leaves high in the air, receive the Palm Sunday blessing, as this occasion marks the beginning of Holy Week.

The faithful remember Jesus' entrance into Jerusalem on his donkey.

MAUNDY THURSDAY (LAVATORY)

On Maundy Thursday, the meaningful act of humility at the Cathedral

Every year, the Primate Archbishop of Mexico, in an act of humility, washes the feet of twelve elderly men to make evident the Lord's commandment,
that is to say, the charity with which we must serve our brothers, and the
purity of soul with which we must approach the altar to receive Holy Communion.

In this mass, the cardinal, the maximum authority of the Catholic
Church, remembers the meaning of Maundy Thursday and consecrates the
Holy Formula. He pronounces the same words which Jesus said during the
Last Supper: *"This is my body."* And he remembers the Lord's prayer when he
established Catholic priesthood.

Pope Pius XII renewed Holy Week, and reestablished the Easter vigil.
On March 21, 1969, the new Roman calendar was issued, with adequate
explanations of the ceremonies during Holy Week.

After celebrating the mass of the Lord's Supper —called the Last Sup-
per— two other masses are celebrated and the faithful receive Holy
Communion. (The Lord's permanence in the Holy Wafer is known as the
Eucharistic Reserve.) The Roman missal has not changed the Maundy
Thursday rites. There is only one change: the people who took Holy Com-
munion during the Chrism Mass on Maundy Thursday morning may take
Communion again at night, at the Lord's Supper.

41

A multitude of faithful Catholics are present at the Visit of the Seven Temples, or the Visit to the Monuments, as they were called in olden times.

To visit the seven temples is a custom which the people maintain since many years ago. A "station" of the Cross, or the entire Way of the Cross is prayed at each church.

VISIT TO THE SEVEN TEMPLES

A Maundy Thursday Devotion

The Christian community in Mexico devotedly continues with the traditional Visit to the Seven Temples to offer their prayers at the Monuments for the adoration of the Eucharist.

One of the most outstanding moments on Maundy Thursday is the institution of the Eucharist, which contains Christ's loving response by giving us his Body and his Blood. For this reason, since the early days of evangelization in the New World, the friars established the visit to the altars in their rites, in memory of the first communities in Jerusalem who commemorated an episode from the Lord's Passion.

The splendor of the altars, together with the popular art in the flower arrangements attract parishioners, who attend with a deep feeling of faith each year.

In Mexico City, the devotion of the visit to the Seven Temples is deeply rooted. Originally, these visits were made to the chapels in the Metropolitan Cathedral, in memory of the first Christian groups and, later, to substitute the Basilicas in Rome.

The pilgrimages through the temples are not considered liturgical acts, but they allow the faithful to meditate about the Lord's action when He bequeathed the Divine Eucharist to His disciples when He blessed the bread and wine which He offered them saying, *"This is My Body and this is My Blood."*

Catholic priests follow the Lord's example, inviting us with the following words: *Do this in My memory.* Even today, the faithful can be spiritually nourished with the Sacred Formula throughout the planet.

Families form true pilgrimages visiting the temples, among which are included: La Coronación (at the Parque España), the Cathedral, San Hipólito, La Profesa, San Francisco and San Felipe, all of which are very traditional in the downtown area of Mexico City.

The Monuments in the churches of Regina, San Loreto, Nuestra Señora del Carmen, San Sebastián Mártir, Santo Domingo and others which are deeply rooted in the people, are found along the pilgrims' way to remember Jesus Christ passing through the places where he suffered: from the Cenacle (the place where Christ and His apostles had the Last Supper), to the Olive Orchard; from the Olive Orchard to the house of Anas; then to Caiaphas' home, from the latter's house to Pilate's Praetorium, then to the house of Herod and then once again to Pilate's Praetorium and, finally, to Calvary.

PROCESSIONS IN OUR COUNTRY

Historical background

The Carmelite priests who arrived in New Spain in 1585 instituted in Mexico City a few years after their arrival, in their doctrine for the Saint Sebastián Hermitage, the Holy Week processions, following the Spanish custom. In fact, chronicles inform us that Father Elias of the church of Saint John the Baptist promoted some of the customs of Sevilla during that period. The Procession of Blood, and the Way of the Cross had an incredible number of participants, ostentation and grandeur in the way they were carried out.

One of the processions, the so-called Procession of Silence, which is held on the evening of Holy Friday, lasted during the Mexican colonial and independent periods and has reached our times in the atrium of the majestic Carmelite Convent and Temple in the San Angel Villa in Mexico City. This tradition, now Mexican, was picked up during Holy Week in 1954, and the paving stones in the streets of San Luis Potosí trembled for the first time under the footsteps of the Nazarene, ladies and penitents who carried the images of Jesus Christ crucified and Our Lady of Solitude on their shoulders.

Origin of the Procession of Silence

This procession originated since immemorial days in the most Christian Mother Country, in the Procession of Blood and the Way of the Cross, which have always been celebrated in the intense and exciting lands of Andalusia, Spain.

43

The traditional Procession of Silence organized every year by the laymen and women in the neighborhood of the church of the Sacred Family in the Roma district, to express their sorrow for the death of Jesus Christ, is truly beautiful.

As its name indicates, silence predominates as an expression of sorrow for the death of Our Lord Jesus Christ, together with Mary's grief for losing her son, Jesus, the Redeemer, on the Cross.

There is a special council for the Procession of Silence, whose members are Catholic, and their idea is to always repeat —like all the faithful— our condolences to our Blessed Mother, the Mother of Jesus.

Tradition has made things seem as though it were a religous rite, but in fact it is merely an offering of the people's religious devotion. Silence is majestic. Candles in the hands of most of the faithful predominate.

After the services in memory of Jesus Christ's crucifixion, long lines of faithful followers form in the central naves in the church of the Sacred Family. Everyone full of faith passes in front of the image of Christ, to touch Him or to kiss His feet.

My hands and my feet have been pierced, and all my bones can be counted.

A car carries the image of the Sorrowful Mother, with around a hundred lit candles of various sizes. Another car carries Jesus Christ crucified, with Mary kneeling by his side. One more car represents Mary, with John, the apostle. And a fourth car carries a glass coffin with the image of Jesus Christ.

The sponsors claim that they have never tried to seek a similarity with the Procession of Silence celebrated in Sevilla, Spain. This is our very own tradition and we must maintain it, because it is part of the Mexican's way of life. We do not wish to imitate or resemble anyone. This was something that originated from the feelings of a people, from a group of persons who wished to express their grief to Christ and to the Virgin Mary when commemorating the Death, Passion, and Resurrection of the Son of God.

At 12:00 noon, led by the priests of the Church of the Sacred Family, the Way of the Cross is celebrated throughout the streets of Puebla, Jalapa, Durango and Orizaba, in the center of the Roma district.

During the procession, people pray. This popular devotion of long tradition with religious fervor, lasts about an hour.

HOLY WEEK IN IXTAPALAPA (MEXICO CITY)

Representation of Judea

Mexicans have always loved spectacular, grandiloquent, massive scenic representations that will allow them to participate, to be part of the plot.

The dramatization of the passages of Jesus Christ's Passion is a typical and complete expression of this preference in Ixtapalapa, where the entire community is transformed in its cast and all the streets become its stage.

The unusual thing about this representation lies in the fact that all the inhabitants represent a certain character: a soldier, a Roman magistrate, Judas, Jesus, the Virgin; musician, script-writer, prompter, or simple member of the crowd, all within the Passion.

This representation is, therefore, the most complete testimony of popular stage tradition in the Valley of Mexico.

The script, written by the church wardens according to their feelings, follows the story in the Gospel and includes: the Last Supper, the Lavation, the Prayer in the Orchard, the Capture, the Trial of Jesus, the Way of the Cross, and culminates with the Crucifixion.

During two full days, Ixtapalapa lives the drama of the Crucifixion.

Ixtapalapa is one of the little towns in Mexico City that still preserves a great deal of the past. It is located at the foot of the famous Estrella hill, where in pre-Hispanic times the Feast of the New Fire was celebrated —a ceremony which consisted of taking to the city of Tenochtitlan the fire which should burn constantly at the Great Teocalli to be taken later to all the natives' homes.

The ceremony of Judea or the Passion of Christ is of great interest, as it endeavors to represent realistic scenes.

The characters dress elegantly. Among these characters, we can find:

Annas	The priests
Caiaphas	Mary
The centurion	Mary Magdalene
Herod	Nicodemus
Jesus	Pilate
Joseph of Arimathaea	People
Judas	Saint Peter
The Jews	Roman soldiers

45

The number of people who take part in this representation is high, and most are inhabitants of the locality. Some people participate due to promises made and have been acting in this ceremony for many years.

It is an outdoor stage prepared in the extensive atrium of the parish with an enormous platform covered with cloth and adorned with greenery and flowers which abound in the region. Besides this great platform, others are built, and these are called Praetorium where Jesus of Nazareth must be taken.

Years ago, the Crucifixion ceremony was held inside the church, where a hill had been formed, with trees and rocks, built as naturally as possible. The crucifixion now takes place at the foot of the Estrella Hill.

The "Judea" begins very early on Maundy Thursday, when the Pharisees run throughout the town shouting that they seek Jesus of Nazareth, who must be judged for being a false prophet and deceiving people saying that taxes should not be paid to Caesar.

The Lavation takes place in the afternoon. In this ceremony, Jesus washes the apostles' feet and then sits by their side to celebrate Easter. A very lively and picturesque dialogue is held between Jesus and the disciples (among which the traitor Judas is found) and Jesus reveals that one of them will deliver Him to his enemies.

Outside the Cenacle, the Pharisees can be seen looking for Jesus and speaking about His capture.

The Olive Orchard is the place where Jesus goes to pray. The person representing the Nazarene —who knows his role and memorizes his part— says a prayer wherein the following words are heard: *Father, if possible, please remove this Chalice, Thy Will be done*. An angel appears to comfort Him and then Jesus rises and looks for His disciples.

A group of Pharisees led by Judas, carrying big lights, for everything remains in the shadows, carry out Jesus' capture. Judas kisses the Messiah as a sign of treason.

The costumes worn by the Apostles are bright-colored tunics with their respective cloaks, especially red, blue, purple and yellow. The table is decorated with old-fashioned wooden cups and the dishes and tableware are typically made of clay with artistic decorations.

The flower arrangement is made of poppies, carnations and *cempasuchiles* (orange marigolds grown in this country), so original that they are worth contemplating.

The final ceremony celebrated on Maundy Thursday corresponds to

"Jesus in the Little Room." He is in prison and various scenes take place there. The Jews mock Him, saying words such as the following:

"Did you say you are King? Where is your power? Where are those who defend you? You are mad, you are an impostor."

Outside the Little Room, Peter denies Jesus, and the cock crows. To highlight the drama of this scene, several roosters are placed on nearby trees.

The clerks, the Pharisees, and the ministers of justice walk through the town, shouting that at last the so-called King of the Jews will be executed.

The different actors who act in the ceremonies: King Herod, Annas and Caiaphas, Pontius Pilate, the governor of Jerusalem with his followers, the clerks and the Pharisees, all go through the town in a procession.

The principal actors are mounted on magnificent horses, and when they dismount after riding through some of the town's main streets, they do so ceremoniously, making these scenes very attractive.

Naturally, in plays of this type, there are always some variations to the true tragedy of Calvary, as the particular taste of the people in charge of the rehearsal is involved in order to provide more importance to the people who, in their opinion, deserve it, and they also improvise new scenes for some of the Passion's most important actions.

The scene where Jesus is taken to Pilate takes place on the big stage. The person who represents Jesus answers with dignity the questions made by Caesar's representative, and the latter finds more than enough reasons to sentence Him, so he sends Him to the Pontiffs.

Annas is on another stage. He is wearing strange clothes; a big crown like the Pope's Roman tiara is on his head, and he has a big beard.

The shouts of the ministers of justice are heard.

At that moment, the *chirimías* begin to play their dismal, melancholic tunes. The instruments include the famous *teponaxtli* (a percussion instrument), a drum, and the horns, which can be heard at long distances.

Then, Jesus goes to the house of Caiaphas, where another scene takes place, and the Pharisees, the ministers of justice, and the townspeople —the masses— shout offensive exclamations towards Jesus, asking that He be condemned. He will appear before Herod, who is in his majestic palace, eager to wield his power. Herod asks Jesus for miracles and establishes a dialogue:

"If you are the Son of God, let us see some of your miracles. Why are you silent? Speak. You are the Son of God. Ask your Father to free you from our hands, if his power is so great."

Once again, Jesus is taken to Pilate's palace, where He is sentenced to death. When the death sentence is heard, the *chirimías* play their gloomy melodies, and an original scene appears. A group of old men, the Nazarenes, can be seen near the raised platform.

They are wearing purple tunics with their respective cloaks and a kind of black hood. They sing, like mournful weepers, verses which say,

> *La muerte del justo*
> *será maldición*
> *al infame pueblo*
> *que lo condenó.* *

In that moment, Judas appears, proudly flaunting a big bag made of *ixtle* (maguey fiber with which rope and bags, among other things, are made), so that everyone can hear that the bags bear the coins which he obtained by betraying Jesus. Judas is wearing a wide vermilion-colored tunic, tied at the waist, decorated with excellent lace on the lower edge; he is also wearing a navy blue cloak, black stockings and *huaraches* (sandal-like shoes).

The spies accompany this character. The spies are wearing fantastic costumes; they carry lanterns which are lit despite the bright sun and lead a few white dogs adorned with colored collars.

The ceremony consisting of taking Christ to Mount Calvary is also impressive. Simon of Cirinea, the man who helps to carry the Nazarene's Cross, appears. In the scene of the Encounter, Jesus sees His Mother, accompanied by the compassionate devout women, Martha and Mary. Jesus engraves the image of His face on the mantle which Veronica shows him and He falls several times under the weight of the Cross.

Barabbas appears and a crowd follows him, uttering words that attack the Nazarene. Another group of natives follow Barabbas, who drags enormous chains.

The *chirimía* plays its dismal melody and the people chant their melancholic songs.

When evening falls, the Redeemer dies; another man is crucified, and the Virgin Mary, Saint John and Mary Magdalene remain grieving.

---

*The death of the Righteous One/will be a curse/to the infamous people/who condemned Him.

The most beautiful ladies in town are chosen for the roles of the Virgin and Mary Magdalene. Mary Magdalene is represented by a young girl with long loose hair.

At night, when the representation has been completed, the mysterios sounds of the *teponaxtles* and the *chirimías* are still heard.

The inhabitants of the town and other neighboring places, people who come from many miles away, as well as other persons in attendance, mainly devout people, watch these representations with a great deal of interest.

In other times, with the intervention of priests, devout acts took place, such as the Three Falls, with a sermon pronounced in the atrium itself. The Sermon of the Lance, and the Condolences, with the true Christ and the Holy Burial, were made with a devout procession at nine in the evening, when the people in attendance appeared with lit candles, providing this act with due solemnity.

In the church, the cornices and towers were illuminated with large torches and oil lamps.

Liturgical hymns impregnated with deep sorrow, with profound grief, highlighted these ceremonies.

Holy Week, Christ's Passion, lived yesterday and continues living today at Ixtapalapa.

CRAFTS DURING HOLY WEEK

Craftsmen's hands interpret exactly the feelings of Mexicans. Paper, cardboard, wood or clay express adequate emotion for the occasion; thus, the workmanship is both a symbol and a message.

The men who make *judas* and saints for Holy Week work all year men round to prepare the work of art which the fire will consume in an instant.

Easter Saturday at Cuajimalpa

The burning of *judas* on Easter Saturday is an old tradition. Popular irony sharpens in all its wit.

But, within this sense of humor, the tradition at Cuajimalpa is unique, since the *judas* are real live men who run desperately trying to escape the whip, and when they are captured and hung, they scatter gifts, fruit and candy.

The festival culminates with the blessing of clear water brought by the children from a nearby spring, as well as fresh camomile to cure illness of the body and of the spirit, as the old people in the locality say.

The Burning of the Judas

To the rescue of an old tradition

Why is the *Patronato Pro-Fortalecimiento de las Tradiciones Mexicanas* (Council in Favor of Strengthening Mexican Traditions), against all odds, so interested in rescuing a tradition that is almost lost? Because aside from being part of Mexico's cultural history, burning the *judas* acts as social therapy: it is an escape from social stress as each one of us —jokingly and harmlessly— burn our own Judas, that is, that person in politics, in art, in culture or simply in our social life who is disagreeable to us; it is an escape from our personal and social stress; people need to get rid of their passions in a positive way.

The burning of *judas* is like the political joke which great statesmen and social leaders —so scarce in our days— have wisely used.

Naturally, everything is against rescuing this tradition, because with the Catholic church's liturgical modifications, Easter Saturday has disappeared, and this was the day in which we burned Judas Iscariot with fireworks —Judas represented in cardboard as our personal "traitor." And, if we add to this the fact that the authorities in our capital have forbidden the use of fireworks due to public safety reasons...

Origin of the burning of the judas

With the Arab domination in Spain, the liking for fireworks and pyrotechnics was promoted and established, and this was particularly emphasized with carpenters who made large figures with the left-over wood. When they created these wooden dolls, they burned them with gunpowder, and thus a tradition was born. This tradition was to become a craftsmen's festival called *Las Fallas de Valencia*. This festivity has great splendor and continues to be celebrated.

Pyrotechnics was at its peak in Spain, and with the spiritual conquest of natives after teaching them the catechism, it was necessary to find impressive methods of evangelizing them; therefore, the Franciscan priests conceived the idea of initiating a festivity similar to that of Valencia during the Holy Week festivities, and they made dolls to represent the death of Judas Iscariot, the traitor.

When Easter Saturday was instituted in Mexico —the liturgical commemoration called by this name because on that day the veils covering the altars were removed, thus meaning that heaven was opened to receive the Redeemer —the custom acquired deeply rooted popularity and church members with their special creative skill and charm— began to make the *judas* with the faces of the Spanish judges and rulers, which provoked the prohibition of burning the *judas* by the viceroys. But the custom was so deeply ingrained in the people, that the Spaniards were unable to end it. However, it began to take different characteristics in some communities, like the Yaquis, who celebrate Easter Saturday with dancers (Chapayecas or Pharisees) who —with masks representing Judas— do all kinds of mischief because, supposedly, when Jesus is in the hands of the Pharisees, evil dominates at that time; at twelve o'clock noon, when "heaven opens," the Chapayecas carry out ritual dances and they burn the masks, which in this case represent the *judas*, and then joy takes place due to the return of goodness.

In the Valley of Mexico, it was necessary to discard the use of political figures, and then the custom began of burning dolls began with the faces of popular characters began. The very first was the *Charro Mamerto* (a rancher who established residence in the capital), as well as many other famous people, until reaching the popular Cantinflas, a symbol of the city's uncouth pauper. This not offensive to anyone because when the people burn their popular heroes, they feel special joy and respect. Naturally, some people burn figures with the faces of politicians and of persons who are not pleasant, but the custom of the popular figure prevails.

This century-old tradition became very important because merchants favored the burning of enormous *judas* hanging on them merchandise from their shops, which the people gathered after the *judas* was burned.

In Mexico City, the *judas* were burned at the *Plaza del Volador* (The Flyer's Square).

EASTER SUNDAY IN MEXICO
AND THE TRADITIONAL SUPPER WITH HOT CHOCOLATE

When the Lenten liturgical cycle ends, which is a time of spiritual meditation, fasting, abstinence and sadness due to Jesus' Passion and Death, joy
and happiness breaks loose because of Christ's Resurrection and thus the
"Easter Cycle" begins. During this cycle, Christian joy abounds, because the
doors of heavenly glory have been opened to all human beings.

As in the case of the Lenten Cycle, the Easter Cycle also lasts forty days,
but during this time everything is happiness and hope. The word "Easter"
(*Pascua*) is derived from the Latin *pascha* and the Hebrew antecedent *pesah*,
whose exact meaning has not been determined. However, the terms clearly
refer to a festive sacrifice that finally leads to a happy result.

Liturgy is filled with "Alleluias," solemn and gay majestic songs. The
organs resound in the churches, shaping the profile of the Easter Cycle
which recalls the physical presence of Christ reborn before his disciples.

This festive mood always coincides with the spring season, and it is
therefore also known as "Flowery Easter," different from Christmas which
is celebrated in the winter. Thus, the altars in the churches are more than
ever full of flowers during these forty days.

In Rome, Italy, there is a tradition to cover the entire flight of stairs in
the Spanish square with azaleas.

The cycle ends with Jesus' ascent to heaven, forty days after Easter Sunday.

Originally, Easter was a shepherds' pastoral, where the first-born lamb
was sacrificed. Later, the flight from Egypt and the liberation of the people
of Israel from the "tenth plague" was celebrated. Thus, it passed to the Jews,
until Christ, with His Incarnation, Death and Resurrection — gives Easter a
definite meaning.

With time, the word "Easter" in Spanish (*Pascua*) has become synony-
mous to joy and happiness; the expression "to be like we were at Easter
indicates this, as it means being happy and joyful, both figuratively and familiarly.

Easter Processions in Colonial Mexico

Since the Easter cycle was the climax of Christian liturgy, during the period
of the spiritual conquest the missionaries were very careful of providing a

great deal of solemnity to the Easter Sunday Festivity, which was celebrated with great splendor during the early years of colonization.

The famous historian, Brother Juan de Torquemada provides complete information in Book XVII, Chapter Eight of his *Monarquía Indiana* describing the Easter procession in 1609 as follows:

"The Procession left from San José, with about 230 litters of golden, colorful images of our Lord and our Lady and other saints. Most of the members of religious congregations participated in the procession, as well as the litters from the four ruling seats, by special command from the King and from those who rule in his behalf. This chapel was always recognized as the Mother and the First. Although there have been, and there continue to be clashes because of this, the opponents do not prevail. Everyone marches together and in order, carrying candles in their hands, and another crowd accompanying them also carry lit candles.

"They walk in order through their neighborhoods, in accordance with the superiority or inferiority which they all accept according to their ancient customs. The candles are all white, like ermine, and since both the men and women are also dressed in clean white clothes, this is one of the most colorful and solemn processions in Christianity, as it takes place at dawn or a little earlier. And the Viceroy Martín Enríquez said that this was one of the most beautiful sights that he has ever seen; everyone who has seen this procession says the same.

"The litters and the members of the religious congregations carry so many flowers and roses in their hands and with wreaths their heads, that by this act alone it can be called Flowery Easter. The procession proceeds through one street until reaching the main church, where it is received by the priests and the cross, with bells pealing; the procession then turns toward another chapel, where mass is celebrated together with the crowd."

Unfortunately, at the end of the XIX century, as Luis González Obregón says in his book, *México Viejo*, "Those processions which were the pride and joy of our grandparents and even of our parents, came to an end."

Since the very nature of the Easter Festival is joyful and familial, the custom spontaneously arose of giving sweets and desserts to family and friends, and to invite guests to the Easter Suppers with hot chocolate, where the hostess served: chocolate, *tamales*, "bride's sighs" (meringue sweets), cakes, *cajeta* (a milk specialty candy), *palanquetas* (candy made with pumpkin shelled seeds, or with shelled peanuts, sweetened with brown sugar), *pepitoria* (candy made with toasted pumpkin seeds in molasses), fine almond and peanut cookies, green milk and sugar specialty candy, nougat, little eggs and animals made of pumpkin seeds, *alegrías* (candy made of amaranth seeds), "nun's sighs," *buñuelos* (fried donut-like sweets), candy twists, almond custards, *rompope* (a type of eggnog), jelly turnovers, brown sugar cookies, *muéganos* (a typical candy made of bread and molasses), bicarbonate rings, *gaznates* (pineapple or coconut sweets), *chongos zamoranos* (dessert made of milk and sugar, originating in Zamora), fine almond and vanilla cookies, rose-flavored *marquesotes* (a type of cake or cookie with very little flour), *carlotas* (a dessert made with ladyfingers), the *borrachitos* (wine-flavored cakes), almond delights and a thousand other homemade delights prepared by the angelical hands of nuns and kitchen maids.

The ancient custom derived from Mexican tradition of giving presents of native candy and desserts, as well as delicious baked fruit, was thus born.

As the result of our communication with other cultures, the customs of other countries have tried to penetrate in Mexico, among which is the custom of giving Easter eggs and rabbits. This was a popular European tradition which was transmitted to Saxon America during the colonization period. The egg symbolizes the creation of the animal kingdom on Earth (this is a symbol for country people —Easter, in its Jewish origins was a country festival). The rabbit symbolizes fertility, which in the spiritual sense, was an attitude of the human mind, whereby the Word of God should be fruitful in order to produce kindness, love and good deeds.

In our times, perhaps it is impossible to return to the old Mexican Easter traditions, with the old characteristics, but it is feasible to maintain the custom of giving the wonderful desserts included in our traditional confectionery, and to revive the wholesome custom of the Flowery Easter Supper, which will provide a home-like tone to the Easter festivities, but above all, will be more in accordance with out ancestral way of life...more like our very own.

FESTIVITY OF THE HOLY CROSS

May 3, traditional festivity of the unions in Colonial Mexico, has almost disappeared and is now celebrated only by bricklayers and masons who place the cross decorated with flowers and crepe paper clippings on top of their construction work.

Milpa Alta is the place which most closely follows the original tradition, and the neighboring towns take their patron saints to visit their neighbors.

A TRADITION WHICH REFUSED TO DIE

The enthusiasm and faith of construction workers triumphed

One of the oldest popular festivities in our country is the celebration of the Holy Cross —also known as the Flowery Cross, due to the bricklayers' and masons' inveterate custom of placing a simple cross on top of their constructions, decorated with flowers and colored crepe paper.

On July 25, 1960, Pope John XXIII voluntarily eliminated the festivity from the liturgical calendar of the Catholic Church, in order to highlight the festivity of the Exaltation of the Holy Cross on September 14. However, in view of the fact that the union of construction workers continued to celebrate their special day on that date, the Mexican episcopate took the necessary steps to allow the festivity to remain in effect in Mexico, regardless of the fact that it had been eliminated in other parts of the world.

The bricklayers' and masons' faith won, and the Primate Archbishop in Mexico heads the ceremony at the Cathedral, where bricklayers and masons from every part of the city arrive, taking their adorned crosses.

Therefore, fireworks will explode in Mexico's sky every year, proclaiming the victory of this beautiful and meaningful tradition.

ITS BACKGROUND

Its origin dates back to the 4th century of our era. Emperor Constantine was facing an imminent defeat by the barbaric hordes of the Danube. When he was weary and exhausted, a shining cross appeared in the sky with the inscription: *In hoc signo vinces* (With this sign thou shalt conquer). Victory

55

favored him when he defeated the barbarians. After Constantine was taught and baptized by Pope Eusebius in Rome, in gratitude he asked his mother, Saint Helen, to travel to Jerusalem and seek the relics of Christ's Cross, whose whereabouts were unknown at that time. The Mother Empress pledged all her passion and efforts to searching for the cross. She investigated during some time, until finally, and after resorting to everything that was in her power, she was able to convince a Jewish sage by the name of Judas, to reveal what he knew. Thus, Saint Helen began to excavate in different sites in Jerusalem, until one day, moved by divine inspiration, she pointed to a place. She made profound excavations with a great deal of faith, despite the words of advice that she received to try someplace else. Finally, she discovered the Three Crosses.

As the inscription on Christ's Cross was found separately, it was impossible to know which of the three was the true cross of the Redeemer. Consequently, the bishop of Jerusalem called a dying woman and asked her to touch the Three Crosses. When the woman hugged the third, she was cured , and the true cross was identified with this miracle. Therefore, this Festivity is also called the *Fiesta de la Vera* Cruz (Festivity of the True Cross).

Judas, the sage, who was a witness of the miracle, converted to Christianism, and as the bishop of Jerusalem died during those days, Saint Helen asked Pope Eusebius, who went to worship the relic, to consecrate the converted Jew and make him a bishop. The Jew took the name of Cirius. Saint Helen remained in Jerusalem and asked Constantine to build commemorative churches, to restore the Holy Places and to give alms to the poor in Jerusalem. Upon her death, the empress asked the faithful to celebrate a festivity annually on May 3, the day on which the Cross was discovered. and this festivity was established ever since those distant days.

The faithful in Spain initiated the custom of making a cross, placing it on top of their homes and adorning it with flowers, and the missionaries took this tradition to Mexico. As many churches were being built, the evangelizers asked the bricklayers and masons to make a cross and place it on top of the building, adorned with flowers and beads. This group of workers accepted this celebration as their very own and each year they celebrate with a great feast at the work site itself, accompanied by their families.

FESTIVITY OF THE HOLY CROSS IN COLONIAL MEXICO

The union of bricklayers and masons celebrate the "Festivity of the Holy

Cross." In an old article, I read that this custom dates back to the times of illustrious Brother Pedro de Gante, founder the first school in Mexico.

Perhaps the cross was placed on the pinnacles and adorned with natural and paper flowers on the early churches built in New Spain, and since that time, the builders of houses devote themselves to preparing the Festivity of the Holy Cross throughout the national territory.

Usually, a cross is blessed by a priest on the eve of the celebration. The cross is then placed at dawn on the most important place in the building, at a regular height, while the fireworks produce great joy. Sometimes, a band of music or a group of philharmonic musicians enliven the celebration.

In other times, until the middle of the century, praises were sung when the Cross was hoisted.

The crosses are decorated with paper, linen, canvas or natural flowers. Sometimes distinguished artists take pride in showing off their talent and carry out the above mentioned decorations with great skill.

During the entire joyful day, fireworks explode, popular songs or dances are played, and at midday, the typical barbecue or turkey *mole* is served with *pulque* (an alcoholic drink made of agave). The festivity ends with a real drinking spree by the bricklayers and masons to celebrate the Feast of the Holy Cross, which is more pagan than religious.

Some native towns follow the custom of making a cross made of *pericon* (wild yellow flowers) grown in Santa María, or field roses, for instance on the day of the Festivity in honor of Saint Michael, and before sunrise the people place these crosses in front of their houses or on some nearby tree trunk, perfuming the crosses with *copal* incense.

The natives also enjoy drinking. In Jalisco, they drink *tejuino*, in Colima and Guerrero they drink *tuba* or *chinguerito* and in San Luis Potosí, *colonche*; in Mexico City and in the states of Mexico and Hidalgo, they drink *pulque*.

Sometimes they also prepare *enchiladas* (stuffed *tacos* covered with a spicy chili sauce) and eat them for a delicious lunch. On that day, they have the offering to the Cross, similar to that made on the Day of the Dead.

The day before the crosses made of flowers will be placed in front of their houses, the people place pumpkin and boiled ears of corn, *chayotes* (a vegetable somewhat similar to the potato), as well as other vegetables which are the favorite food of the natives, on an altar.

The natives are deeply ingrained in their traditions, and there is no way of preventing them from celebrating their festivities. Ever since colonial times, the priests and other religious people abolished bloody rites, but the offerings and the sacrifices consisting of burnt copal in incense continue to our times, as the natives have the belief that if they don't do it that way, the gods will turn angry and great disasters will get into their homes.

In the churches of Santa Cruz Acatlán and the Soledad de Santa Cruz in Mexico City, magnificent festivities took place during the middle of the last century, with a solemn mass, noise on the awning, *chirimías*, fireworks, bells tolling, and a festival in the church atrium. The festival was enlivened by a few typical dances from various parts of the country.

The groups of bricklayers and masons who went to these festivals wore their best clothes; the traditional national *charro* costume with a big-winged hat, a short jacket and tight pants. Although the bricklayers and masons did not usually dress this way, on this occasion they appeared showing off the colorful *charro* costume.

THE BARBECUE RITUAL

This traditional and delicious dish is prepared with mutton wrapped in maguey leaves which are placed in a big pot where the meat juice gathers. The broth contains rice, chickpeas and various chopped vegetables such as carrots, cauliflower, potato and mint. All this must be cooked in an underground hole, which acts as an oven, and is covered with maguey leaves and soil to keep the heat.

The complete ritual of preparing the authentic and traditional barbecued meat of Actopan, Hidalgo, appears below. The people who prepare this dish are called "barbecuers."

- Obtain a ram or sheep.
- Cut and clean the maguey leaves.
- Gather *mezquite* or evergreen wood, as this wood does not smoke when burned.
- Have available black porous rock, or "fire rock."
- After you have all these elements, dig a hole about 80 centimeters deep and 1.20 cms. in diameter.
- At the bottom of the hole, place the mezquite wood first of all.
- Over the wood, place the above mentioned porous or "fire" rock. (It is called "fire rock" because it is porous and keeps the heat.)

- After this has been done, your oven is ready. Light the fire below the wood so that it can become coal and can heat the rock.

- The coal will be ready in approximately two hours, and the rock will be very hot.

- Thus, the oven will be ideal to place the pot which will hold the broth.

- Before putting the pot in the oven, put the following ingredients in the pot: rice, chickpeas, cauliflower, potatoes, carrots, *chipotle* (a hot dry chili), garlic, onion, mint, salt and water for the broth.

- Then, extend the maguey leaves around the pot. The leaves should be roasted and very clean. Put thin mezquite wood over the pot to form a grill.

- Put the mutton meat over the grill made of wood and maguey leaves around the pot, and put more maguey leaves over the meat. Cover with soil and wait six hours for the barbecue to cook.

- Finally, remove the meat and then the broth.

You can now enjoy a delicious dish which is difficult to prepare and is considered one of the best in Mexican cuisine.

CORPUS CHRISTI THURSDAY AT THE CATHEDRAL

et the children come to me, because in truth I say that theirs is the kingdom of Heaven.

And every Corpus Christi Thursday, these little angels, dressed like native Indians go to the Cathedral of old Tenochtitlan to present their ineffable innocence to Jesus.

FESTIVITY OF CORPUS CHRISTI

Month of June

The festivities of *Corpus Christi* or Corpus Thursday are an old tradition which has survived in the enormous capital.

The inhabitants of Mexico City prepare to revive the old tradition of celebrating Corpus Thursday, after defeating the city traffic and forgetting the difficulties in the city streets.

Street vendors have appeared throughout the city, offering picturesque little mules made in different ways, providing a touch of color and joy to the monotonous city life.

The tradition of celebrating Corpus Thursday in Mexico City is almost as old as the capital itself —since 1526, historians have reported on this celebration.

After some time, around the year 1560, the splendid procession which began at the first modest Cathedral and proceeded towards every direction in the city, was already famous. The inhabitants of all the neighborhoods and districts which at that time constituted our capital participated in this procession, one way or another. The procession started at the west door and circulated through the Cathedral's nearby streets, headed by the archbishop, the regular clergy, the religious orders, the viceroy, the audience, the municipal authorities, the different groups and religious associations, the University, the army —one and all dressed in their best finery— and the people in general, who at that time traditionally wore new clothes.

The festivities were always celebrated with joy and devotion. Even the streets through which the procession passed had a luxurious custody which was considered one of the richest in the world. The streets were carpeted and covered with awnings; the houses were adorned, flowers were thrown when the procession passed, and in front of the procession, some people dropped rose petals.

The Main Square was full of a multitude of the capital's inhabitants, and this originated a great fair which congregated craftsmen and traders from different places in the country, who took their merchandise on mule. Basically, they took seasonal fruit and crafts, which they carried in *guacales* (a type of portable square box used to carry on the back). Often, the natives from different regions carried these *guacales* on their backs.

This explains the appearance of the little mules, made of dry banana leaves with little *guacales* with coconut or fruit candy.

Another reminiscense of this fair is the custom of taking the children dressed as native Indians, with *guacales* on their backs.

The first fair in New Spain probably took place during this festivity, with its characteristics of a popular country, where not only producers and merchants gathered to sell their wares, but also they had shows and amusements such as cock fights, bull fights, etcetera. During the early Colonial times, they held the famous Masquerades which were merely amusing parades. All of this lasted throughout the Corpus octave.

We should point out that the Corpus festivities in New Spain originated our theatrical tradition. Along the side of the church, short sacramental plays were presented, so called because the Holy Sacrament presided over the people who stood beside the Cathedral. The sacramental short play was used by the first evangelizers to catechize the natives.

It can be readily seen that this is one of the oldest traditions in Mexico City which, as mentioned before, was famous because it mobilized the entire city, which gladly awaited the celebration of this festivity. This mobilization made the Mexican historians and writers of all times take an interest in these festivities.

It is amazing that even though our Capital city is one of the biggest and most populated in the world, this ancient custom still prevails, and punctually, every Corpus Thursday, thousands of residents, with their children dressed like natives, gather around the Holy Sacrament at Mexico's Cathedral.

And it is exciting to see improvised stalls throughout the city selling little mules, now made of different materials, but maintaining the colorful charm which our craftsmen imprint on their work with their magic hands.

These ancient customs give our city a more human, a more spiritual touch and invite us to think about the fact that we are a people with a history, with spiritual values and with the joy of living.

The faith and the soul of our people explain the existence of this noble tradition. It is the cry of a city telling us about our distant past and reminding us that our capital, our great capital, has been and is a noble, welcoming city of which we should be proud.

THE DAY OF MANUELS WITH PICTURESQUE CORPUS CHRISTI MULES

Corpus Christi Thursday, a religious and colorful festivity celebrated on the day in which good and evil fight symbolically, every Thursday after the Pentecost octave, is held fifty days after Easter Sunday. It is said that the official origin of this day dates back to 1246.

Perhaps the very strength of this tradition explains the recent modification of the liturgical calender, which transferred the celebration of this festivity to the following Sunday. The church authorities decided to accept that, with Mexico City inhabitants' deeply rooted custom of celebrating this festivity on Thursday, they continue doing so. The power of tradition conquered the law!

The center of the festivity was the solemn mass at the Cathedral, followed by an imposing procession which began at the Zocalo, where the Holy Eucharist, carried by the archbishop under a canopy, was escorted by the viceregal authorities, the town council, the religious groups, the army, the clergy and the people. Allusive theatrical plays also took place, as well as special music and wares.

The people began their particular colorful seal on this celebration. This was how the mule drivers initiated the custon of decorating their mules in their droves, so that they might be blessed and thus carry offerings of wild flower and country fruit, while they and their families displayed their best colorful clothes.

The custom of the famous little mules, made of *tule* (a tree) and reeds thus originated, as well as the habit of taking the children to the Cathedral, dressed in their popular costumes, *chinas* and *chinacos* (native gowns), with crates filled with fruits and flowers on their backs, as offerings.

Jointly with the celebration of the Holy Eucharist, the persons named *Manuel* also celebrate their Saint's Day, and this gave rise to the people to freely congratulate them humorously, and giving them a mule, maliciously saying, "Congratulations on your day." For this reason, the festivity is often popularly called "The Day of the Little Mules." (The Festivity of *Corpus Christi* coincides with the celebration of the Manuels' Saints Day, because one of Christ's names was Emmanuel. In the new Catholic calendar of saints' days, the celebration of the Manuels changed date, as was the case with many others in the liturgical calendar. However, as we mentioned, the custom of celebrating both on the same day has survived, so that the local church has had to accept this custom.)

Hopefully, the old custom of the fairs, the theatrical representations and the allusive short plays will survive at the Cathedral's atrium, as this would provide a great deal of joy to the bustling city life.

Day of the Dead and its Celebrations in Mexico

Among Mexicans, death has a unique meaning: sometime it appears like an ingrained tradition which establishes its profound roots in the native past; on other occasions, it seems like a stage where remembered figures move and glide by, receiving various kinds of offerings, such as candy, bread, flowers, and spicy and traditional food. Somehow, the tradition is permanent, but it appears more vigorously —like a spontaneous feeling— on November 1 and 2 each year.

The cemetery summons a friendly familial meeting. Relatives kneel around the persons who are no longer among the living, and with their tears they bathe the soil covering their remains, or the offerings are deposited at their tombs. These two attitudes are the feelings towards the people who no longer walk along the worldly ways of life.

The festivity in honor of the faithful deceased is, within Mexican mourning, full of innocent joy and twilight sadness, adorned with brightly colored flowers which nature has created almost specially for these moments: the slender petals of the beautiful flower, the *cempasúchitl* (or *cempoalxochitl*).

This popular custom plays with people's memories, and grief is transformed into smiling faces through the little sugar skulls, with verses warning the living, with irony and charm, that one day they, too, shall be dead, with virtues and flaws that are highlighted in the irregular poems.

Neither fear nor foreboding destroy the Mexican's sense of humor. The best expression of this feeling is found in the great work of José Guadalupe Posada, who transformed death into a vernacular art.

The graveyards where the deceased's remains are found are illuminated with the presence of numberless persons who carry multicolored offerings in their hands. Transit becomes a chorus of murmurs, and under the spiritual dome, each space occupies a place in that five-century-old itinerary. Thus, the original name of *Mixquic* in the surroundings of the Valley of Mexico, within the geography of lakes which in the past distinguished the Tláhuac region, at the dynamic center of Mexican traditions and customs, survived time and history.

Profile of *Mixquic*

The town of Mixquic is located southeast of Mexico City in the Tláhuac delegation. Its present population is 20,000 inhabitants, distributed among four districts and one neighborhood. The main occupation of its inhabitants is agriculture, producing a large amount of vegetables and legumes.

Etymologically, *Mixquic* means "Place of the *mezquites.*" Antonio Peñafiel and Manuel Orozco y Berra affirm that the name is derived from *Mixcalco: Mizclit (Mezquite)*, *Calli* (house) and *Co* (place). Through metaplasma (physical alteration of a word by adding, omitting, or changing letters) it is pronounced Mixquic.

Other authors consider that *Mixquic* is derived from *Miquiztli*, meaning "death" (due to the tradition of revering the dead). Still others claim it is derived from *Mixtli*, as in *Mixtlán* or *Mixteca* meaning "near the clouds."

Based on the hieroglyph formed by two branches over a house, we feel that its etymology should be derived from the reference to a place or house near the *mezquites*.

This town, like Tláhuac, was established on Lake Chalco. Mixquic appears on the maps, with a mark showing the presence of a pier or wharf. Mixquic is the only riverside center outside of the chronological model in the region, as there are no archaic or Teotihuacan remains. Its history dates back to the Postclassic era which began in Culhuacán; that is, during the time of the Aztec expansion. The men from Mixquic mentioned this later when referring to their Toltec influence.

According to Bernal Díaz del Castillo's testimonies, it is known that during the Conquest, Hernán Cortés spent a night in the town of Mixquic and that its inhabitants, as well as the Chalcas and the Xochimilcas were the conqueror's allies.

The first Roman-type church as well as the convent were built in 1537 by the Augustinian friars, among whom were found Jerónimo and Jorge de Avila. The present church dates back to the beginning of the 17th century (1620), and was also built by the Augustinian priests. The Roman tower from the first construction still survives.

Due to the excavations that have been made, a *Chac Mool* was found, rings for a ball game, columns with the figures of Quetzalcóatl, traces of the *Teocalli* and a kind of calendar which was emptied and converted into a baptismal font.

The Augustinian influence, combined with the Dominican influence are outstanding in the Mixquic church. This church was built in three naves, with a Doric-style ceiling. It also has a central column and four smaller columns, a baroque-style dome, and a main altar with an altarpiece five meters high. A second baroque altarpiece is also found, where Saint Andrew, the town's patron saint, is shown. Frescoes made by the Augustinians are found in the atrium, on the left side. Christ appears in one of these, marching towards Calvary. The Consecration is represented on the dome and on the ceiling, showing the Augustinian influence.

COMMEMORATION OF THE DAY OF THE DEAD

This festivity is of pre-Hispanic origin, as the ancient inhabitants of Mixquic already carried out rituals to revere their dead.

The celebration in Mixquic on November 2 has now reached international fame.

This festivity can be summarized as follows. At noon, on October 31, the bells in the church are tolled twelve times, followed by a solemn ringing of the bells, announcing the moment in which dead children arrive. By then, a table decorated with white flowers, glasses of water and a plate with salt is ready in the house. Each candle represents a dead child in the family. Little clay figures and toys for the children are also placed on the table. The candles and the copal resin incense are also lit.

After 7:00 p.m., supper for the children is served, consisting of bread, *atole* (a beverage made with corn meal) or hot chocolate, sweet *tamales* and fruit. More incense is burned.

On November 1, between 8:00 and 9:00 a.m., breakfast for the children is served, with *atole*, hot chocolate, bread and fruit. At 12:00 a.m., the bells ring solemnly at the church, announcing that the children are leaving. The bells are tolled twelve times again, as a sign that the adult dead are now arriving.

In the house, the offerings are adorned with yellow flowers (*cempasúchil*); black candlesticks with large candles are placed on the table, according to the number of dead in the family, as well as glasses of water and salt.

At 12:00 a.m., the chimes for the souls ring out; the families gather around the offerings to pray the rosary for their dead. Upon completing the rosary, each person lights a candle and places it on the table, dedicating it to a particular deceased person, and prays an Our Father. Finally, a candle is lit for the forgotten souls.

At that moment, fruit, bread, jellies, and *tamales* are offered. A new sleeping mat (*petate*) is placed on the floor —when the table is insufficient— benches and chairs are distributed all around so that the dead may be able to sit down and eat; some people have available a clean, tidy bed so the dead may rest. The dead persons' belongings when they were alive are also placed on the table, such as clothes, pick and shovel, robe, hoe, oars, cigars, matches and bottles of liquor.

At the same time, children between seven and eight years of age gather, carrying a bell and a bag to pray at their relatives', friends' and neighbors' houses. Upon terminating, the owner of the house shares the offerings with them and they all sing, "Bellman, my friend, don't invite me to partake, as it will make me ill."

At 12:00 a.m. on November 2, the bells toll twelve times again, announcing that the dead are now leaving. Food is served in the houses, consisting of rice, *mole*, boiled chicken, and even an appetizer. Plates, spoons and jars are placed on the table.

The tombs in the graveyard are tidied. If the graves are children's, they are adorned with white flowers; if they are adults', with yellow flowers.

At 5:00 p.m. the families gather, carrying copal incense and candles to light the way back for the souls. Thus, each person lights a candle for a dead person.

The exchange of offerings among relatives and godparents begins on November 3. When a family arrives, the owner of the house says, "...These are the offerings which the dead left for you."

Thus, the festivity ends, with a touch of joy and togetherness by establishing a bridge between life and death, between the present and the past.

SO WHAT, YOU BALD SKULL, WILL YOU TAKE ME OR WON'T YOU?*

Literary calaveras **

During the pre-Hispanic era, life had no higher purpose than to reach death. Somehow, the native expected death on every occasion: with their or-

---

¿En qué quedamos pelona, me llevas o no me llevas?

** Although the word "calaveras" means "skull," the literary *calaveras* are short, simple poems highlighting the dead person's virtues or flaws.

67

naments, in their calendar; the indestructible goddess, the desirable goddess appeared in their paintings and sculptures. With the fall of the Aztec people, the rest of the native Indian world also fell, with the fascinating acceptance of death.

But, if the idea of salvation is collective for the native, for the Catholic it is personal. It is the individual who counts; Christ's death saves each person in particular. Europe is now emerging from the Dark Ages. The horrors of hell and the Final Judgment are popular themes in poetry, theatre, dancing, painting and engraving. All these concepts reach us through religious education.

And so it happened that while the rigorously Spanish culture produced sonnets in Mexico, like those by Francisco Cervantes de Salazar or the poetry of Sor Juana, the native Indian found a new superposition in the Christian religion. A new series of legendary celebrities emerge during the colonial period: ghosts, witches... All the joyful excitement when facing the great beyond opens its doors to a fantastically native Mexico.

During the second half of the last century, after the consummation of the Independence, a change occurs. The first publications were made, satirizing well-known popular celebrities mournfully. The image is caricatured in these publications, and many of them are accompanied by allusive verses, which were later called *calaveras*.

Graphically, Santiago Hernández , Venegas Arroyo and José Guadalupe Posada —together with poets and engravers— showed a re-creation of this popular tradition in their art. Henceforth, death loses her entire power to intimidate; she is no longer wrapped in a mysterious cloak; she is no longer able to make us fear the darkness. On the contrary, this time she is the opposite of everything that is terrifying; she removed her old clothes and threw them into the wastebasket; her clothes are now modern and cause joy.

In other countries, the word "death" is never pronounced. The Mexican flatters death, woos her. Perhaps Mexicans feel the same fear that others feel, but we see her face to face. The Day of the Dead clearly reflects our attitude before the phenomenon: it is the feast where people sing, eat, laugh, and dance...with Death. The art of the festivity is almost intact among us. Therein, we show all the luxury, all the lavishness that we lack in our daily life. Because of the squandering, real abundance is expected.

Calabaza*

Ayotli

Together with corn and beans, this plant makes up the basic trilogy. Pumpkin is the name by which various species of cucurbits of edible fruit are known. The plant is called *ayotera*, a word of Nahuatl origin, proceeding from *ayotli*; the suffix "tera" has the Spanish influence. The *ayotera* is an annual creeping and also climbing plant with tendril ramifications (filaments adhered to the soil or to walls). There are many types of pumpkin or squash with different fruits; some are eaten when they are tender while others are left until they mature and they are dried, so they can be kept for a long time.

All the parts of this plant, of pre-Hispanic origin, can be used: the stalks, the vines, the fruit and the seeds.

Remains of the Coxcatlán culture (between 2500 to 500 B.C.) were found in the archaeological zone of Tehuacán, Puebla, with traces that this was the first culture that used domestic corn and later added beans, amaranth and squash.

Squash and pumpkin occupy a privileged position both in the pre-Hispanic native cuisine and in the contemporary Mexican cuisine. The stalks and the tender little squash are used to prepare a dish, accompanied with tender corn grains, *chipoctli* (a Nahuatl word: smoked chili) and maguey worms.

A delicious soup is prepared with squash flowers, slices of *poblano* (a chili originating in Puebla), corn grains , chopped *epazote* (a wild spicy herb), and *quelites* (a wild savory plant); it is served with Oaxaca cheese.

One of the varieties of squash is the *chilacayote*. The red *pipian* (a dish prepared with pumpkin seeds, dry chili and meat, including duck) contains this vegetable. A delicious dish, the green pipian is also prepared with pumpkin seeds. The seeds are roasted without the husk and they are ground together with tomatoes, green chili, coriander and *hoja santa* (a large wild leaf with a great deal of flavor). This is seasoned with turkey fat and a little

---

* *Calabaza/Calabacita* (Pumpkin/squash). The enormous fruits of this cucurbit, of American origin, are used in various ways in Mexico, as well as their seeds, their flowers, and in the tiny version, the *calabacita* (little squash or zucchini). *Calabaza en tacha* is prepared with brown sugar or sugar cane.

broth is added. The broth can be made from turkey, chicken, or pork meat.

Another soup is prepared with squash flowers, *epazote*, and tomatoes ground with onion and garlic. The flowers and the *epazote* are chopped and then fried; the ground tomatoes are added and seasoned; enough water is added and finally, a few balls made of corn meal, salt and chopped *hoja santa*. This is simmered until the little balls are cooked.

The delicious squash flower turnovers (*dobladas*) should also be mentioned. These are prepared with corn flour *tortillas* and stuffed with a dish made with chopped onion and *epazote*, fried in vegetable oil, and then clean, chopped squash flowers are added, as well as salt. The pan is covered and allowed to boil two or three minutes. This dish is accompanied by a green or red hot sauce.

Pumpkin is also present in desserts. For example, pumpkin in brown sugar is prepared mainly for the traditional offerings for the Day of the Death in November. This dessert is prepared by cooking the pumpkin in a brown sugar syrup.

One of the most popular typical desserts is the *calabazate* pumpkin prepared as a glazed fruit.

Mexican herbal medicine uses pumpkin in different forms, the best known being against intestinal parasites. A glass of milk is prepared in the morning with pumpkin seeds, removing the husk (a teaspoon of seeds ground with a little water, consumed during ten days). The pulp of the pumpkin is also used to relieve irritations and burns in the skin, and it is applied in poultices. The patients suffering from kidney stones are given a tea made from the pulp of the pumpkin boiled in water.

CEMPASÚCHIL OR CEMPOALXOCHITL

Flower with four hundred petals, or the twenty flowers

Pre-Hispanic tradition

Cempoalxochitl, the flower with four hundred petals —as it was called by the ancient inhabitants of Mexico— was part of the religious rites since far distant times.

The tombs of the dead are covered abundantly with the *cempoalxochitl*

70

flower, and the altars with the offerings for these festivities are also adorned with the same flowers.

The word *cempoalxochitl* also designates a small bright yellow flower, which in some regions is called *pericón* and is abundantly used, from the beginning of autumn when it begins to bloom, to make small crosses which are placed beside the corn fields so that the crops may be good, and they are also placed at the entrance of houses as a good-luck symbol.

But this flower is not merely mystical. It is also a curative plant which the ancient Mexicans greatly appreciated, as it was used to cure different kinds of diseases and maladies.

This beautiful wild flower grows as a weed in places near the crops in the states of Sinaloa, Michoacán, Mexico, Veracruz, Hidalgo, Chiapas, Morelos, in the Valley of Mexico and in other regions.

This Mexican flower has extended its frontiers to many places in the world, where it appears mainly as an ornate plant. In Mexico, the industrialization of the *cempasúchil* has begun to manufacture food for birds, and is being exported in large amounts.

The *cempoalxochitl* leaves are also used to prepare a mixture to eliminate vermin that attack roots of plants. The flower is crushed, using the same amount of water, and is left all night and then a tablespoon dissolved in half a liter of water is applied on the base of the plant.

HE WHO HAS DIED BECOMES GOD

"...the ancients said that when men died, they did not perish,
but that they started to live again, almost as if they were awakening from a dream..."

Fray Bernardino de Sahagún

*When we die,
in truth we do not die
because we live, we resuscitate,
we continue living,
we awaken.
This makes us happy.*

*Do we really live on Earth?
Not forever on Earth,*

71

just a little while here
Even if it should be jade, it breaks;
Even if it should be gold, it breaks;
Even if the feathers were from a quetzal,
they rip
Not forever on Earth,
just a little while here.

Where shall I go? Where?
*On the way to the Dual God**
Perhaps, if luck would have it, to his home,
to the place of the disembodied?
Or perhaps inside heaven?
Or is Earth the place
of the disembodied?

Nahuatl poem

---

* DUAL GOD: A divinity in the Nahuatl culture, called *Ometeotl*. This deity was composed of: *Omecihuatl* (Lady Dual) and *Ometecutli* (Lord Dual), who live at *Omeyocan* (place of duality).

DAY COMMEMORATING THE VIRGIN OF GUADALUPE

ecember 12: all Mexico gathers for the celebration of the Virgin of Guadalupe, a devotion which transcends the religious scope to become a symbol of Mexican nationalism.

An endless parade of pilgrims from the country's four cardinal points appear with their flowers, chants and prayers for the Virgin. A multicolored gathering of dancers perform in the immense esplanade of the old and new Basilicas. A deep, profound feeling of Mexican roots and essence.

And the altar becomes a glitter of lights, roses and hope...

OUR LADY OF GUADALUPE

Her apparition, her sanctuary and her worship

Worship of the Virgin of Guadalupe is the fervent prayer which the Mexican nation raises; it is the immense sigh of tenderness that resounds on its crystalline lakes and on the crest of its volcanoes, the *Popocateptl* and the *Iztaccihuatl*, and is then extended on the waves of its oceans; it is an endless hymn of its love which, resounding from heart to heart in future generations, will reach the lintels of eternity.

The great Spanish historian, Bernal Díaz del Castillo tells us in his unique language, that in Mexico, Cortés gave Gonzalo de Sandoval the following instructions: "On land, go and put a fence on another road that leads from a town called Tepeaquilla."

In Mexico's town council records during the early times of the Conquest, plots of land and sites were requested to plant vegetables, orchards, and farmlands. These same documents present the period in which the town lost its primitive native name and was popularized into Guadalupe. In the records for December 3, 1563, the name of Guadalupe instead of Tepeaquilla was used for the first time.

That poor and humble place was where the Virgin of Guadalupe appeared, according to the tradition which has been preserved and made known extensively from the Mexican language to our own.

THE APPARITIONS

First Apparition

"In December 1531, Juan Diego, a native of Cuautitlan, married to María Lucía, goes from the town where he lives to the Tlatelolco Convent, to hear the mass celebrated by the religious men of Saint Francis. At the foot of the hill called *Tepeyac* which means extremity or sharp, jutting ridge, he hears soft, delicate music on the highest part of the little hill. He sees a beautiful rainbow, and on it a lovely Lady, as she is presented in her image. She stops him and asks him maternally where he is going. The native Indian replies that he is going to Tlatelolco to hear mass. The Virgin tells him that she is the Mother of God, and that it is her desire that a church be built in that place, and that he must go to see the bishop with her message; that he must tell the Bishop what he has seen and heard."

Second Apparition

"The Virgin waits for the reply to her message and the native appears before her and tells her that he is willing to be at her entire service, but that the bishop does not believe his words. The native thinks that a person with a better representation than his own should take the message. He tells the Virgin that the bishop insists that a sign should be sent to prove his mandate tangibly.

"As the bishop doubts the native's words, he sends trustworthy persons to follow him, but Juan Diego loses these people, and full of resentment, they tell the prelate of the happenings, asking that the native be punished for deceiving them."

Third Apparition

"Juan Diego returns before the Virgin and tells her what the bishop has said and she promises to give him the sign that the prelate requested, indicating that he return the following day. The native does not go as he had promised, because when he arrives home he finds his uncle, Juan Bernardino, seriously ill with *coclixtle* (typhoid fever of typhus) and he goes for a doctor and also to the Convent of Santiago Tlatelolco for a priest. Juan Diego, embarrassed about what has happened, takes another road in order to avoid

74

meeting the Virgin, but she intercepts him and appears again surrounded by a white cloud, as clearly as the first time he saw her.

"The native, ashamed, apologizes and the Virgin comforts him, advising him that his uncle will be well again.

"The Lady appears before Juan Bernardino and he, of course, recovers his health."

Fourth Apparition

"The native, comforted and satisfied with what the Virgin says, asks her for the sign which the bishop requests. She commands him to climb to the peak of the hill and among the ridges and boulders, he will find a garden of Castillian roses, which he places on his coarse robe and returns to show her the flowers. The lady takes the roses in her hands and tells the native that he must present them to the bishop. In that very moment, the painting of the miraculous image was made, through God's power.

"Juan Diego, in the presence of the prelate Juan de Zumárraga, extends the robe and the painted image appears, just as it can be seen today.

"The bishop falls on his knees and is the first to worship the Mother of God."

(Quotations from Higinio Vázquez de Santa Ana)

Professor Ignacio Manuel Altamirano says the following about the naive and poetical Guadalupan tradition: "It is a tradiation so well accepted and beloved, that not only all the races which inhabit Mexican soil are in agreement, but also, surprisingly, all the parties that have stained the country with blood during half a century due to their political and religious beliefs."

The image began to be worshipped in the bishop's private chapel until Christian piety built first an hermitage and later several churches, among which the Illustrious National Basilica is outstanding, presently our old Basilica of Guadalupe.

THE ILLUSTRIOUS NATIONAL BASILICA

On July 15, 1746, Pope Benedict XIV gave his superior approval for the erection of the Collegiate, and on March 6, 1749, the Archbishop of Mexico, Manuel Rubio y Salinas carried out that commandment.

Not less than six million pesos were spent in building the Basilica, and all that money came from the alms of the faithful.

The old temple was a wonder of art, and surprised observers due to its magnificence, splendor and grandeur. In another period, Vázquez de Santa Ana said:

"The church glows with the donation of all the faithful, and its wealth amounts to two million pesos, either in the construction of the superb sanctuary, or in the silver objects such as candlesticks, bouquets, and other pieces, and in the magnificent corridor that joins the presbytery with the choir.

"The series of sacred glasses, tabernacles, chalices made of rich stones, chandeliers for candles and lamps were also very valuable, and in order to appreciate the value of these ornate objects, it would be necessary to say that one of the lamps alone weighed seven hundred silver marks.

"The Basilica has three spacious naves, it is beautiful and vast, the construction is solid and severe; superb pillars support the slender arches and the high-rising domes and the image of the Virgin of Guadalupe is found in the magnificent tabernacle mounted on a silver frame."

THE VIRGIN OF GUADALUPE'S CORONATION

The Virgin of Guadalupe's coronation was an outstanding event which took place at the Basilica of the miraculous image.

The Roman See granted the corresponding authorization to place a golden crown on the image and his Eminence, Doctor Próspero María Alarcón y Sánchez de la Barquera carried out the solemn ceremony, accompanied by all the prelates of the Mexican Church, as well as others from different American countries. This solemn ceremony is without precedent in our history.

The royal crown was made with the gold and silver donated by Mexican ladies and, according to experts it is without equal as a work of art in the, New World and even surpasses the famous crown of Charles the Great in Europe.

Antonio Plancarte y Navarrete, abbot of the Collegiate, was in charge of performing the magnificent Coronation of the image.

GUADALUPAN TRADITION IN COLONIAL MEXICO

The festivity of the Virgin of Guadalupe is no doubt the most splendid of

76

all in the country. Two famous Mexican writers, Manuel Payno and Ignacio Manuel Altamirano describe it as follows:

Payno states:

"The crowd of pilgrims arriving from all over the national territory to the *Villa de Guadalupe* is admirable; the city is emptied and everyone goes to the country to enjoy a picnic filled with joy and lasting pleasure, half profane, half religious.

"After hearing mass, exactly in the Collegiate or directly outside, due to the large crowds, they go to the *Capilla del Pocito* (Chapel of the Little Well and drink a great amount of briny, sulfurous water in copper jars. From the *Capilla del Pocito*, they go to the Hill and there they commend themselves again to the Virgin; then they have lunch in the midst of the thistles and the rough mountain ground. Lunch consists of dry goat legs, called *chito*, with a hot chili sauce prepared with *pulque* which they call *borracha* sauce.

"After lunch, they sleep a *siesta* under the shade of a boulder or an old wall, and at sunset they go down to the square to buy little cakes made of ground corn with sweets, the size of a coin; these little cakes are not made in any other part of country, except at the temple, and they are known as *gorditas de la Villa*.

"In the late evening, all the families return walking, some will be praying the rosary, other singing and all of them loving the Virgin of Guadalupe, carrying branches of poplar, a pitcher with sulfurous water, and their handkerchiefs and pockets full of *gorditas*, all of which are the trophies which they bring back from the pilgrimage and the gifts that the children and relatives who remained at home are anxiously awaiting."

Altamirano says:

"One of the most important festivities in Mexican Catholicism is celebrated on this date, certainly the most important due to its popularity, its universality, as both natives and educated people participate. Juan Diego or Don Quijote, Martín Garatuza and Guzmán de Alfarache. Everyone is equally enthusiastic, all are filled with exemplary piety, and on that day they go to pray to the Virgin, to eat *chito* with *borracha* sauce in the fortunate Tepeyac Hill, and to drink the white nectar of the Apam plains.

Positively, anyone who wishes to see and study an authentic description of Mexican life, whoever wishes to become acquainted with one of the most constant traditions of our people, should go to the *Villa de Guadalupe*.

"Mexico Ciy moves to the foot of the Sanctuary, from morning to evening, forming a confused, jumbled, multicolored, picturesque crowd, difficult to describe.

"All the races of the ancient colony are present, all the different classes, all the lineages who live in our democracy; all the costumes of our civilization, all the opinions of our politics, all the varieties of vice, as well as the masks of virtue in Mexico.

"The aristocratic lady wearing a Spanish shawl or a feathered hat mingles with the tangled native woman from Cuautitlan or Azcapotzalco; the elegant young man blends with the rough, bearded muleteer from Ixmiquilpan or the half-naked native from the regions of Texcoco, Coatepec or Zumpango, or with the dirty leper from Palma or Santa Ana. And there are no social considerations: everone walks and mixes among the crowd. The lady crushes her dress against the humble daughter from the people, with the trousers of the pilgrim coming from afar. It is impossible to enter the church, except by pushing; it is impossible to circulate through the square, except by being led by an inevitable stream.

"After the twelve o'clock solemn mass, accompanied by an orchestra of voices celebrated by a Pontifical representative, and with the presence of the Collegiate priests and by the abbot who worships the Virgin of Guadalupe, during which the natives dance with their Indian costumes, with the odd ornamental coverings of ancient eras, that is, feathered headgear and bright-colored fantastic costumes, the crowd disperses through the town streets, or the Villa, which is traditionally called *Villa de Guadalupe*, and has officially received the name of Guadalupe Hidalgo, a name which has not caught on, and then the people return to Mexico."

OUTSTANDING EVENTS THAT HAVE
HAPPENED AT THE *BASILICA DE GUADALUPE*

On July 11, 1794, the illustrious Count of Revillagigedo delivered a command to the Marquis of Branciforte at the *Villa de Guadalupe*.

—The picture frame with the image of the Virgin of Guadalupe was taken from the Church of Atotonilco, and was the liberator Hidalgo's banner with his troops shouting, "Long Live Our Lady of Guadalupe!" "Long live Ferdinand VII!" "Long live America!" "Down with the bad government!"

—The illustrious leader, Jose María Morelos, officially recommended worship of the Holy Virgin of Guadalupe, and sent an incognito emissary to the Collegiate to pray at the feet of the Virgin, offering a valuable gift.

—The first president of the Republic, Félix Fernández, changed his name and surname to the symbolic name of Guadalupe Victoria when the War of Independence broke out, and carried this name until his death.

—Agustín de Iturbide, the liberator, created the Order of Guadalupe.

—The Council of the Collegiate of Guadalupe gave the First Constitutional Congress a copy of the original image to augment devotion to the Native Virgin. This copy remained in the Hall of Sessions of the Chamber of Representatives for several years.

—On August 11, 1859, the president of the Republic, Division General Antonio López de Santa Anna reestablished the Order of Guadalupe.

—The government of Juárez issued a decree signed by Melchor Ocampo on August 11, 1859, eliminating religious festivities, and leaving only the festivity of December 12.

—The Battle of May 5th is waged at the Hill of Guadalupe in Puebla, where the Virgin's Sanctuary is found. The Republican army is victorious, under the command of General Ignacio Zaragoza.

—Emperor Maximilian makes an official visit to the Collegiate, accompanied by Empress Charlotte Amalia, and the Order of Guadalupe is reestablished on April 10, 1865.

—The new Basilica of Guadalupe, where the image of the "Patron of Mexico" is still worshipped, is inaugurated on December 12, 1976.

BLESSING OF THIEVES' HANDS

"We are all God's children!" proclaims with conviction and certainty the priest of Mexico's slums: La Merced, Tepito, Candelaria de los Patos and other similar places.

And in the light of this divine truth, which is the basis of universal fraternity, the paradox crumbles and no one is surprised that the native thief resorts to the loving care of the Virgin of Solitude in a private ceremony, seeking understanding and protection.

ABOUT THE AUTHOR

Attorney Sebastián Verti —citizen of Sinaloa by birth, and ex-student at the Universidad Militar Latinoamericana— was oriented towards the social communicaions area and, within this area, towards the transmission of Mexico's folkloric values since the early stages of his life. This explains why the author of this book first explored the area of artistic and cultural publications jointly with his university studies in Law and Communication Sciences.

He travelled to Europe after obtaining his degrees, to carry out postgraduate studies.

He took various courses on American pre-Columbian and viceregal culture in Spain. Thus, he reaffirmed his decision to devote himself to disclose vernacular art and culture.

He returned to Mexico upon completing his higher education and dedicated his efforts to the production of children's books. For this reason, he created the "Cycle of Shows for Recreative Initiation," a program with a bro-ad sense of aesthetic education designed as a complement to school lessons. Since then, this well-known Mexican nationalist has desired that all his activities carry a message of optimism.

Later, as a theatrical producer and stage director, Sebastián Verti has directed his efforts towards the promotion of shows with an eductional content, tending, as well, to strengthen national unity. This work has been possible owing to the sponsorship of various cultural organizations from the private sector and from the Government.

At that time —the seventies— attorney Miguel Alemán Valdés, ex-president of Mexico, invited him to collaborate with the National Tourism Council, an institution where attorney Verti directed a cultural program for more than ten years. In this program, the following cycles were outstanding: "The Mexican Literary Tradition" and "Conservation and Diffusion of National Traditions and Customs."

In view of the benefits contributed by the program to the revitalization and conservation of folklore, attorney Verti has received countless awards from national and foreign institutions. These distinctions include, among others, his designation as international delegate of the Bethlehem Association in Madrid —belonging to the Spanish Bethlehem Federation (Federación Española Belenista [FEB]), with a silver medal from the Most Excellent City Council— from the *Universalis Foederatio Praesepística (Un Foe Prae)*. Owing to this distinction, he was able to found the Bethlehem Association of Mexico, the Board in Favor of Strengthening Mexican Traditions and the First Alliance for the Defense of Traditions in Mexico, organisms which he presently presides and where, naturally, he participates actively to promote Mexican nationalism.

Supported by the media —where he is a radio and television commentator, attorney Sebastián Verti has devoted twenty-five years of fruitful work in favor of maintaining our country's cultural legacy.

Festival dedicated to the Christ Child, celebrated in the old neighborhood of Coyoacán (Mexico City).

(Left) The three kings: Mechior, Gaspar and Baltasar.
(Below) Spectacular Mexican Ring-Shaped Cake of the Kings decorated with poinsettia flowers, presented in Paris, France.

The sentimental tradition of the Blessing of the Little Animals.

The celebration of Candlemas.
(Right and *below)*

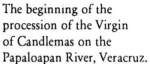

The beginning of the
procession of the Virgin
of Candlemas on the
Papaloapan River, Veracruz.

The Christ Child who plays and
sings, rises from his crib to look
for his toys in the darkness,
the Niñopa of Xochimilco.

The Altar of Sorrows, prelude to Holy Week. It commemorates the suffering of Jesus Christ.

The refreshing, sweet water
of the woman Samaritan.

Lent cuisine, legacy of the pre-Hispanic culinary tradition.

(Below) The sublime ceremony of the washing of feet. *(Above)* The visit to the seven houses.

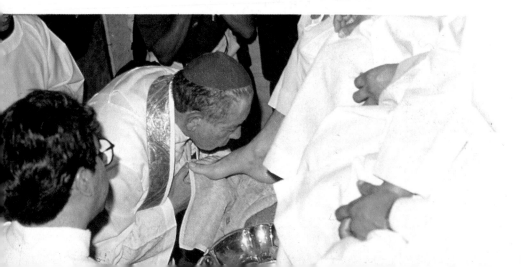

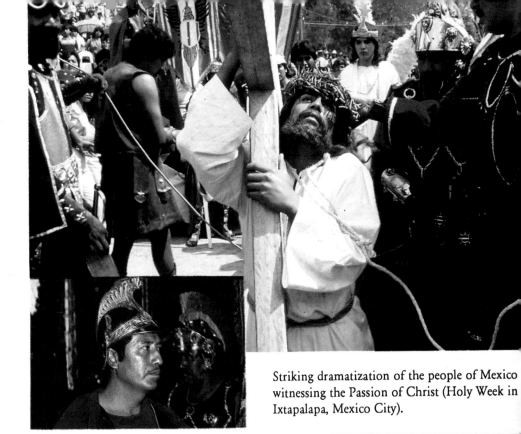

Striking dramatization of the people of Mexico witnessing the Passion of Christ (Holy Week in Ixtapalapa, Mexico City).

Holy Week crafts.

Papier maché Judases before they are blown up.

Panorama of the Mexican
Suppers with chocolate of Easter.

Delicious sweet *tamales*.

Home-made, freshly baked country cookies.

Tiny picturesque mules from the Thursday of Corpus Christi.

The traditional Day of the Dead "Catrina," the seductive skeleton.

Dramatic Day of the Dead setting, illuminated by candlelight.

"So what, Bald Skull (Death), will you take me or won't you?"

Food prepared for the dead who return from the otherworld to feast.

Empress of America.
The Virgin of Guadalupe,
the symbolic Mother of all
Mexicans.

Praying to the Queen of Mexico.

The Piñata, originally a
tool used to teach
the Christian faith.

Strength and character of Mexican clay (ceramic pots).

Mexican craftsmen, as if with magical hands, create a variety of figures for crèches.

The fantasy and color of Christmas decorations.

Sculptures made of radishes in the state of Oaxaca.

MEXICAN CHRISTMAS

HE *POSADAS*: THE HISTORY OF A TRADITION

Meaning of the nine Posadas

The *Posadas* are festivities created for the purpose of provoking expectation towards the birth of Jesus. Therefore, they are held during nine days which, according to religious tradition, represent the nine days between December 16 and 24, and the request for shelter and human warmth which Mary and Joseph made while awaiting the coming of the Child Jesus.

The *Posada* is a colorful community festival, with the songs of litanies and carols, breaking the *piñata** and a banquet with a variety of dishes, desserts, and punch.

These nine days were initiated with the Christmas masses which the Augustinian priests celebrated in their convents during Colonial times. Later, they moved from the churches to the *haciendas* (farms) and ranches that had a chapel, and then to the mansions of the wealthy and finally to the neighborhoods. They acquired their present form in the early nineteenth century.

To ask for *posada* (shelter) has been one of the most important aspects of the Christmas festivities since days gone by, as it constitutes the difficult journey of the Holy Pilgrims from Nazareth to Bethlehem. This began when the singers sang a Christmas carol and then the litany to the Virgin began. A few children carried the Holy Pilgrims with the angel and the indispensable little mule, and when they arrived at one of the homes, they asked for *posada* (shelter) and prayed. At the end of the journey, the *piñata* was broken.

Although foreign customs and rites have influenced Mexican traditions, Christmas in our country will never die because it represents one of the most profound expressions adopted by the natives, from the time in which the coming of the Child Jesus was commemorated, with carols, Christmas litanies, *posadas*, Nativity scenes, *piñatas* and the use of the poinsettia (the Christmas Eve flower) as an emblem.

---

* Further ahead, on page 88 an entire chapter is devoted to these spectacular and festive handicrafts.

Today it is difficult for us to know the way in which a *Posada* was celebrated when our grandparents and our parents lived: nine days (from
December 16 to 24) symbolizing the wait for the coming of the Child Jesus,
and the petition for shelter and human warmth which Mary and Joseph
made more than two thousand years ago; nine days where the representation of the Holy Family was not missing, as well as the *piñatas,* sweets, candy,
and a variety of dances to complete the event. But allow the testimonies of
other times speak to us in detail about how the *Posadas* were in Mexico.

Testimonies

Antonio García Cubas in *El libro de mis recuerdos* (The Book of My Memories) (1904) recalls the *Posadas,* the Nativity scenes, the Christmas masses and
the Midnight mass, as well as the Pastourelles; he refers to an era which by
then was long past: the time of his own childhood in 1832.

There is an important difference between customs today and those of
1920, and those celebrated in 1840, described by García Cubas, which almost coincide with those masterfully described by José Tomás de Cuéllar,
born in this same Mexico City only two years before the author of *El libro
de mis recuerdos.*

The origin of these celebrations can be considered immemorial. Mari-
ano de Carcer in his 1945 article "Posibles orígenes de las típicas Posadas
mexicanas" (Possible Origins of Typical Mexican *Posadas*), he merely affirms
that they came from Andalucía and that it was a worship "bequeathed by
the colonizers, and celebrated during many centuries in private homes and
convents." However, it is possible to imagine that this celebration perhaps
coincided with a festivity of the ancient inhabitants of Anahuac —as the
same thing happened in the case of the festivity of the Virgin of Guadalupe— as this is the only means of explaining the deep, extraordinary and
exceptional roots that these festivities have achieved among our people,
especially in the past, and expressed with an enthusiasm which is missing in
other festivities, for example Pentecost or Corpus Christi —which are much
more celebrated in other countries. There is no information available regarding the popular commemoration of these nine days, which make this
festivity particularly Mexican, and we would say, pertaining to the Capital,
as Christmas is celebrated in other parts of the country, as in Querétaro, for
example, but the *Posadas* are not.

Investigator Germán Andrade Labastida claims that the *posadas* originated in the small village of San Agustín Acolman, that is, almost under the shadow of the pyramids in Teotihuacan, the sacre place of our native forefathers. He writes that: "The Aztecs celebrated the birth of *Huitzilopochtli** with a great deal of splendor. And, according to Doctor de la Cerna, this ceremony took place precisely during the Christmas season. All night, and during the following day, a celebration was held in every home, where the guests were invited to partake of delicious food and some small statues or idols made with an edible paste called *tzoatl*, prepared with blue corn, ground and roasted, mixed with black honey from the *maguey*."

Marchioness Calderón de la Barca describes the last Posada that a family in Mexico City celebrated almost one hundred and fifty years ago, in her famous letters regarding Mexican life:

"This is the last evening of the so-called *Posadas*, a strange combination of devotion and amusement, but a very tender picture: an army of children dressed like angels joined the procession; their gowns were made of white feathers, an abundance of diamonds, of gauze and white satin shoes embroidered in gold; young men dressed as shepherds and a wonderful Nativity scene. We all returned to the parlor: angels, shepherds and other guests, and there was dancing until dinner time."

The problems which the country might be facing did not matter even in the worst political or economic crises, Mexican families continued celebrating the Christmas festivities. Sometimes the setting was limited to the privacy of the home, but on other occasions the streets, the small plazas and the city squares became the ideal place to reaffirm our national customs. No family, regardless of how poor it might be, did not decide to be a host for one of the nine *Posadas*.

The group of people who went out on the streets, together with the musicians in order to prolong the festivity, were described in detail by the newspapers of the period, and since so much passion prevailed, the people who attended the *Posadas* made an appointment for a "Godparents' Dance," which was generally held on the first Thursday of the following year.

Andrade writes:

"The surprising similarity of this Aztec ritual festivity with the festivity which recalls the birth of Jesus Christ, made the Augustinian priests use it

---

* *Huitzilopochtli*: Aztec war god, the most important. His name means Southern Hummingbird, Sinister Hummingbird or Left-Handed Hummingbird.

to instill the new religion on the Aztecs. Therefore, during the same days which the Aztecs used for their Christmas festivities, the priests represented plays during each of the nine days prior to December 25, with people dressed in costumes recalling those of Titus Vespasian's and Tiberius' times, the different journeys that the patriarch Joseph, the carpenter, made with his wife Mary, in order to comply with the precept of the census to which all the Jews were submitted. Thus, the home festivities known as *Posadas* were born."

Religiously, the nine journeys also symbolized Mary's nine months of pregnancy. Andrade adds, "The religious Augustinian friar, Diego de Soria, prior of the Saint Augustine Acolman Convent, obtained a papal bull from Pope Sixtus V during his stay in Rome, to celebrate the so-called Christmas masses in New Spain. These masses should be celebrated from December 16 to 24 each year.

But it seems that eventually, people began to refuse to celebrate these festivities in the atriums of the churches or in convents —perhaps due to the season's cold weather, and gradually they went back to the native custom of celebrating the festivities at home, with characteristic traces of the pre-Hispanic rites, such as gifts of little figures and the distribution of candy and sweets, (such as those which we have sometimes seen), ending with the final ceremony of breaking the *piñata*, about which Andrade explains:

"The symbolism of breaking the *piñata* is the following: the colorfully dressed pot represents Satan or the spirit of evil, who with his appearance attracts humanity. The candy found inside the pot represent the unknown pleasures which Satan offers man in order to attract him to his kingdom; the blindfolded person represents faith, which must be blind and will be in charge of destroying the evil spirit. Altogether, the struggle which man must wage, availing himself of faith to destroy evil passions."

Substitution of one festivity for another is neither new nor strange to our customs, although we cannot claim that it is exclusive. The secular power of the *Tonantzin* festivities on the Tepeyac hill constitutes ample proof of the above, as they explain the impressive rigor of the worship of the Virgin of Guadalupe.

We can consider another example from a distant country. When the Americans occupied Spain at the end of the Second World War, they wanted to eliminate the worship which was essentially military, towards Emperor Meiji. Nevertheless, nowadays a great "Festivity of Culture" is celebrated precisely on the same three days of the year and at the same place where the warrior was formerly remembered and worshipped. Therefore, it is not surprising that the "Festivity of Culture" is so successful.

Mexico's ancient history is full of anecdotes about priests' discoveries of little idols buried under the Catholic altars. Thus, the new worship leaned on an ancient one, on an old tradition, on a deeply ingrained custom. A single explanation of this kind would suffice to justify the great power which the celebration of the *Posadas* had in Mexico during centuries.

A few years ago, the *Posadas* were celebrated in theatres, in night clubs and dance halls, and not only in private homes; and a mere specter of these Posadas was still maintained in the churches.

During the 20's and the 30's, the stalls with *piñatas,* sweets, pilgrims, toys for gifts, moss, hay, dry fruit, candy, peanuts, limes, oranges, *tejocotes* (a small juicy fruit) which García Cubas saw in the Zócalo (the main square of the City in downtown were installed in the northern part of the Alameda Central, from San Diego to the National Theatre which later became *Palacio de Bellas Artes* (Palace of Fine Arts). This large marketplace had mechanical games for children, merry-go-rounds, and the wheel of fortune. At some time during the administration of President Abelardo Rodríguez, who enjoyed gambling, they even had cardboard bingo. When these stalls disappeared in La Alameda, they were established for a short time on the street Ejido (now the western part of Avenida Juárez), from *El Caballito* (the Little Horse which is the popular name of the sculpture of Carlos IV) to the Revolution Monument, which was formerly the unfinished Legislative Palace. Then, the *piñatas*, the fruit and all the other things for the *Posadas* were withdrawn from this place and taken to the San Juan marketplace, which has disappeared, or the San Cosme marketplace, which has moved.

Those who have written about the *Posadas* often regret that the religious portion has been disappearing, at the expense of the social aspect.

Also, it is too bad that the dancing, the banquets and the drinking which the *Posadas* originated began to be forgotten and started to disappear. The tenants of the neighborhood apartments no longer gather to distribute the dates for the festivities, the children of a single patio no longer exchange invitations to cover the nine day-festivities.

García Cubas ends an account of wandering through the patios and halls of the house: "Once the litany ended, during which firecrackers were thrown into the air, the procession stopped and asked for the *Posada* (for shelter). To this end, the singers, usually beautiful young girls, were divided in two groups, one of which remained in the chosen room and the other group with the walking group and with most of the crowd."

The following classification was published in the newspaper *El Monitor* in 1886:

Posadas *for praying*

Grandmother with her spectacles, or the best aunt in the family calls all the inhabitants in the house to come near her; they pray the litany, the nine-day prayers, the rosary...and off to sleep go the children, after kissing Father's hand. Those who are present at these posadas do not perceive even the smell of sweets.

Posadas *for children*

The litany is sung, one or two jugs are broken, sweets and candy are eaten, a little conversation, and then to wrap up, as the nights are cold.

Private Posadas

Small dances, where everyone jumps to the rhythm of the piano; every once in a while, a clavichord joins the music. The evening is spent this way: there are no sweets, nor cold water, nor sugar cubes for the cough.

Posadas *for the area*

These are now mostly legends. The *Jornadas* (day's journey), as they were also called, had nine consecutive nights of festivities in a celebration which was originally entirely religious and later became a joyful combination of angels, shepherds, guests, *piñatas*, gifts and dancing.

The Posada *Fair and the* piñata *in the State of Mexico*

Acolman, a small municipality in the State of Mexico, of only 87 square kilometers, is internationally famous because it is near the archaeological zone of San Juan Teotihuacan and because the outstanding Augustinian ex-Convent was located in its territory, an architectural jewel of the 16th century that has now become a museum and is a rare example of the Plateresque architecture in Mexico.

This beautiful Augustinian building has striking altarpieces and mural paintings, where various icons and craftsmen's work from native communities are combined.

Its facade shows an interesting series of ornamental elements, beautifully carved with the region's flora and fauna. In the first section of the nave's left wall inside the church, the mural painting of an ornate altarpiece, made a tempera, is outstanding. Beautiful paintings, executed al fresco representing saints, bishops, cardinals and popes are outstanding on the dome.

Its main cloister is contemporary with the church's facade, Renaissance style, with pillars decorated with vegetable motifs, interpreted in the native way. The cross at the entrance is outstanding, located in front of the main entrance and is an interesting sample of native interpretation with the symbols of Christ's Passion.

On August 5, 1586, Diego de Soria, prior of the convent which sheltered the Augustines, obtained the Papal Bull (*Apud Sanctum Marcum*)* granting authorization to perform the so-called Christmas Masses, which were carried out from December 16 to 24 each year (dates in effect in our times), and which we now call *Posadas*. It became a custom for the priests to invite the people to break the decorated jugs, symbolizing evil, when the masses ended. The jug should be destroyed by hitting it with a stick so that the fruit and candy, symbols of goodness, could be enjoyed by the people present. Thus, our *piñatas* were born.

Evidently, the masses were the origin of the beautiful December traditions in our country.

A de luxe program

The tradition of the *Posadas* and the *piñatas* has been maintained for many years. In 1985, the first *Piñata* Fair took place. Many people from different communities gathered to participate in the creation of *piñatas* and cultural and athletic events. This custom still continues, and is organized with more projection and force.

---

* Meaning "according to Saint Mark." The name of papal bulls is taken from the words with which the document begins thus, the name of the event.

Each year, this tradition takes place from December 14 to 23, under the name of *Feria de la Posada y la Piñata* (Fair of the *Posada* and the *Piñata*). To this end, careful research was made of the traditions and origins of these December festivities, and the investigators reached the conclusion that, in effect, the *piñata* was born as a result of the *Posadas*; thus, the name of the event.

During the fair, bullfights are held, the bird-men of Papantla, Veracruz, fly; Nativity scenes and Pastourelles are exhibited; groups of regional dancing perform, and our traditional *palenque* (a typical Mexican fair with cockfights and other amusements) and popular dances are not missed, in the evenings; typical restaurants and stalls with typical Mexican food participate; crafts as well as colorful *piñatas* and products from the region are exhibited and sold.

Very near the capital

San Agustín Acolman is located only 40 kilometers from Mexico City, on kilometer 38 of the highway leading to San Juan Teotihuacan. You take *Avenida Insurgentes Norte* to the city limits, passing through *Indios Verdes*; from this point, you travel around 15 kilometers to the place where the new booth and the old free highway are separated from the toll superhighway. The route is shorter and it is more convenient to follow the signals indicating *cuota* (toll). If you follow the free highway, you will pass through interesting places. Acolman is located on the old highway, but it can be seen from the superhighway, and the detour is on kilometer 38.

Acolman has sixteen communities and eight neighborhoods, showing that it is one of the biggest towns in the State of Mexico and has deep historical roots dating back from the pre-Hispanic era.

THE PIÑATAS

The Mexican *piñata* is the most attractive and influential toy in Mexican families during the Christmas season.

The *piñata* stimulates unrestrained high spirits, due to the particular joy derived from a collective conscience —acknowledgement of the Savior of the World, by remembering and celebrating the birth of the baby Jesus.

The *piñata* is a wonderful, beautiful and spectacular toy, unfortunately short-lived, considering its manufacture requires time and effort to achieve its beauty and perfection in order to be present during the Christmas festivities, with its enormous power of unity and joy.

The *piñata*, taken form the verb *apiñar* (to cram, tie, join or amass) is derived from the word *piña* (pineapple), which with the passing of time intended to imitate animals and fruits, and anything else that the imagination could conceive.

The Italian *pignata* was present during the first Christmases in New Spain. The magical hands of Mexican craftsmen took the clay pots and transformed them —with crepe paper— into *mameyes*, guava apples, oranges, *papayas*, radishes, carrots, onions, dahlias, stars, birds, ships, and many other objects.

Julio Prieto declared: "A certain oriental influence is noted as far as the decoration with crepe paper is concerned." This could be true, because from the beginning of colonization, there were certain contacts with lands in the Far East.

Salvador Novo in his book *Acta sobre piñatas* (Report on Piñatas) helped to clarify the hypothesis regarding the origin of these Mexican works of art, with this valid question as a reply, "Doesn't it seem that the handling of the *piñata* by a person who pulls the rope that sustains it to keep it as far away as possible from its attackers has a bit of the Mexican kite (*papalote*) in it?"

At the same time amusement with artificial butterflies also formed part of the first Pastourelles and crèches organized with living people during the period when religious principles were taught (catechism).

Based on the above, some historians locate the origin of the *piñatas* in China, and point out that they were taken to Spain and Sicily by the Arabs, and then to America during the 17th century, in the commercial fleet known as *La Nao de China* (Merchant Chinese Ships).

Regarding the *piñatas* with which the *Posadas* ended in Acolman, these *piñatas* started to be broken in the homes of the people until they became simple domestic ceremonies that intended to carry the following message:

THE CLAY POT, COLORFULLY DECORATED, REPRE-
SENTS SATAN OR THE SPIRIT OF EVIL, WHO WITH HIS
APPEARANCE ATTRACTS HUMANITY.

THE SWEETS SYMBOLIZED THE UNKNOWN PLEA-
SURE WHICH HE OFFERS MANKIND TO ATTRACT HIM
TO HIS KINGDOM.

THE BLINDFOLDED PERSON IS LIKE FAITH, WHICH MUST BE BLIND, AND WILL BE IN CHARGE OF DESTROYING THE EVIL SPIRIT.

THIS IS THE STRUGGLE WHICH MAN MUST SUSTAIN, AVAILING HIMSELF OF FAITH TO DESTROY EVIL PASSIONS.

Artemio Del Valle Arizpe declared that in Spain *piñatas* were broken during the so-called "*Piñata* Sunday," after Ash Wednesday, and he assumes that a Spaniard brought the custom, which he managed to implement here, and was later transfered from Holy Week to another religious celebration.

Thus, the *piñata* was established in Mexico, as the result of a combination of pre-Hispanic and European traditions, whereby the struggle of good against evil is implicitly present.

The evolution of the form and content of *piñatas* offers curious information. During the 19th century, *piñatas* were not broken, as they were made in pieces, tied with colored ribbons which should be pulled, so that the gifts and sweets might be within the reach of the people present. Another type of *piñata* was filled with white doves, and another kind, for fun and pranks, containing confetti, flour, water, mice or black *sapodilla*.

THE PASTOURELLES

Teaching and amusement

The Pastourelles together with the Posadas constitute the prelude of the Mexican Christmas.

The Pastourelle is a lovely, tender and naive scenic representation, festive and joyful, which refers to events prior to the coming of Jesus and culminate with the innocent splendor of the manger and the shepherds' worship.

The living images of the "Nativities" in churches, plazas, and gardens which the followers of Bethlehem (*belenistas*) place in all the corners of the city, are an example of this tradition.

The Pastourelle, as a scenic and literary genre, had its roots in the Spanish religious theatre which was in fashion during the 16th century. It was used and adapted by the missionaries as an instrument to evangelize the natives of America.

90

You must remember that the Spanish religious theatre follows, or is at least inspired by the classical Greek theatre, which is a splendid combination of divine and human characters within the framework of a dramatization whereby the destiny of the gods and men occupy the theme's main role.

With this inspiration, Spanish dramas integrate God, the Holy Spirit and the Virgin as the main characters in their relationship with human beings, impressing upon them a religious moral, and a message for the purpose of exalting Christian faith.

The first missionaries who arrived in Mexico noticed that the natives of Anahuac lacked a real writing system and had to face this problem. They solved it through the use of graphic means which were familiar to our ancestors. Thus, they perceived that the religious theatre was a wonderful instrument for their purpose, as it met a didactic function.

The representation of the birth of Jesus was initiated by the Franciscans in the Acolman Convent in 1528 as a living scenic image, creating the proper atmosphere with preaching and songs.

The transition from the scenic image to the Pastourelle found its explanation in these facts. It was not a formal theatrical performance, but rather a popular representation of the events surrounding the birth of Christ. Certainly, the fundamental point spun around the characters and the divine happenings, but native ingenuity was combined with their humorous nature and in this way celebrities were born which would become classical, such as Gila, Bato, Bras, Menga, Celfa and others, with the common characteristic that they are all shepherds · are the first to worship the Child Jesus in the manger in Bethlehem. And that is why they are called Pastourelles.

The Pastourelles are humorous and joyful, with an innocent, country humor where even Lucifer and his court of "little devils" appear with naive wickedness, who provide special tenderness to these representations, to awaken noble feelings of love towards our fellow men, as well as universal fraternity.

This is the reason why this genre has spread throughout the towns as a representation in open spaces. This genre has been rescued from the streets by valuable writers, such as Joaquín Fernández de Lizardi, *The Mexican Thinker*, for the purpose of imbuing it with dignity.

THE BRANCH IS HERE!

Typical Christmas tradition in Veracruz

The Branches are a popular tradition which are mainly located on the leeward region of the State of Veracruz (Medellín, La Mixtequilla, Alvarado, Tlacotalpan, Cosamaloapan, Tesechoacan, etcetera), although this expression has spread throughout all of Veracruz and has even reached some towns in Chiapas and Tabasco.

It is difficult to determine its origin in space and time. However, like many of our expressions, it is the result of the permanent interrelation between Hispanic, Mesoamerican and Negro cultures.

Originally, and in some places where the tradition has been maintained, this festivity began on December 16, by selecting, cutting and decorating the Branch (of *otate* <bamboo>, orange or pine tree).

The decorations, according to the region, are usually made with colored tissue paper, palm leaves and fruit, shaping chains or lanterns in different forms and sizes. Some Branches are illuminated with candles placed inside the lanterns.

The group carrying the Branch is made up of children, young people and/or adults who walk from home to home, singing the carols announcing the birth of the Child Jesus. The musical accompaniment is performed with small guitars, harps and regular guitars, with a lively rhythm, rattles and tambourines. These *soneros* or *jaraneros,* as they are called, stimulate the festivity or *fandango* which is organized at the end of the "party."

The vibrant, festive rhythm begins with a tune at the house where the people arrive. The praises and carols refer to fruit, food and to the season's customs; thus, oranges, limes, lemons, sweets, peanuts and *piñatas* parade in each verse.

The festivity ending with the Branch in this region becomes even more animated when the hostess offers fritters and pastry sprinkled with warm molasses. Liquor aged with the region's fruits: *nanche, jobo,* soursop or simply the famous *toritos* (a mixture of lemon, syrup and liquor), clear the throats to continue singing.

The rhythm and the way in which this tradition is adopted in every corner of Veracruz reveals the temperament of its inhabitants. Therefore, in this sample we can hear different kinds of Branches, both the melancholic and the gay lively tune, sometimes accompanied by some type of heel-tapping dance.

THE NATIVITY

The Bethlehem or Manger

The first Nativity was set up more than seven centuries ago

All the characteristic symbols and rites of the Mexican Christmas festivities have different origins. This is the case of the Bethlehem, also called Manger or Nativity, a visual representation of the coming of the Messiah, whose origin is difficult to determine exactly.

Some sources affirm that the first presentation of the Manger dates back to the beginning of the Christian era, around the year 345, in a tomb in Letrán, while an ancient Bethlehem is mentioned in the 17th century in *Santa Maria Maiore* in Rome, where a small chapel existed, whose structure was similar to a manger's cave.

However, the popular custom of representing Nativities, either with figures or with persons, began with Saint Francis of Assisi, the true prompter of this legendary custom, who definitely promoted this unique way (for those times) of celebrating Christmas, between the years 1220 and 1226.

With the permission of Pope Honorius III, at a place donated by Giovanni Vellita, Saint Francis' friend, in Rieti, in front of the city of Greccio, the latter made an altar in front of a cave, as well as a manger. The shepherds in the vicinity arrived on Christmas and so much joy was derived, that the Franciscan order adopted this practice.

Owing to painting, sculpture, the theatrical representations and the Franciscans' diffusion, the Manger was introduced in Spain during the 14th century, but it was not until the 17th century when the mangers reached their definite adoption.

The city of Naples became the head of this movement. It was governed by the Spanish monarch, Charles III, King of the Two Sicilys, who in 1743 built the Capodimont porcelain factory. He was the key person to spread this tradition.

In Mexico, this custom was introduced by the friars who accompanied the conquerors, and they used this custom as a valuable tool to convert the natives. And thus, with subtle adaptations to native ideas, the missionaries introduced the Nativities, in the manner of theatrical representations, and as sacramental rulings where the converts themselves participated.

Friar Pedro de Gante taught the natives to make the figures, with the details of the Nativities for these processions at the school which he founded in Texcoco. Later, the Spanish and Creole families set up their own Mangers with tiny European figures, modelled by the craftsmen's skillful hands.

During two centuries, this tradition was practically hidden, and it was not until the middle of the 19th century when the Nativities reappeared, this time with greater popular force.

The high demand for little statues originated their manufacture in series, until reaching the prestige of works of art, as in the case of those made during the beginning of this century in Tlaquepaque, Jalisco, especially by the Panduro, Zacarías and Ortega families.

A Christmas of illusions and miracles
at the Sierra Tarahumara, Chihuahua

A Tarahumara Nativity

A poet, seated in front of a child from the immense ravines in the Tarahumara Mountains, lets his lyrical fantasy fly to the sky, and taking the coppery, fluttering hands of the small Tarahumara boy, between his own, the poet, full of love, says softly, "I'm going to tell you a story."

The cold Christmas this year in the Tarahumara Mountains is not the same as other Christmases with blue skies and white snow: the echo of primitive drums, the musical song of the rustic reed flutes that join the unequalled sound of the wind, are a prelude to an unusual, miraculous and sublime event.

The Child Jesus asked His mother and the ever kind and exemplary Joseph, to appear with the red skin of the Tarahumara Indians during this Christmas celebration.

The Virgin's face became illuminated with a smile and she wore the white flowery gown of the Tarahumara mothers, made by the magical hands of the women of this race, with a primitive cloth. She also sketched the Child Jesus' diapers.

Thus, Joseph dressed in the Tarahumara way, with his carpenter's hands, and helped by the birds that work the same way manufactured the humble manger that would receive the Child Jesus, sheltered from the highest rocks in the ravines.

The name of the main ravine is *Cobre* (Copper); copper is the skin of

94

the native Tarahumara, and copper is the face which, during this Christmas of miracles and illusions, the Child Jesus will have. He is the Redeemer in all the mountain chasms.

The Yamury set out on their fast race to be the first to worship the sweet Child with the wonderful eyes, and they climbed ridges and rocks to the sound of flutes and drums. The sacred women, stoic and beautiful, hurriedly gathered corn, tender squash and fruit from the mountain to place them in their dream basket, palm filigree made with their own hands. And history is repeated: the first to worship the Child were the good shepherds from this legendary copper race who live in the Tarahumara Mountains, and the cliffs were filled with prayers, rolling of drums and sweet melodies from reed flutes.

The hearts of the little nuns and the missionary friars burst in thanksgiving, and the Child Jesus' infinite love ran swiftly through the mountains and cascades of the Tarahumara Mountains until it reached the sea, at the Topolobampo, Sinaloa Bay. And the entire mountain range and its birds, its deer, its pine trees, evergreens and mountain flowers sang together the angels' song:

Glory to God in Heaven and peace to men of good will.

NIGHT OF RADISHES AND *CALENDAS*

Christmas in Oaxaca

In the times of Colonization and with the arrival of the Evangelizers, the friars introduced the abstinence market, for the purpose of rationalizing the consumption of meat during the days established by the Church. Only vegetables and fruit were sold in this market, therefore in order to obtain the participation of the vegetable and fruit growers, and so that the faithful would carry out the ordinances, the friars organized contests and awarded prizes to the largest vegetable gardens. The fame of the vegetable gardens in the *Trinidad de las Huertas* district, an area well supplied with water at that time, was thus born. The vegetable gardens reached huge sizes. The radishes were especially outstanding due to their odd shapes and great length, which encouraged the vegetable growers and the craftsmen to mold them in human or animal forms.

On December 23, 1889, owing to the initiative of Francisco Vasconcelos Flores, who was a celebrity in Oaxaca, the first vegetable and flower grower's fair took place in the halls of the Government Palace. Eventually, the following fairs would have several favorable modifications. At this time, this fair is carried out in the city's *zocalo* in front of the Government Palace. A large number of artists participate, and the most detailed and colorful stalls are awarded prizes. Furthermore, Nativity scenes, dancing, Biblical or historic scenes, etcetera, can be admired. Once the fair is over, and after the prizes have been awarded, the craftsmen can sell their articles to teh public.

There are two kinds of articles that enter the contest: the immortal flower arrangements and the figures made of *totomoxtle* (dry corn leaves that are used after soaking them in water to make *tamales* and to manufacture crafts). This provides more novelties to Radish Night, an evening where the craftsmen in Oaxaca can show off their creativity.

This is a very special evening in the city of Oaxaca. The people and the tourists gather around the stalls, with a great deal of curiosity to observe the craftsmen's work. In the meantime, at the kiosk, the state band plays its best tunes, and the gay rhythmic melodies mingle with the enthusiastic, simple noise of the crowds who enjoy the delicious food in the stalls.

The Calendas

The *Calendas* are popular and public demonstrations organized to celebrate the Saints' festivities. The *Calendas* are full of Oaxacan folklore: they present typical adornments in the colorful, joyful cars, a band of music, fireworks, people from different districts who often wear typical costumes from the region and carry caps and lanterns and the famous *Calenda* dolls representing people from the town.

Each neighborhood and each church prepare their *Calenda*. The procession formed by each *Calenda* leave the godmother's house where all the participants gather and then they are organized in the following way: in the first place, the people who make and operate the fireworks with their happy noise and their colorful lights, "the musicians with their band and orchestra follow", and then the "*Calenda* dolls" and all the men, women and children from the corresponding neighborhood, each with his or her lantern, which provides a special style to each group. Each Calenda has its own route, with its own luster. The *Calendas* pass through their respective church, where the Nativity scene of the Child Jesus is found.

96

THE *CUETLAXOCHITL* CHRISTMAS FLOWER

Symbol of new life

This flower originating in Mexico, which Friar Bernardino de Sahagún described saying: "...a flower called *cuetlaxochitl* from a tree with bright red leaves."

Cuetlaxochitl is a Nahuatl term meaning "a flower with petals as resistant as leather," from *cuetlax-tli* (hide or leather) and *xochitl* (flower).

The ancient Mexicans, like most of the Mesoamerican people, gave great importance to the cultivation of flowers and plants, to the point that the conquerors were very surprised with the botanical gardens they found, among others, those in Chapultepec and Oaxtepec. Flowers were irreplaceable to our forefathers, both in day-to-day life and in religious life. The people considered flowers as a symbol, not only to represent the physically beautiful things, but also the beauty of expression. They called poetry "Flowery Words," and in pre-Hispanic writing a poet was painted with the symbol of the word —the speech scroll— surrounded by little flowers.

The *cuetlaxochitl* is known as the Christmas Flower (the Poinsettia) due to its beautiful color, and because it blooms mainly in December.

This flower is called poinsettia in some countries, a name which the ambassador of the United States in Mexico at that time, Joel R. Poinset gave it. It is said that he liked the flower so much that it was his favorite and that is why he baptized it and sent it to the United States and later to Europe. At this time, this flower is grown in different countries and is used largely as an ornamental plant.

It has been so well accepted that, since the last century, it can be seen in the December festivities in European churches. It is reported that in December 1899, the Basilica of Saint Peter's in the Vatican was adorned with *cuetlaxochitl*.

As for medicine, this plant also occupied an important place. According to the information provided by the Spanish doctor, Francisco Hernández, it is known that during the 16th century it was used to increase wet nurses' milk; at this time it is still used for this purpose in some parts of our country. It is also used as a cataplasm and in poultices against skin rashes and other skin diseases.

But in pre-Hispanic Mexico it was not only a medical and ornamental plant, it was also a symbol of the "new life" that the warriors who died in battle reached.

Furthermore, the crushed petals, mixed with *oxtle** and other substances were used to dye hide and some textiles.

CHRISTMAS CUISINE IN MEXICO

Many Christmas festivities throughout the world are cold and simple; in Mexico there is a large variety of dishes that make up our Christmas Eve dinner, enriched with the multiple, impressive foliage of our pre-Hispanic era, merging the Spanish cauldron and the species arriving from Chinese ships. Present-day Mexico assimilates any influence whatsoever.

We enjoy the following heritage in our country, and it extends beyond our borders: guava apple, *nopal* (prickly pear), *maguey,* corn, beans, chili, avocado, vanilla, *cacao* (cocoa), pumpkin and squash, *chayote, mamey, papaya,* chocolate, tomato, and turkey, to mention just a few, are all a significant part of international gastronomy.

The Christmas cookbook for present-day cuisine has been enriched in its variety and its elements due to contributions from Anglo-American countries, but given the strength of our culinary tradition, these contributions take a typically Mexican accent. Needless to say, the dishes which continue dominating our tables during the Christmas family gatherings are those which we inherited from our native ancestors: *manchamanteles* (an elaborate dish prepared with chicken and a variety of fruits and nuts), the *mole* with rosemary leaves, the *tamales*, kings of delightful morsels and of family gatherings in Mexico and, especially, his majesty, the turkey. The Child Jesus surely blesses Christmas tables in the homes of every Mexican.

Glory to God in heaven
and peace to men of good will!

---

* OXTLE. Derived from the *oxtli*, a Nahuatl term. It is a semi-liquid resin extracted from pine trees.

DAY OF THE INNOCENT*

HE *INOCENTADAS*** ON DECEMBER 28

A tradition that is disappearing

Beware! Don't become an "innocent." Today, December 28, if someone remembers that on this day you can borrow something and it will not be returned because it is the Day of the Holy Innocents, this joke can be played on you.

The origin of this tradition is unknown. The only known history was pointed out in Antonio de Robles' *Crónica*, indicating that the order of the Bethlemites —established in Mexico in 1673— celebrated its festivity on December 28, 1703: "Today, the Day of the Holy Innocents, the corresponding festivities were celebrated in the Church of the Bethlemites, with the corresponding treats, and the inauguration of the altarpiece in the main altar..."

In 1820, when this order was eliminated, the festivity was no longer celebrated.

This custom (the Day of the Holy Innocents), with which a commemoration is humorously made of Herod's instructions to kill all the children in order to destroy the newly born Jesus, also exists in other countries on different dates. For example, in France it is celebrated on April 1 and it is called *Poisson d'abril*.

In Spanish-speaking countries, this tradition is disappearing, like many other traditions that are now merely part of the past.

On December 28 of other eras, the day was full of charm and ingenuousness in our country. Good humor reigned in the jokes, and thus, neighbors, friends, and relatives sent each other messages borrowing something and then, for a reply, they sent a little basket with sweets and tiny figures for children, indicating the joke, with an inscription reading

Inocente palomita que te dejaste engañar
*sabiendo que en este día nada se debe prestar.****

---

* The Day of the Innocent is similar to April Fool's Day in the United States.
** Naive mistake or blunder (April Fool's joke)
*** Innocent little dove who allowed yourself to be deceived/knowing that on this day nothing should be lent.

The *inocentadas* also consisted of persuasively disclosing news which would be impossible to believe or to happen, so that the person might believe it and be deceived; this was part of the fun.

Beware! Don't become an Innocent!

Another variable approach that has disappeared consisted of giving away little tin trays with miniature toys prepared for the occasion, when the borrowed object was returned. Little cards with the following words were delivered with this gift:

> *Herodes cruel e inclemente, nos dice desde la fosa*
> *que considera inocente al que presta alguna cosa.**

You can probably find the miniature gifts for this day in some of the marketplaces in our city, although the majority of people do not link them with the Holy Innocents.

December 18 is undoubtedly a special day when the Mexicans' creativeness is expressed to make the most incredible jokes, deceiving their friends. Therefore, remember that on December 28 you must not lend anything, nor believe uncommon things that may be told to you, so that people won't say: "Innocent little dove who allowed yourself to be deceived, knowing that on this day, nothing should be lent."

---

* Herod, cruel and ruthless, tells us from the tomb/that he considers the person who lends things to be an innocent.

CHEERFUL
MEXICO

CARNIVALS IN MEXICO

ARNIVALS ARE CELEBRATED A WEEK BEFORE ASH WEDNESDAY

The carnival is one of the most unrestrained, colorful and popular celebrations in Mexico. As in other big cities throughout the world —like Venice and Rio de Janeiro — in some places in our country people take to the streets on those days to give free rein to their joy.

The carnival is pre-eminently a festivity of fun. All the rules may be broken during carnival, all the limits may be surpassed, and fantasies can not only become reality, but they are the norm. Hidden behind the wildest disguises, or barely covered by a simple mask, we can sing, dance, laugh aloud. The most important thing is to become transformed, to contradict everyday order. To be not what we always are, but what we have always wanted to be. During carnival anything is possible.

The most famous carnivals in Mexico are carried out in the ports of Veracruz and Mazatlán, following the tradition of joy and hospitality characteristic of the inhabitants of the coasts. Here, the carnival festivity is multitudinous and popular and it attracts a large number of visitors. Several days before the festivity begins, the streets are adorned with ribbons, paper decorations and colored lights. The most distinctive feature is squandering. Resources are not spared so that the festivity may be brilliant and luminous. It is the custom to elect a Queen of Beauty and an Ugly King who will preside over the celebrations. The most important event is the parade of masquerades and floats, for which the inhabitants of the different neighborhoods have been preparing months in advance. The festivity takes place all day and all night. The bustle, the unexpected meeting, the spontaneous friendship, the warm sensation of celebrating with all the city, the same joy, are continuous.

But carnival in Mexico is much more. In nearly all the towns in our country, carnival festivities are celebrated with their own personality, even though they may not have the same massive and unrestrained nature of urban carnivals, and even though they are much more traditional, intimate and folkloristic.

103

CARNIVALS IN TLAXCALA, PUEBLA AND MORELOS

In San Juan Totolac, as in many other towns in the state of Tlaxcala, it is a tradition to "hang" a person. This is a character that symbolizes the community's sins, so the people take him prisoner, judge him and declare him guilty. Condemned to die, he gives an account of his actions and distributes his belongings among his "widow" and his "children." Then, a rope is tied around his waist and he is hung between two stakes. When he is "dead," he is taken for burial, but then the "hanged man" is resuscitated and begins to distribute lashings right and left.

Huejotzingo, Puebla

Huejotzingo, in the state of Puebla, is famous for its carnival festivities, where the struggle of the Mexican people against the invading army during the French intervention is recalled. Legend narrates that in order to take revenge on the invaders, one of the famous "bandits of Río Frío" kidnapped a French lady during the 1865 carnival, took her to the mountains and wedded her. In the present representation, the kidnapping is staged, as well as the Frenchmen's attempts to rescue her and the battle between the Mexicans and the foreigners. Part of the inhabitants play the part of Mexicans and the other part is disguised as Frenchmen. In order to reproduce the uproar of the battle, fireworks are used and the public participates actively, following both factions throughout the city streets.

Carnival in Tepoztlan, Morelos

The carnival in Tepoztlan, in the state of Morelos, where famous "*chinelos*" dance the Jumping Dance in the town square is particularly interesting. The *chinelos*' main attraction lies in their lovely silk tunics and in the impressive masks with which they cover their faces. These characters also dance in the neighboring town of Yautepec, where the *Burial of Bad Humor* takes place each year, consisting of throwing into the river a box where a dummy has been placed, while the "widows" weep and cry.

NATIVE COMMUNITIES

It is important to mention that the carnivals carried out by some of the native communities in the country combine Christian rites with pre-Hispanic traditions, resulting in ceremonies full of power, symbolism and religiousness.

Carnival of the Chamulas

In San Juan Chamula, Chiapas, a native village of Mayan origin, the carnival begins on Sweeping Saturday, when all the streets in the town are cleaned, and ends on Ash Wednesday. According to anthropologists these days correspond to the five lost days in the Mayan calendar.

For the *Chamulas*, carnival is much more than a joyous festivity. There are changes in the government administration on those days, and people ask for heaven's blessing so that everything may turn out right for their civic and religious authorities. In addition, various ceremonies and rites take place, where each participant has a specific function and a different disguise. One of the most spectacular festivities is carried out on Shrove Tuesday. A straw corridor is formed in the square, in front of the church, where no one is allowed to pass. At two p.m., the straw is lit and the new authorities will have to pass running over the fire. Smoke envelops their silhouettes, reminding one of mysterious beings from other times.

The boisterous carnival, full of symbolism emerging from popular and even religious tradition, has as many facets as there are communities in our country. This is merely an introduction to that magic space which creates these festivities during February. A world into which you can enter to abandon for a moment your regulated everyday life.

The Papaquis Carnival in Jalisco

The carnival has arrived with its uproar, its animation and bustle, its masks, its music: with everything that means pleasure, life and pleasantness.

Since Shrove Tuesday morning, everyone in all the towns in Jalisco have left their home to enjoy themselves and to have fun.

One of the most alluring, most interesting, one of the most typical numbers is the *Papaquis* act. This act will take place outdoors.

To this effect, a large square has been chosen, a wide street, or the courtyard of a church —even though it may have been used in the past as a cemetery and still contains crosses and mounds of earth where the dead reside.

105

The *Papaquis* consist of encounters simulating merciless, relentless wars formed by factions when the festivity begins, with the elements that have been prepared to amuse hundreds of curious persons who will not only be mere spectators, but will also participate in the merriment.

The warlike material in the improvised battles will be thousands of beautifully decorated eggshells, painted with good taste and delicacy and before covering them, the "love," that is, different colored tissue paper, has been combined with tinsel.

Although most of the eggshells have been stuffed with "love" some contain colored liquid, and others are stuffed with colored dyes to stain clothes, or with rotten eggs to scatter a bad odor in the midst of the merriment and bustle of the crowds. Furthermore, it would not be strange to see eggshells stuffed with ashes, chili or even with an inflammable substance.

The battle begins and it will last three or four hours. The factions are multiplied, the fighters are replaced, and there are moments when even the most indifferent spectators are infected with the crowd's happiness, with that gathering of hundreds or thousands of individuals who also participate in the festivities.

There are no ages, no sexes, no social ranks: it is all a true democracy.

Songs that are sung to the rhythm of the music — often when the fighting begins or at the beginning and end of these acts — also receive the name of *Papaquis*.

Among the group of fighters there is a standard-bearer who acts as master of ceremonies and leads the choirs.

CARNIVALS IN OLD JALISCO

Mezquitán, Atemajac and Zoquiapan

The land where the famous *Chimalhuacanos* settled in days of yore is undoubtedly one of the places that are proud of conserving some of their many typical customs of the past.

The people of *Tecuese* origin have made the most original carnival festivities reach us, full of good taste, which they carried out in their towns.

The Release of the Devil is presented with strange costumes. The devils wear the indispensible *sompantle* mask, with horns so huge that sometimes each horn reaches forty centimeters long.

When the devil began his activities, he hurled into the four winds flames of fire through a special system.

Once this devil was released —he was tied with a big chain which other groups called minor devils dragged— he made somersaults which caused admiration due to his skill and ability; he had to be a good dancer in order to perform this main role perfectly, which was so attractive in that masquerade.

The typical instruments used were the *teponaxtle* the *chirimía* and half a dozen rustic drums, with which a deafening noise was made, which sometimes simulated a thunder storm —those storms that are so common in the typical *Tapatía* city and in the neighboring regions.

The Papaquiteuhtli

On the Saturday prior to Carnival Sunday, the main natives gathered in the Mezquitán courtyard —where traditional customs have prevailed. These natives took part in the "Release of the Devil." The old man who would preside over the meeting was among these natives, where the *Papaquiteuhtli* or the King of Good Humor would be elected.

The main Devil received a whip, a Moorish gown, a great roll of tissue paper and an enormous knife. Then, accompanied by the *chirimía*, he would go from house to house, asking if the people had an image of Saint Michael.

If they answered affirmatively, he would enter the place where the saint was found, kneel before him and say aloud: "*With my Lord's permission.*" Then, he would strip the archangel's Lucifer who was chained, and when he was unable to practice this operation without damaging the statue too much, or when it was a chrome, he was content with covering the image of the saint with tissue paper, leaving the image of the devil uncovered, pretending to break his chains.

After his work was done, the old man returned to the electors to tell them that all the devils were now loose, and that the *mitote* (rumpus) could now begin.

Then, the electors took his knife, gathered the remaining tissue paper, and placed a black mask with natural hair or agave on his face, and gave him a little sack full of flour. With the *chirimía* in front of him, and surrounded by all the people's *nigua* (merriment), he wandered through all the main streets.

In the meantime, the crowd waited anxiously in front of the parish church, until the King of Good Humor returned. When the King saw the crowd pretending to enter the church, he lunged furiously against them, pretending to lash the people.

There is a picturesque and sparkling conversation among the principal actors of this gay and appealing farce which highlights the ingenuity and liveliness of the actors, who usually improvise words or phrases that provoke laughter among the spectators when they begin their performance, and which often allude to some of the people attending of certain social importance.

While the people began to run helter-skelter, one of the youngest masked boys faced the old man, shouting in a loud voice:

"Aaaaa, coopaaaa!"

The King of Good Humor, alternating the syllables of the vowels in a high-sounding voice demanded:

"Qué ereqete us?" (What do you want?)

The bold young man responded:

"Your permission to *mitotear* (make a fuss)."

The *Papaquinteuhtli* then made a gesture of surprise, he rolled the whip violently, and changing his tone of voice said:

"Ah, yo bacrei las con tasbia arapa uar-re!" (Oh, I thought you came with the old women to pray!)

"No, no!," added the young man. "We want *mitote*, as tomorrow is Carnival, there's flour and *pinole* (fine ground corn), the *Papaquis* can be heard and the *mariachi* is playing. We do not want to pray, we want *mitotear*, we want a bustle, we want *fandango* (dancing and music), there are lots of beautiful girls who are waiting for their sweethearts to start dancing. The devils are loose, its time to *fandanguear* (to dance)...Woe!"

"Oh, my father! Oh my mother! It's now Carnival time!"

The old man put one foot forward, as if wanting to interrupt the boy, and exclaimed:

"Nobue, nobue, tebas ya, musguadia!" (All right, all right, that's enough, let's go!)

And the people in a chorus responded:

"Amen, amen, amen!"

The King of Good Humor then joined the crowd, the musicians played the *teponaxtle* and the *chirimía* again, and the jokes, the merriment, the dancing, the practical jokes, the mischief, the wrestling matches, and the *Papaquis* combats began. The next day, almost all the natives were drunk with wine, love and pleasure. It was a grand Carnival night!

When Ash Wednesday arrived, all those who had participated in the Carnival festivities were getting over their hangover, some of them were now pretty well, and those who had been injured were vowing to the devil himself that he would never again be allowed to be loose in the *carnestolendas* (carnival).

Someone jokingly said, referring to the carnival festivities in Mezquitán, Atemajac and Zoquiapan, that not many ashes were used on Ash Wednesday, because, since the drunken spree was generalized, there was no one who would get up to receive the ashes.

The carnival festivals from old Jalisco last to our days in Mezquitán, Atemajac and Zoquiapan.

Xochimilco

THE FLOWER *SEMENTERA**

Long ago, long before beauty contests were in fashion, Xochimilco celebrated the festivity of *La Flor más Bella del Ejido* (the Loveliest Flower in the Region).

The luxurious *trajineras* decorated with flowers, depart from the *chinampas*, on their way to this festival, where native maidens compete for the prize.

Dark faces, tanned by the sun and made up with the soft aroma of the flowers and the vegetable gardens; multi-colored dresses reflected in the eternal mirrors of the canals, as if proclaiming the pride of their race; the musical word of their original language resounding; and the imperishable blue of the sky sheltering the setting of this romantic Xochimilcan tradition.

FESTIVITY OF *LA FLOR MÁS BELLA DEL EJIDO*

A Festivity of Joy and Tradition

The festivity of *La Flor más Bella del Ejido* emerged from the Xochimilcan culture itself, in tribute to the Aztec gods of dancing and flowers: *Macuilxochitl* and *Xochipilli*.

THE CELEBRATION CONTINUES

After a period of transition, the Viceroy de Gálvez gave a new meaning to the festivity in 1785. It was celebrated at the *Canal de la Viga* under the name of Flowery Friday, with popular dances, the sale of flowers and vegetables, meals accompanied with *pulque* (a fermented drink made of maguey), as well as contests with *charro* and *china poblana* costumes.

In 1897, the festivity was newly promoted, and it was called Spring Friday. After a series of interruptions during the Revolution, president Lázaro Cárdenas resumed the festivities in 1936, with the name of Flowery Friday.

---

* *Sementera*: A portion of land where some types of vegetables are sown to be transplanted weeks later on a larger surface.

This was the first time that a beautiful young woman was elected as "the loveliest flower in the region."

RENEWAL OF THE TYPICAL FESTIVITY

Today, this festivity is the most important in Xochimilco. It includes rowing competitions (*acalli*), decorated canoes, typical gastronomic contests, exhibits of crafts, cultivation of *chinampas*, flowers and cattle raising. All of this is enlivened by *mariachis*, fireworks, and musical and dancing shows.

THE LOVELIEST MAIDEN: A FLOWER

And in this setting of festivity and joy, the contest of *La Flor más Bella del Ejido* is outstanding, where all the participants wear typical costumes from the Valley of Mexico, consisting of: *chincuete*, a white blouse with brightly colored embroidery, held around the waist by a *rebozo* (a silk or woolen shawl) or by a *tlazincuillo* (a sash) or a *huipil* (a small knitted cape). They also wear adornments made of flowers, fruit, or bird cages.

The most beautiful contestant is elected for her personality, her ethnic characteristics and for the way in which she wears her finery.

COME TO THE FESTIVITY!

The political delegations who still have *ejidos* (common or public lands) participate in these celebrations: Alvaro Obregón, Coyoacán, Cuajimalpa, Gustavo A. Madero, Iztapalapa, Magdalena Contreras, Milpa Alta, Tláhuac, Tlalpan and Xochimilco. The election of "the loveliest flower in the region" is carried out in the downtown area of Xochimilco on the Friday before Holy Week.

111

THE OLD OUTINGS IN SANTA ANITA

anta Anita was one of the places where life slipped by gently, softly and quietly. It was a delightful place for lovers, just as Xochimilco continues to be.

Every Sunday, all year round, the townspeople organized amusing tours through the canal which has now disappeared. Several families got together at the pier. They took a canoe and there were many funny scenes: a sixty-year old woman who did not want to get her new shoes wet; or a young girl who was afraid of jumping into the canoe, or another who was the opposite and boldly put half a leg in the water and showed more than half of the other leg; a man who almost made the canoe capsize when he jumped in the canoe; a lad who, boasting that he could row, got completely wet; the light canoe would then begin to navigate gently rocked by the soft waves; the strings of a guitar were heard and after a little while, the soft and sweet voice like sugar belonging to Mariquita, who sang a melancholic song.

And the songs continued, both the old and the modern songs, and there was drinking of the white nectar of the black dreams invented by Queen Xochitl.

But the most typical aspect of Santa Anita was Sorrowful Friday, the actual day of the Verbena (festival).

The canal presented an unusual aspect since dawn. A long series of huts with canvas roofs were seen, from the pier to La Viga, where bonfires were found, as well as stalls with *enchiladas, pulque,* fruit, *tamales, atole,* (beverage made of corn flour and different flavors), *carnitas* (deep-fried pork meat), barbecue, heads, combined *tortas* (a Mexican sandwich made with French-style bread), *chalupas,* small boats loaded with flowers, *trajineras* (vehicle to carry various objects, generally applied to the canoes navigating through canals), tables with weak coffee and orange leaves, ice cream cones, sweets, wind-instrument music, music with chords, organ grinders...People from all walks of life gathered here to have a good time, to enjoy themselves, to pass the time, from the elegant lady in her powerful automobile to individuals who took taxis costing fifty cents to take them to their destination, or the bus paid with a ticket or ten cents. Young revelers, people on bicycles, *charros,* the military, bullfighters, girls dressed in the *china poblana* costume, prostitutes, thieves, beggars, and, in general a world of people, since rare was

112

Exquisite Mexican Christmas Cuisine (*romeritos*, rosemary and crab cakes in a *mole* sauce).

Exquisite Mexican Christmas Cuisine (*bacalao*, codfish prepared with a tomato sauce).

Delicious strawberry-flavored *atole* is a typical Christmas beverage.

Famous and typical dessert known as "Capirotada."

Lively Mexico, "castles" made of fireworks.

Spectacular Carnival celebrations in the state of Puebla.

Carnival with an indigenous flavor in the state of Tlaxcala.

Typical Carnival mask used in Tepoztlán, state of Morelos.

The clamor and color of Carnival in Puebla.

Masked "Chinelo" dancer from Carnival in Tepoztlán, state of Morelos.

The fantasy and color of miniature *trajineras* or rafts of Xochimilco.

The beauty of brown-skinned faces of our indigenous women.

(Above) The Eternal Ices of Xochimilco.
Desserts from the Aztec imperial table. Exotic ices.

(Below) The greatest spectacle in Mexico
—the Guelaguetza

The most important national fair in Mexico –the Aguascalientes Fair.

Children in a typical Mexican kitchen.

Pre-Hispanic splendor and grandeur of Mexico —a finely carved Maya stela.

Some dishes fit for the table of Emperor Moctezuma.

(Below) Maguey worms for adventurous palates. *(Right)* The Maguey plant and, on the back, the God of Rain, the magnificent *Tlaloc.*

Some of the ingredients of pre-Hispanic cuisine.

(Below) Intricate featherwork worn by pre-Hispanic peoples.
(Right) Detail of ankle rattles.

(*Above* and *Below*) Fine and
magnificent samples of
pre-Hispanic art.
(*Left*) Tasty and nutritious *nopales*
(cactus leaves).

Flavored *pulques* (fermented beverage made from the agave).

(Left) The *nopal* cactus, strange desert plant, king's dish and heraldic symbol from the Mexican coat-of-arms.
(Below) One of the great variety of dishes made from *nopal* leaves.

the social class, the union or the profession that had no representatives for the occasion.

All the people who are devoted to writing about our folkloric customs have described this great colorful and gay festivity.

Rafael Heliodoro Valle writes the following in his book, *México Imponderable* (Inponderable Mexico):

"Yesterday, the *trajineras* were fit to reach the end of the world. Sorrowful Friday must be spent in Santa Anita, listening to the bustle of the radish and poppy sellers at ridiculously low prices, otherwise this is not Mexico or that *rebozo* (shawl) is not the typical polka-dot shawl. 'Where is the King?' shouted the *carcamaneros*. 'What is the *Casarín* and what did he do to us and what did he place in the Reforma before we were brought here?' sighed the marvelous *indios verdes* (green natives). Throughout the canal, the natives went here and there, with the oars' rhythm, with old-fashioned guitars inside, and the young ladies wearing their *china* costumes forgetting everything in front of the doll salesman.

"Cupid is here! The great king of love! A big factory that makes ten thousand cupids a minute. Only fifty cents!

"When I arrived at six, the women were making so much noise that even the locust disappeared. With all the plucking, no one knew where the King was. Trains from Ixtapalapa, colorfully decorated with radishes, cabbage and lettuce began to arrive through the La Viga Avenue.

" 'We need two more five cent coins,' shouted the guitar player from León de los Aldamas. 'But these must be paid, otherwise my companion will not continue singing.'

"And then, at the surprise of the people who circled him, the boy added, 'No credit is allowed!'

"And the singer began his tender song when we had completed the thirty cents which he asked for his singing.

"The festivity reached its height at noon. People came and went through all those places. There were contests for canoes decorated with flowers, the *charros* showed off their abilities holding the bulls by the tail, musicians competed. Everybody ate *mole*, barbecue, stuffed peppers, beef belly and head, offal, *enchiladas* and all kinds of fried food offered in the little restaurants and stalls. There some *charros* were drinking a pint, here a very painted woman was bargaining for the price of the poppies and the radishes. The strange voices of the merchants could be heard in the midst of unceasing noise, in the midst of the bustle."

The notes of a national *jarabe* (national hat dance) could be heard emerging from some of the huts. The *mariachis* from Cocula played the *Golondrinas* (a farewell folk song); the low class people shouted their witty comments; the proficient individual joked at any naive person; the fresh young men who had barely cracked their "eggshells" walked arm in arm with their improvised loved ones, making poetry; a daring young man passed near a fussy middle-aged woman and, pinching her, heard her uttering a litany of phrases: "vulgar, ordinary, bastard..."

The stroll became heated, and in the evening, at sundown, the shadows were poor advisors: the revelers, the brave, the prostitutes, the masses, everybody enjoying themselves; without limits, without barriers, everyone was owner of the place and therefore did as they pleased. And then, all kinds of scandalous scenes took place: the people got drunk, they insulted each other, they fought, boxing entered the scene, tools were exhibited, blood was shed, the outing ended with what the brave considered the best: several dead and hundreds of wounded.

THE ETERNAL NIEVES OF TULYEHUALCO

T he *nieves** of Tulyehualco. Are they a pre-Hispanic tradition? Was it a dessert at Moctezuma's table? Was it a dessert at the Aztec Imperial Table?

The verbal tradition in Tulyehualco —a beautiful, ancient village at the feet of the volcanoes, dating back to the pre-Hispanic era— proclaims that the *nieves* in Tulyehualco, like the snows in the volcanoes, are eternal. In effect, the oldest settlers in this ancient town, when asked about the origin of the "ices" with a thousand flavors that have made the town famous, reply proudly that their native ancestors had the custom of bringing the snow from the volcanoes in their *trajineras* (canoes) when the heat got worse, to serve them at the tables of the grand noblemen, and they also stated that the custom originated, spontaneously and naturally, to mix the snow with wild honey from the *tuna* (prickly pear), the *maguey*, from the bee, and from corn, for the purpose of making it more pleasing to the taste.

In fact, the oldest makers of "ices" (or sherberts) remember that these ices were made with snow from the Ixtaccihuatl and the Popocatepetl, instead of manufacturing it with artificial ice.

This oral tradition originated due to the proximity of the town with the so-called eternal snows of the volcanoes; logically, it provoked the desire to consume them on hot days and enjoy them with the natural fruit they had handy. In truth, this explains the infinite variety of what I call the Eternal Ices (sherberts) of Tulyehualco.

When I first heard the story of this tradition from my dear Xochimilcas, the emotion and the romantic candor of the tale moved me, but after all, I am an investigator of traditions, and after a time, it provoked my desire to analyze and study the basis of this romantic legendary tradition. I

---

* *NIEVE* (Sherbert) When one speaks of *nieve* for table use, it does not refer to the condensed vapor when the weather is cold, which is properly called *nieve* (snow), but it refers to any liquid, mainly water, artificially converted into a solid body, and it is sometimes crystal clear due to the intensity of the cold weather transmitted by the wet *nieve* mixed with saltpeter or common salt. In this sense, it is called Lemon *Nieve* (Sherbert) Pineapple *Nieve* (Sherbert), etcetera, although it would be more proper to call these liquids, frozen by the cold, "ices."

From *Nuevo cocinero mexicano en forma de diccionario, 1888*
(New Mexican Cookbook in the Form of a Dictionary, 1888).

now have first-hand information that there is no reference or mention of this tradition in traditional written or graphic sources (chronicles or manuscripts). Nevertheless, there is a clear and specific documentary reference from the last century that qualified the ancestral tradition of enjoying the delicious ices in the Xochimilco area, particularly during Lent, and this is the only permission granted under the rigid austerity which Colonial Mexico lived during that period of penance, when families observed fasting and penance rigorously and, according to their custom, this was not violated when people consumed a delicious ice in the afternoons at the squares.

The famous traditional fair is celebrated a week before Holy Week, and this explains why I took the literary license to baptize the fair with the name of the Fair of the Eternal Ices.

It is impossible to end this section without a special mention to the most infinite and delicious variety of ices (sherberts) known in all the world. To prove this, suffice it to mention just a few of the varieties which you could personally enjoy when you visit the fair: pineapple, cantaloupe, strawberry, mango, *mamey*, custard apple, banana, peach, apple, *tejocote* (a small fruit similar to the prune), pecan, pine nut, guava apple, coconut, and *cajeta* (a sweet made of milk), just to mention a few.

Exotic Ices

Faustino (Tino) Sicilia Mora is the creator of the "exotic ices": rose petal, beet, carrot, crisp pork rind, rosemary, *mole*, celery, prickly pear, *tequila*, brandy, cheese, avocado, cucumber, lettuce, tomato, mint, oyster (recently emerged), and many others.

A conclusion is imposed: the ice-making tradition in Xochimilco is old, it has certain character and is deliciously beautiful, but especially, it is a unequalled testimony of the gastronomic genius and creative imagination of the makers of Mexico's immortal culinary tradition.

Fairs in Mexico

One of the social customs in Mexico's festive tradition are the fairs, which —as the word expresses— are festive events, many of which are religious, where an important event is commemorated in the community. In Mexico, there is always the presence of a public market of greater importance than that which is commonly and daily used to supply the community with its requirements.

The traditional fairs in different regions in Mexico originated in the famous *tianguis* (marketplaces) carried out by different groups of natives in Mexico, a custom which was renewed by the priests who evangelized New Spain, who made extraordinary use of it to promote devotion to the community's patron saint.

If we are to believe the historians of the Conquest —such as Bernal Díaz del Castillo, Cortés himself, and later historians such as Torquemada— the festive, gay nature of the fairs, their folklore, as well as their peculiar aspect and regional accent come from afar and, undoubtedly, have been the source of many folkloric and artistic expressions in our country.

The fair, dear friends, has occured forever, an event having great social significance for the enormous range of communities in our country, since all the members of the town show up, with their best clothes, and in their best state of mind, which strengthens the relationships of social solidarity among the residents, provides them with a sense of belonging to the group, and strengthens the ties to their customs and traditions.

Furthermore, the fairs make it possible for the community to show the abilities of its craftsmen, and to make known the region's products and merchandise.

Thus, the fairs have become a matter of pride for the towns organizing them; therefore, they form part of their traditions. They are not frivolous acts, in an unimportant and circumstantial explosion of euphoria; on the contrary, they are a legitimate expression of the social and cultural aspects of people who express themselves joyfully in the fairs.

117

JANUARY
    Jojutla, Mor. *Regional Fair of Jojutla.*
Commercial and artisan.
Matehuala, S.L.P. *The Kings' Regional Fair.*
Commercial and industrial.

León, Gto. *Fair in León.*
National porcine, agricultural, commercial, artisan, cultural, and sports show.

Almoloya del Río, Mex. *Day of the Lord of Burgos.*
Folkloric festival.

Ciudad del Maíz, S.L.P. *Regional Fair.*
Agricultural and livestock industry, industrial and commercial.

Chiapa de Corzo, Chis. *Regional Fair.*
Agricultural and livestock industry, artisan and commercial.

Taxco, Gro. *Festival of Santa Prisca.*
Popular religious festival.

Throughout country. *The Day of the Three Kings.*
Popular religious festival.

FEBRUARY
    Santa María del Tule, Oax. *The Candlemas Fair.*
Popular religious festival.

Mexico City. *House and home fair.*
Commercial and industrial.

Zitácuaro, Mich. *State fair.*
Commercial and artisan.

FEBRUARY	Almoloya del Río, Mex. *Masquerade parade.* Popular festival.
	Mérida, Yuc. *Mérida Carnival.*
	Mazatlán, Sin. *Mazatlán Carnival.*
MARCH	San Miguel de Allende, Gto. *Day of the Lord of the Conquest.* Popular religious celebration.
	Huauchinango, Pue. *Flower Fair.* Floral, agricultural, artisan, cultural, sports.
	San Cristóbal de las Casas, Chis. *Regional Spring and Peace Fair.* Agricultural, livestock, industrial, commercial, artisan, and cultural.
	Tapachula, Chis. *National Fair.* Agricultural, livestock, industrial, artisan, and cultural.
	Irapuato, Gto. *Strawberry Expo.* Agricultural, commercial, and cultural.
	Coatzacoalcos, Ver. *Regional Coatzacoalcos Fair.* Agricultural, livestock, industrial, artisan, and sports.
	Texcoco, Mex. *International Horse Fair.* Livestock expo, commercial, and artisan.
	National Celebration (throughout the country). *Holy Week.* Popular religious celebration.
APRIL	Cuernavaca, Mor. *Flower Fair.* Floriculture and crafts.

119

| APRIL | Xochimilco, D.F. *Flower Fair.*
Floriculture and crafts.
"The Most Beautiful Flower in the Land" Contest. |

Villahermosa, *Tab. Regional Tabasco Fair.*
Agricultural, livestock, industrial, commercial, cultural, and sports.

Morelia, Mich. *Michoacan Fair and Expo.*
Agricultural, livestock, industrial, and cultural.

Tuxtla Gutiérrez, *Chis. San Marcos Fair.*
Agricultural, livestock, artisan, and sports.

Puebla, Pue.
National and International Participation Fair.
Agricultural, livestock, industrial, commercial, artisan, and tourist.

Aguascalientes, Ags. *San Marcos Fair.*
Agricultural, livestock, industrial, commercial, cultural, and tourist.

MAY

Linares, N.L. *Regional Linares Fair.*
Agricultural, livestock, industrial, and commercial.

San Luis Potosí, S.L.P. *National Potosí Fair.*
Agricultural, livestock, industrial, artisan, and tourist.

Loma Bonita, Oax. *Pineapple Fair.*
Agricultural and livestock.

JUNE

Papantla, Ver. *Corpus Christi Fair.*
Livestock expo, commercial, cultural, and sports.

Cd. Juárez, Chih. *Juárez Expo.*
Commercial, cultural, sports, and tourist fair.

JUNE	San Juan del Río, Qro. *Regional Fair.*
	Agricultural, livestock, industrial, commercial, and artisan.

JULY   Guasave, Son. *Cotton Fair.*
        Exhibit of regional products.

        Actopan, Hgo. *Barbecue Fair.*
        Gastronomical, commercial, artisan, cultural, and sports.

        Cd. del Carmen, Camp. *Carmen Fair.*
        Exhibit of regional products.

        Parras, Coah. *Grape Fair.*
        Agricultural expo.

        Tulancingo, Hgo. *Expo-Fair.*
        Agricultural, livestock, industrial, commercial, and artisan.

        Santa Ana Chiautempan, Tlax. *National Serape Fair.*
        Artisan and commercial.

        Cuetzalan, Pue. *Traditional Fair.*
        Folkloric.

        Oaxaca, Oax. *Hill Monday (La Guelaguetza).*
        Folkloric festival.

AUGUST Zacatlán, Pue. *Great Apple Fair.*
        Fruit growing, industrial, artisan, and commercial.

        Durango, Dgo. *National Durango Fair.*
        Commercial, industrial, and artisan.

        Santa Clara del Cobre, Mich. *National Copper Fair.*
        Artisan and commercial.

        Juchitán, Oax. *Candle Festival.*
        Popular, cultural, and folkloric celebration.

SEPTEMBER	Zacatecas, Zac. *National Zacatecas Fair.* Commercial, artisan, cultural, and sports.
	Huejotzingo, Pue. *Great Traditional Cider Fair.* Agricultural, livestock, industrial, commercial, artisan, and tourist.
	Temoaya, Mex. *Charro Day.* Popular festival, *jaripeos* (somewhat similar to rodeos).
	National celebration (throughout the country). *Independence Day.* Civic event.
OCTOBER	Pachuca, Hgo. *Hidalgo Fair.* Industrial, commercial, and artisan.
	San Pedro Actopan (Milpa Alta, D.F.). *The Mole Fair.* Gastronomical and artisan.
	Mexicali, B.C. *Sun Fair.* Agricultural, livestock, industrial, and artisan fair.
	Colima, Col. *Colima Regional Fair* Agricultural, livestock, industrial, commercial, artisan, and tourist
	Tlaxcala, Tlax. *Tlaxcala Fair.* Agricultural, livestock, industrial, commercial, artisan, and cultural.
	San Luis Colorado, Son. *Cotton Expo-Fair.* Agricultural, industrial, and commercial.
	Guanajuato, Gto. *International Cervantine Festival.* Cultural and tourist.

OCTOBER	Guadalajara, Jal. *October Festival.* Agricultural, livestock, industrial, commercial, artisan, and tourist fair.
NOVEMBER	Jilotepec, Mex. *Jilotepec Expo.* Agricultural, livestock, industrial, and artisan.
	Guanajuato, Gto. *Festival of Illumination (Lights).* Popular celebration.
	National celebration (throughout the country). *All-Saints' Festival Day of the Dead.* Popular religious celebration.
	Taxco, Gro. *National Silver Fair.* Artisan and commercial.
	National celebration (throughout the country). Anniversary of the Mexican Revolution. Civic event.
DECEMBER	Tuxtla Gutiérrez, Chis. *Chiapas Fair.* Livestock, commercial, and artisan.
	Querétaro, Qro. *Regional Expo.* Livestock, commercial, and artisan.
	Celaya, Gto. *Christmas Fair.* Industrial, commercial, artisan, and cultural.
	Vicente Guerrero, Dgo. *Corn Fair.* Agricultural, livestock, industrial, and commercial.
	Morelia, Mich. *Christmas Fair.* Commercial and artisan.
	Oaxaca, Oax. *Radish Night.* Exhibit of regional horticulture, popular festival.

National celebration (throughout the country).
Posadas (Mexican Christmas).
Popular celebrations.

The exact date on which local fairs are celebrated is not the same every year.

Therefore, in consideration of the visitor who is anxious to attend any of these splendid events, we suggest that he or she contact the Representative of the State of the Republic (in Mexico City) in which he or she is particularly interested. These departments will provide all the necessary information, with full details.

THE NATIONAL FIREWORKS FAIR IN TULTEPEC, STATE OF MEXICO

Month of March

Tultepec, in the state of Mexico, is the most renowned fireworks center in the Mexican Republic, as proven by the fact that during more than 25 years, the craftsmen have manufactured the artificial fireworks that form part of the national festivities in the Zócalo (the main plaza) in Mexico City, as well as the fireworks, crackers and firecrackers that enliven the festivities and fairs in many regions in the country.

Tultepec is located on the plains belonging to the lake regions and volcanoes of Anáhuac. The climate is moderate, with rains in the summer, and a surface irrigated by a few streams from neighboring regions.

Tultepec, located 45 kilometers from the capital through the Mexico-Querétaro superhighway, has adequate soil for agriculture with irrigation, such as pastures.

Economically, it depends on the cultivation of corn, lima beans, and beans, and raising pork, cattle, sheep, horses and goats, as well as on the mining of sodium nitrate for powder for the fireworks.

The National Fireworks Fair is celebrated year after year, sponsored by the municipal authorities who, aside from backing the fair, promote a fireworks contest for the craftsmen from seven states in the country.

Cockfights, sports events, as well as cultural and artistic events, popular *verbenas*, and exhibits of crafts are ever present, following the tradition of every fair, where miniature fireworks and different toy fireworks are outstanding.

Tultepec has a population of 70,000 inhabitants, among which native groups are still found, such as *Mazahuas, Nahuas* and *Otomíes* as these groups predominate in the region.

On the other hand, it is important to point out that the Sanctuary of Our Lady of Loreto, an architectural jewel dating from the 16th century, is found in this place. The facade is made of stone with native and Spanish motifs, a lateral tower, Solomonic pillars, and a unique altar with walls full of images of pink angels.

The fair offers the public a wide view of the craftsman's work and, due to the contest, representatives from the states of Guanajuato, San Luis Potosí, Querétaro, Hidalgo, Puebla, and Tlaxcala also attend to promote their pyrotechnical art.

THE GREAT NATIONAL FAIR OF SAN MARCOS IN AGUASCALIENTES

The San Marcos National Fair is now a legendary event in our festive tradition, a wonderful, polychrome synthesis that presents the joyful face of our province and of our country.

Mexico has a beautiful festive mosaic which is adapted to all the fairs celebrated in our territory throughout the year.

The Aguascalientes fair is outstanding among all the splendid fairs, as it is the most representative of what I like to call Mexico's festive tradition.

The fairs are deeply rooted in national sensitivity; they are a free and natural expression of Mexicans' taste.

Although the custom of celebrating these fairs is of Spanish origin, its sense of belonging among us is due to the fact that the Aztec *tianguis* (market), was very similar to the Spanish fairs, as Bernal Díaz del Castillo pointed out. That is why our fairs, from the very beginning, had a notable Mexican accent.

Our fairs, similar to those in Spain, were initially formed by unusual markets to trade merchandise from various Mexican regions and from Europe and Asia. However, the most important fairs among those that are still celebrated are based on spiritual reasons.

This is the case of the San Marcos Fair, which owes its origin to the devotion and reverence towards the patron saint in a humble village of *Chichimeca* natives, at that time near the proud Villa of Our Lady of Assumption of Aguascalientes, founded in 1604 under the protection of Mark, the illustrious evangelist. Because of its history, it is one of the oldest in Mexico.

Because the San Marcos Fair emerged from spiritual emotions, it continued growing and, with the passing of time, it was to become the prototype of what the Mexican fair is and should be: a spontaeous and fes-

125

tive expression of the national spirit that forms its profile with various elements: spiritual feelings, as well as art, culture, gastronomy, folklore, and the trade of agricultural products, crafts, industrial, and cattle-raising products.

Thus, the San Marcos Fair is a national tradition which constitutes a full expression of what all Mexicans are and wish to be in provincial life, even when we abandon our daily tasks.

But don't think that the fair is an informal act; on the contrary, it is a social event that is formally attended and cared for. During centuries, the residents of Aguascalientes have done their best to refine it and surpass it, because they are aware that it is a way of sharing life pleasantly, that it is a mirror reflecting the people of Aguascalientes' hospitality.

Thus, throughout its history, the different generations of people in Aguascalientes have imprinted the feelings of their times. It would suffice to read the chronicles written by Alejandro Topete del Valle, to realize that each version of the fair has been a reflection of those who organized it, and of the period in which they lived.

This is how the 18th century was outstanding for its profound, religious sense and community splendor. During the 19th century, in Independent Mexico, its regional flavor was stressed and nowadays, in the 20th century, it maintains its fundamental traces of a splendorous past, so that it is a great expression of today's vigorous and industrious Aguascalientes.

History is more than a mere anecdotal breviary of dates and information; each chapter has a social and human content. Therefore, at the end of this 20th century, the Fair in Aguascalientes is a vibrant echo of the spirit of Aguascalientes, decanted and purified by time. But, above all, it is still a magnificent expression of what all Aguascalientes means to Mexico: a national and historic pride, vigorous improvement, and the joy of feeling and being Mexican.

The National Fair of San Marcos has been, is and will continue to be a genuine expression of Mexican emotions and of our festive tradition.

That is why it is not by chance that Aguascalientes is represented in the Plaza of the Three Cultures in the ancient Aztec capital, by a replica of the San Marcos Gardens.

And, should this not be enough, like every fair of noble lineage that boasts of being famous, the San Marcos Fair has its own train: the *Sanmarqueño*, which travels from Mexico through the rails en route to the city of Aguascalientes, just as López Velarde thought: "a gift from the toy shop."

A tree without roots is destined to die, and similarly, the towns that survive throughout history are those who cultivate their roots and therefore love the history of their ancestors.

Hopefully, the new generations will learn from the people in Aguascalientes to feel the pride of conserving and enriching this beautiful expression that emerges from popular feelings and emotions, as well as its traditions and customs.

The Mexican people have many faces, and the fairs —as we have said— are the gay, fierce and romantic face, where Mexican feelings explode.

It is the gentle country, "cupboard and bird cage" of a "vigorous race of hat dancers," proud of their history and of their characteristic personality.

VALLARTA LIVES THE MAY FESTIVALS

There are geographic spaces in the world with an innate vocation for luminous destinies: Vallarta, Puerto Vallarta confirms this idea because it is one of these privileged locations.

During many centuries, this beautiful place on the Pacific, originally called Las Peñas, awaited the fulfillment of its destiny, ever since Captain Francisco Cortés de Buenaventura, nephew of the Conqueror, saw the sea from the mountains, as well as a lovely valley inhabited by "bellicose" natives, and so he asked for the possession of these lands. This captain imposed the name on one of the largest bays in the world, *Bahía de Banderas*, in 1527. Thirteen years later, Pedro de Alvarado disembarked his troops on the coasts of Vallarta and described them as "beautiful beaches and drilled rocks emerging from the sea." For this reason, they were identified as *Las Peñas* (The Rocks) since then.

Certainly, the history of this heavenly place has yet to be written, but owing to the investigative efforts of illustrious residents of Vallarta, we can learn something about the history of Puerto Vallarta. It is only fair to pay homage today to that desire to preserve Vallarta's historic tradition.

Numerous illustrious explorers have witnessed the legendary beauty of this place, which also acted as a refuge for pirates and as an oasis for ships from the Orient. Nevertheless, Vallarta awaited patiently, and unknown, for its complete universal fulfillment.

It was not until the middle of the 19th century, when Mexico was now an independent nation, that a determined young man from Jalisco, born in Cihuatlán, decided to establish a city together with his wife. Guadalupe

Sánchez Torres and Ambrosia Carrillo thus took the first steps in Vallarta's history. And they, like the old explorers, gave a name to this town, *Las Peñas de Santa María de Guadalupe* on December 12, 1851. Vallarta decided to be born as Jaliscan and as Mexican precisely during a period in which the Mexican nation was shaped in its purest profiles.

And from then on, slowly but surely, and breaking off with adversity, Puerto Vallarta began its way towards progress. At the beginning, it leaned on the trade of salt; then in agriculture and cattle-raising and later, on marine trade until it finally discovered that rich human and economic lode —tourism. On his basis, Vallarta fulfilled the universal destiny to which it was entitled, because of its vocation, and owing to nature's good graces.

A paradise such as this could not remain ignored by the world, but in order to emancipate it from its hiding place —such are the laws of human happenings— it was necessary for a group of ingrained pioneers who loved their city to build its destiny. Illustrious Catalina Montes de Oca de Contreras, who adopted Vallarta as her native city, narrates all this in her simple and beautiful prose, *Puerto Vallarta en mis recuerdos* (Puerto Vallarta in my Memories). Almost unknowingly, but naturally and continuously, Puerto Vallarta emerged like its rocks, like the mountain ranges surrounding the city, into Mexico's light and finally into the entire universe. Today, Puerto Vallarta is a universally famous destination of great renown throughout the world, and we can affirm this without a shadow of a doubt.

It is safe to assume that the first settlers who founded *Las Peñas de Santa María de Guadalupe* had an unbreakable faith in their fate, because they were in daily contact with nature in their city.

The city's development was gradual and natural: first it reached the category of a political station; then it became a coastal trading port and then it had a customs house. Later, during our century, on May 31, 1918, it became a municipality and acquired the name of one of the most illustrious Jaliscans —Ignacio Luis Vallarta.

When things follow their natural course, it seems as if their fulfillment had emerged from mystery and enchantment; however, this is not so, it has a historical explanation which deserves to be focused on the essence and on the courageous human tenacity of the pioneer settlers, a beautiful social treasure which gives shape and an urban profile to traditions in Vallarta.

This basis of human value is what has made Puerto Vallarta what it is today: a center of universal coexistence that offers the world not only the beauty of its beaches, the wealth of its ocean, the coolness of its mountain ranges and the perfume of its flowers, but also the valuable hospitality of the Vallartans.

A few sociology critics adduce that tourism, a modern human industry, disfigures the original profiles; Puerto Vallarta is a testimony to the contrary. While it has become one of the main tourist centers in Mexico, Vallarta has reaffirmed its profile of a Jaliscan province and of a Mexican ancestral home. In praising the community, it must be said that the Vallartans have made a great effort to bring back the rich cultural and social Jaliscan tradition, which has allowed them to reaffirm Mexican values. Congratulations for this, and hopefully the new generations will concentrate on this spirit of struggle to conserve their authenticity and their regional values, without diminishing progress and modernity.

The May festivals participate in this spirit precisely, as they originated in the region's customs, whose purpose consisted of pleasing the pilgrims who went to visit the Virgin of Talpa, and who extended their route to take "sea baths" in Vallarta.

The May festivals were and still are a new way of showing hospitality, expressed by the gay feelings of the Vallartans, who are, ultimately, Jaliscan. The Vallartans are hospitable by nature and this is why they have been able to fulfill their touristic vocation spontaneously and naturally, but in doing so, they act as the Vallartans and Jaliscans which they are, and also as Mexicans. Congratulations to the Vallartans for this praiseworthy desire to conserve their typical aspect of a Jaliscan province, and for the efforts they have made to maintain their original values. The May Festival program demonstrates this purpose amply.

Present-day Mexico, the great proud and centralist capital, now turns its eyes towards its provinces to find in these the country's richest treasures.

Therefore, we must exhort the Vallartans, citing López Velarde's thoughts, to always be faithful to their daily image, because the bird is fifty times the same and is happier and more complete. Thus, we Mexicans will joyfully attend the May Festivals, because Velarde's sentence is fulfilled, when he says that in Vallarta's land, "the Mexican nation gives herself to us completely."

Querétaro yesterday and today

Mexico, our Mexico, owes its historical presence within the universal concert —as all of America— to two great discoveries.

The first, which has not always been recognized as it deserves, perhaps because it was lost in the remote origin ot time —refers to the discovery made by America's first settlers, who subdued its fertile soil and made our great native cultures and civilizations prosper, from the splendid Olmec civilization, to the culture of the Aztec empire, whose magnificence and grandeur are highly praised by historians. America's first conquerors accomplished a great feat when they established their civilization on our country's territory. Certainly, they were anonymous conquerors, but undoubtedly deserve our gratitude, because later, the new conquerors would establish upon their legacy what we now are.

The other great feat was Christopher Columbus' discovery, as he opened the routes on which the Spanish conquerors would travel to found viceregal Mexico.

The face and the national identity of a new culture would emerge from the melting pot of these two grand feats: our Mexican culture. The fusion of these two cultural springs —the native and the Spanish springs— infiltrates all the cultural, artistic, and social expressions of our people, and we are therefore heirs and legatees of two generous sources of traditions and customs.

Consequently, it is not surprising that all our gastronomic tradition is a reflection of this fusion, which resulted in a rich variety of high-quality gastronomical delights having a strong personality which identifies this variety as a national accomplishment.

Two facts explain why Mexican gastronomy, with a unitary and national profile, also accept regionalization: Mexico's viceregal territory was more extensive than the Aztec Empire, and the explorers and conquerors of the various regions in Mexico came from different parts of Europe.

Thus, we can properly speak of Queretaran cuisine, Yucatecan cuisine, Northern cuisine, and many others typical of any particular region. In Queretaran cuisine, we find many of the dishes normally served throughout the Mexican Republic, but when the Queretanos assimilate these, they acquire their own seal and aspect and become something new. To mention an example, Querétaro has more than 20 varieties of our famous *carnitas,** which one way or another are a generalized dish in all the country.

---

* *Carnitas*: Fried meat, generally pork. The *carnitas* tacos are some of the most popular and delicious. From *Cocina Mexicana* (Mexican Cuisine).

Since Querétaro is located in the heart of our national territory, and due to its proximity to the capital, and as Querétaro was capital of the Republic on two occasions, its regional culture is undoubtedly magnificent and refined. Its gastronomy, a daily necessary expression of its civilization, participates in these characteristics.

It is not surprising that the Queretaran cuisine has been qualified by some experts as "the dining table of surprises" because Queretaran women —and we must remember that Mexican cuisine exists because of our women— make a creation out of every dish. The recipes are traditional, but when they prepare the dishes they use their imagination and thus —as in the case of the *carnitas*, the variety is almost infinite: their *tamales*, their *moles*, their sauces, their *enchiladas*, and even their tacos have a particular accent and flavor.

Their culinary fruitfulness is still in effect. The endless variety of cheeses and wines, the most recent contributions made by this famous state of the republic to our national cuisine are an example of this. The manufacture of cheeses was a European contribution to Mexican cuisine, as the pre-Columbian natives had not tasted the delights of milk products until the arrival of the Spaniards. It is preferable to reflect upon the following: the European continent is famous for its cheeses, but if we were to analyze the different types of cheeses, we would realize that the variety in each European country is not very extensive. On the other hand, the variety of cheeses from a single region in Mexico can be seen at the Cheese and Wine Fair. Not only do we learn soon, but, based on what we have learned, we enrich the variety. For this reason, it is necessary to mention creativity and fruitfulness when referring to the Queretaran cuisine, which constitutes a pleasant surprise for the most refined and demanding tastes.

The National Cheese and Wine Fair is carried out in Tequisquiapan, Querétaro, during the last week of May.

CANDY FAIR AT SANTA CRUZ ACALPIXCAN

From June 17 to 26

Currently, Xochimilco fervently maintains its traditions, legends and customs in a deeply rooted way in each of its fourteen towns and sixteen neighborhoods which form the political contours.

More than four hundred festivals are celebrated each year, where the characteristic Xochimilcan people's hospitality is transmitted. One of the most traditional and ingrained towns is Santa Cruz Acalpixcan, whose name in Nahuatl means "caretakers of canoes." This beautiful town is located approximately 15 minutes away from the southeast of downtown Xochimilco, through the Xochimilco-Tulyehualco highway, and joyfully celebrates the Candy Fair, a unique festivity which celebrates its sixth anniversary on this occasion, providing the visitor the opportunity to enjoy the region's most delicious candy, known as glazed candy, among which the following can be mentioned, yam, fig, *pepitorias* (candy made with pumpkin seeds), wafers, lemon, peanut and pumpkin seed brittle, coconut candy, milk toffee, and *necuatole* (pumpkin candy).

Besides enjoying the different candy from the region, you can have fun with your family at no cost, with the presentation of artists, contests, and popular dances which have been prepared to make your visit more enjoyable. The festivities are part of Xochimilco, so become acquainted with them and share our traditions.

You can also know and discover a great variety of tourist attractions in this picturesque town, among which the following are found: Xochimilco's Archaeological Museum —a beautiful building of the Porfirio Díaz era, exhibiting around 480 archaeological pieces. This museum can be reached by land or through the lake— it is located on Tenochtitlan Street on the Xochimilco-Tulyehualco highway. The Cuailama archaeological zone —a place that conserves interesting petroglyphs showing the Xochimilcan people's historical happenings— is located at the end of 2 de abril Street, approximately ten minutes away from the museum.

The inhabitans of the town of Santa Cruz Acalpixcan invite you to share a different fair from June 17 to 26 every year.

THE FLOWER FAIR (FERIA DE LAS FLORES)

The Flower Fair is held every year around July 10 in San Angel

The Flower Fair has been held in San Angel since more than 132 years ago. Its purpose is to safeguard the traditions of this place, formerly known as "*Tenanitla.*"

The nature of the flower festivals is purely native, as it emerged as worship which the ancient inhabitants of *Tenanitla* —which means "under the volcano"— offered each year to Xochipilli, god of flowers.

This festivity includes the exhibition and sale of flowers, painting contests, balconies and gardens, the election of the queen of the fair, *callejonadas* (singing by troubadours in the streets), *charreadas* (horsemanship and roping by *charros*), cultural activities (concerts, dances, theatre, exhibitions), popular *verbenas*, fireworks, gastronomical samples, as well as the festival for the closing ceremony.

The great festival —between July and August in our calendar— was devoted to the god Xochipilli, to thank him for the crops of flowers and fruit.

In the course of time, religious syncretism gave this festivity a "profane" nature, although a sacred touch was still imparted, since the barefoot Carmelites decided to preserve the ancient tradition, linking it to the worship which they offered to the Virgin of Carmen, patron saint of the locality.

The Fair's Origin

The Carmelites had a special worship towards the Mother of God, in her appearance as the Virgin of Mount Carmel —our Lady of Carmel— whose festivity is celebrated in July.

Since then, they made good use of the month with great solemnity, because it coincided with the native celebrations in honor of the god Xochipilli. As the years passed, it became a fair where different divinities were present, as well as cockfights, betting, bullfights, and fireworks.

During a few years in the 19th century, the festivities were interrupted, until a neighbor in San Angel organized a special meeting in 1885 to revive the festivities in honor of the Virgin of Carmen and rescue the ancient worship of the Lord of Flowers. In 1940, the authorities of the Alvaro Obregón neighborhood decided to combine the events to make them a single festivity and called it the San Angel Flower Fair, taking the native and Catholic aspects instilled by the Carmelites.

A Traditional Festivity

Thus, the festivities which are now celebrated in San Angel date back from the past century. They have gone through several uninterrupted stages: the pre-Hispanic, the Colonial, the Reform, the Revolutionary stage and the present stage.

The Flower Fair, one hundred and thirty two years old, is the most important traditional festivity in Alvaro Obregón, in the San Angel area, which was since the viceregal period the political and administrative center, first of the municipality and later of the area, until 1987.

This festivity is the result of the union of religious, economic, and social elements, as these were fundamental factors for the organization of the fair from the beginning.

The first fair was organized in 1857. During several years the fairs were held in different places and their duration was variable. Ever since that time, a series of activities were organized, where the people participated.

San Angel is not very old. Its primitive name was Tenanitla, an unimportant hamlet, near very important towns, such as Coyoacán and Tizapán. As mentioned before, Tenanitla means "under the volcano" in Nahuatl and undoubtedly refers to the rocky terrain originated by the eruption of the Xitle volcano, which was close by.

THE GUELAGUETZA

A Multicolored Spectacle

The term *Guelaguetza* described an act of courtesy or kindness among the ancient *Zapotecas* of Oaxaca. Later, the word was also used to designate the traditional system of mutual aid established in the native communities for sowing and harvesting, and to provide assistance given to young married couples and ill relatives. Finally, it referred to the ceremonial and ritual acts where offerings were presented to Centeotl and Xilonen, god and goddess of agriculture and corn, and to Huitzilopochtli, god of war. Incidentally, these acts were always accompanied by music and ritual dances.

The *Guelaguetza* became an act of courtesy to receive celebrities and to celebrate the day of the Virgin of Carmen, during the viceregal era, owing to the influence of evangelizers.

This is the background of the present *Guelaguetza*, a festivity celebrated traditionally near the city of Oaxaca, and known as Hill Mondays and the Hill has virtually taken possession of the name.

These Hill Mondays are held on two Mondays after July 18, date in which the anniversary of the death of the illustrious Benefactor of the Americas, Benito Juárez, is commemorated. The festivity has become the most important folkloric spectacle, not only in Oaxaca, but even throughout the Mexican Republic, due to its musical wealth, its choreography and

134

dancing. The variety of rhythms, the colorful costumes, the excellence of the performers, all make this show one of the most beautiful choreographic groups with the highest artistic value of international fame.

The choreography —the heart and soul of this show— was integrated in a natural way to the traditional music and dances of the seven regions forming the beautiful native mosaic of Oaxaca.

These regions are:
1. The coast: Pachutla, Jamiltepec and Pinotepa.
2. The ravine: Teotitlán del Valle and Huautla de Jiménez.
3. The *Mixteca* region: Tlaxiaco, Huajuapan, Chicahuaxtla and Copala.
4. The Isthmus: Tehuantepec and Juchitán.
5. The valley: Mitla, Tlacolula, Ocotlán and Ejutla.
6. The Atlantic slope: Tuxtepec, Ojitlán and Valle Nacional.
7. The mountain range: Yalalag, Choapan and the Mixe area.

This show begins with a parade including all the participants, who show off their regional costumes. The development of the show includes:
1. The *Jarabe del Valle* (the Valley Hat Dance), performed by Oaxacan maidens.
2. The mountain songs and the *Jarabe de la Botella* (the Dance of the Bottle), from the Juárez mountain range.
3. The *Flor de la Piña*, (the Pineapple Flower), from Tuxtepec.
4. The *Mazateca* songs (*Jarabe Huauteco* <the *Huauteco* dance>, *La Flor de Naranja* <the Orange Blossom>, *Anillo de Oro* <Gold Ring>) from Huautla de Jiménez.
5. The dances: *El Perro* (the Dog), *El Quirio*, *El Zopilote* (the Buzzard), *El Cotón* (the Shirt).
6. *La Chilena*, (the Girl from Chile), *La Malagueña* (the Girl from Málaga), *El Son* (the song), *El Rumbero* (the Rumba Dancer), *La Vaca y El Pandero* (the Cow and the Tambourine), from Pinotepa Nacional
7. *El Jarabe Mixteco* (the Mixtecan Hat Dance), from Huajuapan.
8. *La Sandunga y la Tortuga* (the *Sandunga* and the Turtle) from Tehuantepec.
9. *El Jarabe Chenteño* (the *Chenteño* Hat Dance) and *El Palomo* (the Male Dove) song from Ejutla.

These numbers are all accompanied by regional bands, especially from the Zacatepec-Mixe regions, outstanding for their excellence. The festivity ends with the Plume Dance, where all the participants carry enormous multicolored plumes on their heads, decorated with mirrors.

135

FAIR OF LIGHTS AND MUSIC IN SANTIAGO, ZAPOTITLAN

An expression of tradition, legend and customs of a people, a race and a country, Tláhuac Region, from July 23 to 31

The Fair of Lights, celebrated in the town of Santiago Zapotitlan in the Tláhuac region is, since time immemorial, a typical Mexican fair, where the inhabitants of this beautiful town, a suburb of the state capital, all splendidly and proudly show the characteristics of their daily life: the pyrotechnical fireworks, in order to celebrate the day of the festivity of their patron saint.

We should mention that at this time, the manufacture of fireworks is one of the best known and highly paid professions in the world, since, aside from technical knowledge, creative imagination and love for the work are required.

Certainly, pyrotechnical games, and therefore, the profession were introduced in Mexico by the Spaniards. Undoubtedly, the love of artificial lights was modified by the relationship which our country had with the Far East throughout centuries, by way of the Philippine Galleon, as we must not forget that powder and artificial lights come from China.

All Mexicans are fascinated with "burning the castles" in village celebrations, because the powder that other people use to kill is employed by our marvelous makers of pyrotechnical fireworks to express their joy and to transmit happiness to their fellow countrymen.

Who among Mexicans has not enjoyed the starlit sky in village fairs, competing splendidly with the skies invented by our pyrotechnical fireworks, filling the nights with thousands of stars proceeding from the magical hands and the creative minds of our manufacturers of fireworks?

They are authentic short-lived murals that elegantly adorn all the fairs in Mexico. Imagination, illusion, polychrome poetry from Mexico's pure soul, our pyrotechnical fireworks are undoubtedly the recreation of our country's popular soul.

And thus, we not only enjoy the luxury of dressing all the fairs in Mexico elegantly, but at the same time, the inhabitants of the town where the descendants of the ancient Mexicans live have been invaded by this splendid spectacle, a gift without equal, called the Fair of Lights.

136

CULINARY
LEGACY

PRE-HISPANIC FOOD

The art of gastronomy began from the moment in which fire was used. Most of the recipes with which we are familiar were transmitted verbally. We do not know who thought of preparing a sauce for the first time, nor when the first *tortilla* was made. But, because of the need in the first place, and because of the mainly feminine creativeness and dedication, we now have an incalculable number of pre-Hispanic recipes.

Before the arrival of the conquerors, the *Mexicas* had well-balanced and varied nourishment.* It has been said that the people were undernourished because their diet had no dairy products, nor meat in the European style. However, this theory has been refuted. Due to our present knowledge, we

---

* *Acociles*: From the Nahuatl term *acocilli*. A species of sweet-water small shrimp

Achiote: Seasoning obtained by crushing and grinding the seeds of a fruit bearing the same name. Aside from using this as a seasoning, it is also used to dye red.

Ahuautli: Whitish eggs from a lake mosquito. From Nahuatl root of *atl* (water and *huautli* - (literally, tiny bit): bits of water.

Ajolotes: From the Nahuatl *axolotl*. Mexican amphibian.

Capulín: From Nahuatl *capollin*. A small dark fruit, which is eaten fresh or in preserves. Similar to the cherry.

Cutícula: The cuticle from the maguey is extracted from the center of the plant. It is a very thin white membrane, which was used as paper to write or paint during the pre-Hispanic period. It is also used to wrap meat which has been previously prepared with a chili sauce and steamed. This dish is called *mixiote*.

Chapulín: From Nahuatl *chapollin*. Mexican grasshopper which is generally bred in the cornfields.

Chayote: From Nahuatl *chayotli*. A pear-shaped fruit, with a sweet, soft, watery pulp; the rind is hard. It can be smooth or spiny, according to the variety.

Chicozapote: From Nahuatl *xicotzapotl*. A fruit with brown rind and pulp, with shiny black seeds. It is eaten fresh or in desserts.

Chirimoya: A green, heart-shaped fruit, with black seeds. The white pulp has a pleasant sweet flavor.

Escamoles: From Nahuatl *azcamolli*. Ant roe. It looks like puffed white rice, and is eaten in a prepared dish or in *taquitos* (stuffed tortillas) with *guacamole* (crushed avocado with minced onions and chili).

Guanabana: A fruit very similar to the *chirimoya*.

Itzcuintli: A hairless dog which was fattened to eat in different forms.

Izote or *yuca*: From Nahuatl *iczot* meaning tree. It is a type of palm with edible leaves and flowers of a creamy white odor and pleasant aroma.

are aware that a combination of food based on corn, beans, and amaranth produces enough amino acids to provide good nutrition. The *tortilla* is a far better nourishment than bread, because processing the corn with lime and heat (*nixtamal*) is a fundamental process to improve the nutritional value of the grain. This procedure incorporates calcium —which is so necessary and is usually missing in human diets— and it also increases the contents of assimilable iron. The number of dishes based on corn that can be prepared is extensive; for example, we shall mention a few: *tortillas, tlacoyos, tamales, pozole,* turnovers, *pinole,* etc.

On the other hand, the *Mexica* people consumed proteins originating from different kinds of animals, both by hunting or fishing, and from domestic animals. Among the hunted animals, we can mention a few, such as the armadillo, the wild boar, the *tlacuache,* the hare, the rabbit, the *tuza* (a variety of dog). From fishing in sweet or salt-water lakes and lagoons, they obtained fish, frogs, *ajolotes,* turtles, shrimp, *acociles.* Among the domestic animals, they ate turkeys and *itzcuintles* (hairless dogs). The people also consumed edible insects, and roe from a lake mosquito called *ahuatli* considered Mexican caviar. They also consumed *teocuitlatl,* an alga rich in proteins. This plant floated on the water, where the people gathered it, and then dried it, to add to different dishes.

They prepared their food in a variety of ways, baked, boiled, steamed, or as we now know, barbecued, cooking it in a hole on the ground. They used very little fat, which they obtained from the wild boar or the turkey.

A good diet must include vegetables and fruit, sources of vitamins and

---

Maguey, agave: Agave is a Latin voice meaning "admirable." It is a plant with long spiny leaves. *Aguamiel* is extracted from the center of the plant, and when it is fermented it becomes *pulque.* The worms that grow there are highly appreciated. The leaves are used to wrap meat to prepare barbecue, and *mixiotes* are prepared with the cuticle. The fiber is used to manufacture sacks, *ayates,* bags, etcetera.

Mezcal: A strong liquor made with the *aguamiel.*

Octli: Name by which the old Mexicans called the drink which they extracted from the maguey, which they later called *pulque.*

Pitaya: A vine with beautiful flowers and fruit bearing the same name.

Pulque: Drink derived from the fermentation of the maguey.

Quelite: From Nahuatl *quilitl.* An edible herb.

Tepeizcuintli and Tepezcuintli: From Nahuatl meaning "mountain dog," which is nourished with fruits and vegetables. It formed an important part of pre-Hispanic food.

Tlacoyo: A long, thick *tortilla,* stuffed with beans.

Xoconochtli: A Nahuatl term meaning acid *tuna* (the fruit of the *nopal*).

minerals. Among the vegetables, we can mention *quelites* (a leafy vegetable), squash, *nopales, huautzontles, xoconochtles, chilacayotes, chayotes,* mushrooms, *huitlacoche* (a fungus that grows on ears of corn), squash flowers, *izote* flowers, maguey flowers, and many other vegetables. Among the fruit, we can mention the following: *sapodilla, mamey, tuna,* avocado, pineapple, guava apple, wild prunes, capulin, *chirimoya, guanábana, tejocote, jícama. Achiote,* vanilla, honey, maguey honey, *hoja santa* (a large perfumed leaf), *epazote,* (small perfumed leaves), coriander, *chipilli,* etcetera, were used as seasoning.

The *cacao* (cocoa bean), the maguey, the chili (peppers) and *huautli* should be specially mentioned.

Cocoa was so highly appreciated that it was also used as money. To prepare it for a hot or cold drink, the beans were first roasted and ground with corn. Then they were dissolved in water, and sweetened with honey; vanilla was added, then the mixture was whipped with a whisk, or it was served in calabash cups from high above, in order to obtain foam.

The word *agave* is a Latin term that means "admirable." From this vegetable (the *maguey*), everything is used. A drink called *octli* is obtained from the *maguey,* later known as *pulque,* which was consumed in daily life and in religious festivities. *Mixiotes* are prepared with the cuticle. Fabrics and ropes are made with the fiber. White worms with the lower part of the body red are grown on this plant, and these worms are very nourishing. The maguey's pineapple, and the thick part of the leaves can be baked, obtaining a delicious sweet called *mezcal.*

Chili, indispensable for the preparation of numerous dishes, can be consumed fresh or dried, and there is a large variety of these hot peppers: *poblano, cuaresmeño,* green, *chilaca, pasilla, ancho, mulato, chipotle, de árbol, guajillo, piquin,* etcetera. If used with moderation, hot peppers are excellent to stimulate the appetite, and they contain vitamin K as well as ascorbic acid.

The *huautli* or amaranth seed was roasted and mixed with honey. Figures were formed with this paste (*tzoalli*) and these were consumed in various religious festivities, and they are presently known by the name of *alegrías.* Amaranth is used to prepare various dishes such as cookies, *atole* (a thick corn beverage with different flavors), and sweets in general.

As we can see, food in pre-Hispanic Mexico was well-balanced, as the people always sought harmony among cold and hot dishes. They ate twice a day, without excess, and they ate with deep respect and in silence, avoiding any discussion. The variety of dishes was extensive, and some of these dishes still exist.

The reason for the tradition of eating different and special dishes during the Mexican's festivities

Friar Diego Durán, historian, said the following when describing the festivities that were celebrated in Tenochtitlan during a year: "Eating different food in their festivities was a rite and a ceremony to distinguish the tasty dishes, and to eat a different and new tasty dish during each festivity, which this festivity allowed."

The people offered these meals to their gods.

Imperial Aztec Cuisine and Moctezuma's Table

It may seem strange to some people to talk about an Imperial Aztec Cuisine, referring to a select, very fine and varied gastronomy. But this is not a simple metaphor, it is a historical reality. People usually have the wrong impression that pre-Hispanic cuisine consisted merely of corn, beans, and chili. Some anthropologists have even considered this as the trilogy of the eating habits of our native ancestors, but fortunately this is not true. Certainly, they constitute the three usual elements, but in no way were these the only things used by the great native cooks, creators of the wonderful Mexican Cuisine.

Suffice it to recall the great amazement with which the Spanish conquerors described the native markets in Tlaxcala, Chalco-Puebla, and finally, Tlatelolco. In his Second Report to the emperor Charles V, Hernán Cortés, as well as Bernal Díaz del Castillo, Friar Francisco de Aguilar and, particularly Friar Bernardino de Sahagún, were first-hand witnesses who visited the famous *tianguis* (markets) in the native kingdoms.

Based upon what Hernán Cortés and Friar Bernardino de Sahagún stated, we shall mention some of the merchandise sold in those markets. In the old native markets, there was a street exclusively dedicated to the sale of all kinds of birds, either hunted or domestic birds: turkeys or double-chinned roosters, hens, partridges, quail, wild duck, fly-catchers, garganey, turtledoves, pigeons, birds in cages, *papagayos* (a variety of parrots), eagles, falcons, sparrow hawks, kestrels, and ducks.

In another part of the market, quadruped animals were sold: rabbits, hares, deer, small dogs fattened to eat castrated, armadillos, monkeys, and raccoons. In another street, fresh fish, salted and cooked fish, *ajolotes*, snails, shrimp, and all kinds of seafood were sold.

142

Among vegetables, the following were found: *nopales*, tomatoes, *quelites*, green tomatoes, *huitlacoche*, squash, green beans, mushrooms, *chayotes*, *huauzontles*, avocados, izote or yucca, *xoconochtli*, as well as the following fruits: *papaya, tuna, mamey*, pineapple, *guanábana, chirimoya, capulines*, wild prunes, black, white and yellow *zapote (sapodilla), chicozapote, nanche*, guava apple *pitahaya* and *tejocote*. As for tubers: sweet potatoes, potatoes, *chayote* roots, *jícamas*. Beans, corn and by-products: *tortillas, tlacoyos, totopos, pozole*, turnovers, *pinole, tamales, atole*, pop-corn. Green or dry chilis: *ancho, pasilla, mulato, guajillo, morita, de árbol, catarina, piquín, poblano, habanero*, green chilis. Beverages: chocolate, *aguamiel, pulque*, fruit-flavored water drinks, *atoles* sweetened with honey and perfumed with vanilla. Candies and sweets: pumpkin seed and peanut brittle, *pinole* (ground corn meal), pop corn, sugar cane and corn syrup, syrups mixed with amaranth seeds, honey, *maguey* ho-ney, *tuna* syrup, *biznagas* (candy made of *maguey*), *mezcal* baked sweet potatoes.

All of this was what made Hernán Cortés exclaim that our markets were far better than those in the East, and even those in Constantinople; this was the merchandise that the inhabitants of the great Tenochtitlan had within their reach, merchandise that originated the Aztec cuisine, which culminated in the wealth and variety of Moctezuma's imperial table. If we call it Imperial Aztec Cuisine, it is because not only its preparation, variety, and taste were exquisite, but because the service ceremony was quite refined and elegant, a requisite for a cuisine to be considered authentically imperial, and always better than that of the royal cuisine.

We should also mention that Moctezuma II is described as a man with a strong character, cultured, intelligent, charismatic, and with a profound religious feeling. This was why his personality was also reflected in his eating habits. He was the author of a rigid culinary ritual.

This was what Bernal Díaz del Castillo said in this respect:

"Let us go back to the way in which he had at his service the time for eating. If the weather was cold, he had a live coal fire burning (red embers), from wood taken from barks of trees that did not produce smoke, and the aroma of the bark was quite strong. And, so that the fire would not produce more heat than he desired, the servants placed a sort of screen in front of him, engraved in gold (with other figures of idols), while he sat in a low soft chair, in front of a low table, made exactly like the chairs. There, they placed the white tablecloths and some long napkins made of the same cloth, and four very beautiful and clean women gave him a washbasin, something like deep agaves which they called *xicales*.

"They placed more agaves underneath the table to gather the water, and other like plates, while two other women took *tortillas*, and when he began to eat, they placed in front of him something like a wooden door painted in gold so that no one could see him eating, and the four women stood at a certain distance. By his side stood four big, older men, with whom Moctezuma chatted once in a while or asked them questions...and when he finished eating, he gave them a plate of the food that they had liked best."

The historian also mentions that a kind of butler presented the dishes, and Moctezuma indicated the dish he preferred with a little wand. The tableware (dishes) were only used once.

"The dishes were made of red and black clay from Cholula, and more than three hundred dishes were placed on individual braziers, filled by young native noblemen.

"In the parlor, behind the folding screen, the priests, the judges, the ministers, and guards were assembled in silence (without speaking). Sometimes, when Moctezuma was in the mood, he listened to music and a type of jester —bent, ugly, deformed because their bodies were small, coarse, clownish— danced and sang for him. And, at the end of his meal, the women returned and gathered the tablecloths and gave him water to wash his hands; he then dismissed the four older men and, after smoking his pipe, he remained there, resting. Then the remaining food was distributed among the members of the court and his guards, which according to historians, were more than a thousand. This was the protocol."

We shall now see some of the dishes that Moctezuma was offered, based on Friar Francisco de Aguilar's chronicle, who also says:

"His service was very great, as befitted a powerful prince, like he used to say —the dishes filled the hall in rows: the birds were cooked in various ways: boiled, broiled or baked; another row consisted of enormous turnovers; they had the different varieties of *tamales* which also contained birds, roosters and hens. Another row of quails and pigeons also occupied their place; all kinds of fish from the river and the sea; a casserole with green chili, casseroles with green, red, yellow and black *mole*, green and red *pipian* (a variety of *mole* with pumpkin seeds); barbecue prepared with birds, boar and *tepezcuintli* and *techiches* dogs; casseroles with *maguey* worms and *escamoles* and other insects such as grasshoppers and locust; dishes prepared with *nopales*, *quelites*, *verdolagas* (a leafy vegetable similar to spinach), hard boiled eggs from different birds, quail, hens, pigeons, and turkeys.

"Frogs, *ajolotes* and a rich variety of *tortillas* also had their place, all of

144

which were greatly enjoyed by the conquerors. There were served all kinds of local fruits, as well as fruits from all the regions. The variety of desserts was very special, among which we can mention: ears of corn sweetened with syrups, *capulines*, honey, sugar cane; fruits: *mamey*, black and white sapodilla, *chicozapote, chirimoya, pitayas, tejocotes, capulines* and *tunas*."

According to this description of Moctezuma's table, it is readily seen that the figure of three hundred dishes is not exaggerated. Is not this a great imperial cuisine? If not, which cuisine could be imperial?

We must clarify that the abundance and delicacy of Moctezuma's table does not mean that he was an exaggerated glutton. On the contrary, he always behaved like a disciplined man, as historians always point out specially that he ate very little and did not indulge in excesses; that is, he was a gentleman worthy of such a table. Consequently, the refinement of his great cuisine was merely the reflection of his people's tradition, and of the highest degree of culture and spiritual character.

We should be very proud of our historical past, because as from our native roots, all the cultural expressions denoted a civilization integrated with such an identity and force of character, that even today, after five centuries, the Mexicans' cultural expressions continue prevailing. This is why the subject of Aztec Imperial Cuisine and Moctezuma's table, the direct and still-in-force background for the present Mexican cuisine, is really interesting. Even including modern tendencies, the thing that should fill us with pride is that the native woman created this wonderful cuisine which has been and continues being the leader of our gastronomy. Because it reached imperial levels prior to the Conquest, it stamped its seal and bequeathed its greatness to the future typical Mexican cuisine, together with the combination of our pot and the Spanish cauldron. The present table in Mexican homes is a direct descendant of Moctezuma's imperial table.

TECUITLATL

Spirula Alga

Pre-Hispanic food which the Aztecs ate regularly. It is a microscopic blue-green alga, presented in the form of a helicoidal filament. It lives in strong alkaline water.

Within natural foods, this alga has the largest content of proteins, and like vegetables, grows through photosynthesis. It is a multicellular organism that lives in aquatic crops having a high concentration of inorganic salts, which with the sun's rays develops its protoplasm with a high content of excellent quality proteins.

Friar Toribio de Benavente, better known with the name of Motolinia, arrived in the Valley of Mexico in 1524, and he said the following about the spirula alga: "...there was a certain kind of very fine mud on the water of Mexico's lake, and during a certain time of the year, when the layer of mud had thickened, the natives gathered the algae with fine nets, until they filled their canoes with this clay; they then deposited it on land or on the beach's sand in knolls about two or three fathoms wide and a little less in longitude. They left the clay to dry a bit and then they made cakes about two fingers thick, which were completely dry in a few days; they were shaped like bricks. The natives ate this a great deal and they obviously liked it and it satisfied them. This product was bartered with merchants from inland, just as cheese is bartered among us. It has a strange, salty taste..."

The *tecuitlatl* is a low-cost, highly nourishing food, and consequently it can help to solve the entire world's malnutrition.

Chemical analyses reveal that this alga contains 65% to 70% proteins, the highest percentage ever found in a natural food; furthermore, it contains eight essential amino acids: leucine, isoleucine, valine, threonine, lysine, methionine, phenylalanine, triptophane. It also contains some minerals, such as: calcium, potassium, iron, phosphorus, and sodium; unsaturated acid fats and seven vitamins: A1, B1, B2, B6, B12, C, and E. This alga is easily digested.

A century after the arrival of the Spaniards, the *tecuitlatl* had disappeared from the markets, but the natives —who have lived on the shores of Lake Texcoco— have continued consuming it.

There are two important reasons to really value the spirula alga:

a) It is completely digestible and does not cause side effects. During its long history of use as a human food, there has been no evidence of complications.

b) It can be produced with low-level technology and intensive work. It is recommended to take along when travelling or on tours, as it is a highly concentrated food, and is light to carry, in comparison with other heavy, voluminous foods.

Some people use it as a fertilizer for plants that grow in the shade. Due to its high content of chlorophyll, xanthophyll, carotene and vitamins A and B, it produces amazing results as hair and skin conditioner.

Currently, the company Sosa Texcoco is producing it with advanced industrial technology. Since 1967, as the result of scientific investigations carried out in Mexico on this alga, Sosa Texcoco built, with the collaboration of the French Petroleum Institute, an industrial production unit for this product, where a program was carried out for growing this alga in a controlled way.

We hope that very soon, this food will truly be within the reach of every budget.

THE CULTURE OF CORN AND THE CIVILIZATION OF CHILI

The eating habits of different people are, undoubtedly, an anthropological fact essentially linked to geography, to the people's territory, and to their culture. Thus, culinary art proves to be a natural expression of a people's civilation.

The way in which eating habits are transmitted is precisely the tradition, which is merely the transmission made daily, from generation to generation, of the uses and customs of food.

It is therefore correct to refer to the Mexican culinary tradition, which is certainly formed by the so-called regional cuisines, because, as previously mentioned, the cuisine is linked to geography, and since Mexico is a country formed by various regions, when we speak of the culinary tradition, we have to understand that it refers to a large number of cuisines, which are necessarily regional.

But it is valid to speak of a national culinary tradition, since within the historical process of Mexico's cultural integration, as far as cuisine is concerned, various elements of general acceptance are combined in all the national territory.

Such is the case of corn, tomatoes, green tomatoes and, basically, chili.

Some anthropologists tend to mention the Culture of Corn, in order to express symbolically the habits of Central American cultures; in the same sense, the Civilization of Chili could also be classified, because it is a universal ingredient in Anahuac's nourishment.

Chili is an ingredient originating in Mexico, whose function consists of providing character, taste and color to Mexican dishes, an authentic culinary accent, a certain seasoning —if the usual term is preferred. When mentioning that it is an accent, this does not necessarily suggest the characteristic that it is a "hot" spicy food, because Mexican dishes have evolved,

147

and gourmet cuisine has endeavored to eliminate it, or at least tends to soften it, so that the taste may become more universal. Rather, it is the result obtained from handling chili, which stamps a special flavor on the dishes.

The enormous variety of chilis, with their respective characteritics in color, taste and preparations, provide Mexican sauces with enormous variety and richness, to be used as a garnish for dishes with a Mexican origin.

The great Mexican culinary discoveries are based upon the use of the ingredients and their combination with other elements and ingredients, whether of Central American origin, or contributed by other civilizations —as in the case of spices, vegetables and animals brought from other countries.

In Mexico, chilis, including all the different varieties, have been used during a long time as a basic ingredient in the preparation of dishes; that is, if the history of Mexican cuisine were to be analyzed, it would be seen that for a long time chili has always been included as a complement or companion of the substantial or main part of the tasty dishes.

It can therefore be appreciated that it is correct to speak about a civilization of the table, because food is the expression of the culture with which people identify themselves.

His Majesty the Chili and the Divine Sauces

This product is of pre-Hispanic origin. Some researchers consider that the cultivation of chili came before corn, beans, and squash.

Two places in the Valley of Mexico prove the use of chili in the high plateau since the Preclassic era: in the underground debris in the excavations of Loma Torremote, Cuautitlan, Mexico, carbonized chili seeds, of the conic trunk type were found, dated between 2950 and 2250 B.C., as well as remains of chili in the form of carbonized seeds in almost all the chronological sequence of Teotihuacan.

Chili is an indispensable ingredient in the preparation of most Mexican dishes. It is used fresh (green) as well as dry; the variety is extensive.

The *Codex Mendocino* —named after the first viceroy in New Spain, Don Antonio de Mendoza, because he had it painted to report to emperor Charles V of the wealth of the new conquered lands— mentions the products and the amounts that should be delivered to Mexico by the subdued people, in the list of tribute.

Chili is also mentioned in children's education, as it is said that when a child deserved punishment, he was forced to breathe smoke from roasted chili, with which he promised to behave.

Many of the dishes which we enjoy nowadays that contain chili are of pre-Hispanic origin, such as *chileatole, tamales,* turnovers, and *tlacoyos* with the different types of sauces; red and green *pipian,* (with ground pumpkin seeds), *escamoles* (ant roe), *charales* (tiny dried fish), *ahuautle* cakes, shrimp cakes, *mixiotes,* squash with sliced peppers, and many others.

Combination of the Clay Pot with Spanish Cauldron

With the arrival of the conquerors, our cuisine became more varied, since by combining the different types of food which we had here with those that were brought, the cuisine of the mixed races appeared, which was greatly appreciated by natives and foreigners and occupies third place in the world due to its delicious flavor, its high nutritious value, its variety, and presentation. We shall mention a few examples of this cuisine. The *mole* from Puebla is in the first place, followed by the black *mole* from Oaxaca, the red snapper *à la* Veracruz, the traditional rosemary with shrimp cakes, the famous green peppers in walnut sauce, the *tinga* (shredded pork meat) from Puebla, *mole de olla* (pot mole), the *pozole* (dish made of corn and pork meat), *pancita* (beef belly cooked in a spicy stew)...the list could be endless. And we cannot forget to mention the *piquín* chili in powder which, mixed with salt is sprinkled on fruits and vegetables, on boiled or roasted ears of corn, and on different fried foods.

Chili is a very familiar ingredient among us, and its name is present in different puns and songs.

It is said that during the Middle Ages, Europeans appreciated spices, but they did not have enough seasoning or stimulants, which became a decisive factor to seek new routes to India in order to obtain spices. During this search, they arrived at America, and although their contribution to Mexican cuisine was determinant, ever since that time they too found new cooking elements, among which the most important were chocolate, vanilla, chili, etcetera.

Chili can be eaten fresh or dried. It generally has a different name when it is dry from its name when it was fresh. For example the *chilaca* chili is known by that name when it is fresh, and *pasilla* chili when dry. When the *poblano* chili is dry it is known as *ancho* or *mulato*; the *cuaresmeño* is called

149

chipotle when dry; the fresh *morita* chili is called *serrano* or *de árbol*, according to the type.

The chilis that are left to dry on the plant are the best quality. This type of dry chili is called *pasera*, although most of the chilis are now dried in ovens and they are immediately sprinkled with water in order to pack them in sacks. The chilis that are dried in the sun are recognized because their stem is not burned.

Although there is a large variety of chilis, the expert housewife knows how to distinguish the flavors.

The degree of hot spicy chili ranges from very little to a great deal. The largest concentration of spiciness is found in the chili's transverse section; therefore, small chilis are "hotter" than the large ones.

Among the least spicy chilis, we can mention: the *mulato, ancho*, big *guajillo*, the bonnet pepper; and among the spiciest: *de árbol, pulla, piquín, serrano, morita* and *habanero*.

When speaking of chili, we should mention the term in the Nahuatl language, *molcaxitl* (plate or bowl for the sauce), as it can be ascertained that the most delicious sauces are those made in the *molcajete* (a special stone), although to save time, the blender is now used most of the time.

Mexico is an important producer of different types of chilis, as this product is present in many dishes, from soups, such as the *tortilla* soup, the *caldo tlalpeño* (a chicken soup with vegetables and *chipotle* chili); in dishes such as *moles*, sauces, and even in sweets such as fruit pulp and lollipops, to mention a few products. However, most of the production is absorbed by industry, as canned chilis have a great deal of demand in the country and in other countries, especially marinated chilis.

If consumed moderately, chili stimulates the appetite. Furthermore, chili contains vitamins A, C, K and ascorbic acid.

Friar Bernardino de Sahagún, in his book *Historia general de las cosas de la Nueva España* (General History of Things in New Spain), mentions chili for medical uses:

a) As a remedy for dental problems.
b) For sores on the tongue [as an antiseptic].
c) For problems in the digestive system.
d) For coughs
And others.

Chili is used in contemporary popular medicine, although it is considered a household remedy.

When people know how to eat chili, it is delicious, but for those who are not familiar, it can become painful or a new experience.

We should now mention the Mexican tradition of chilis (green peppers) in walnut sauce.

Stuffed chilis, and the famous peppers in walnut sauce mark a degree of cultural avant-garde evolution in Mexico's general civilization, represented in eating habits In effect, as we had mentioned, prior to the creation of the stuffed chili in walnut sauce, peppers had a complementary function, or were used to accompany dishes. However, when this dish appeared, chili surpassed the function of merely being a seasoning; it became independent and imposed its sovereignty and its personality in the Mexicans' table, becoming an important tasty dish.

Strangely enough, the invention of chilis in walnut sauce coincided with the era of our national independence, and the reaffirmation of Mexican sovereignity. This chili not only obtained its independence from its former function, but it was presented plastically with the colors of the recently born national flag as well, plus the fact that the monastic fantasy offers it as a symbol reasserting our nationality, which was the reason why it was presented with the national colors: green, white and red of the national emblem. Chilis in walnut sauce is a representative dish during the commemoration of the national holidays.

CHILIS IN MEXICO

Fresh chilis are:

JALAPEÑO CUARESMEÑO. Measures between 3 and 6 centimeters. It is meaty, with a round point. Used to marinate, and to stuff.

JALAPEÑO CHICO. There are smaller varieties (between 2 and 3 centimeters, and they are spicier.

SERRANO OR *CHILE VERDE.* (Green chili) Pointed and small. It is only eaten in raw or cooked sauces, marinated, and in stews.

POBLANO. Large and green, the most commonly used to stuff. It is also sliced and ground for soups. It is roasted and peeled before using. A variety of the small *poblano* is called *chile de agua* (water chili).

DE ARBOL. Very small and hot. For sauces and marinated.

CHILACAS. Dark green, long and smooth, very hot. It must be roasted, peeled, removing the veins. Used to stuff, sliced and marinated.

151

MIRASOL. Its flowers always look at the sun. It is not used very much when fresh.

PIQUIN. This is the smallest chili, the best known and perhaps the hottest. It is green and turns red when mature. Used in many sauces. Other names by which it is known: *chiletepin, pulga, amash* (in Tabasco), *enano, tichusni* (in Oaxaca) and *guindilla* (in Spain).

TROMPO. Spherical, small. Used in fresh sauces. It is also called *bola* or *trompita.*

GÜERO. Yellow or light green. In the Southeast it is called *ixcatic.* Aromatic and fine. Used in dishes and stews, or for stuffing; used in sauces or marinated, and can be canned. Other names given to this chili are: *caribe* and *caloro.*

HABANERO. Very aromatic, and the hottest of all. Exclusively grown in the Southeast. Used in stews and other dishes.

DE AGUA. Similar to the poblano, but smaller, light green. Grown in Oaxaca.

The same chilis, when dry, bear another name:

CHIPOTLE. It is dried by smoking it. It is dark red, wrinkled, aromatic and hot. Used in sauces, *adobos,* and (whole) in stews and soups. When it is dry and unsmoked, it is called *meco.*

MORITA. Reddish, aromatic and hot. Other names by which it is known: *chilaile* and *mora.*

SERRANO SECO. (Dry *serrano*) Used in sauces and *adobos.* When ground it is used for seasoning fruits and salads.

ANCHO. Brick-wine color. Comes from the light *poblano.*

MULATO. Intense red. Comes from dark *poblano.* Used in *adobos, moles,* and sauces. It can also be stuffed. Another name given to this chili is *chino.*

DE ARBOL SECO. (Dry) In powdered form, it is used to garnish vegetables and fruits.

PASILLA. Long, wrinked, dark red, aromatic, with a sweet spicy flavor. It can be stuffed, or used in *adobos* and sauces. Also called *achocolatado* (chocolate-like).

GUAJILLO. Long, smooth, thick skin, fleshy and aromatic. When it is smaller, it is hotter.

NOTE. When speaking of "sliced" chili, this generally refers to sliced *poblano* chili.

PIQUÍN SECO. When dry, it is a purplish-red color. It is the basis for numberless garnishes, among which is the *Tabasco* sauce.

CASCABEL. Has a spheric shape and sounds like a rattle or small bell. Hot, with a strong aroma.

RED. From the Southeast. It is the basis for *chilmole*.

CHILHUACLE. Dark sepia color. It is a necessary ingredient for the black *mole* from Oaxaca.

MOLE, A GASTRONOMICAL MONUMENT

Much has been written about *mole** just as it happens with important things in life, and even more has been said about it.

The truth is that it is an ancient dish, originating in the lands of Anahuac, where it used to be a main dish at the Aztec emperors' table. Historians have testified to this and, should it not be enough, suffice it to remember the origin of its name: it comes from the Nahuatl word *mulli* with which the chili sauces were designated.

Thus, the humorous anecdote referring to the origin of the *mole* from Puebla loses its wit, as it asserts that the word originated from a nun's exclamation, when she observed her companion, Andrea de la Asunción, preparing a recipe created by the former, and she said, bewildered, "But how much is ground (*mole*)." And her companions immediately stopped her, saying, "*Muele* (the correct way of expressing the verb 'to grind') sister, not *mole*."

But joking aside, the origin of the *mole* or *moles* —to be more exact— is undoubtedly pre-Hispanic. It was a dish served and enjoyed by the people in Central America, and it could not be otherwise, because although it is true that as far as a culinary tradition is concerned, we are usually known as

---

*MOLE. The Aztecs used to say *molli* when referring to sauce. Nowadays, *mole* is understood to be a thick sauce based on chilis and spices. The *moles* from Oaxaca and Puebla are famous, and the latter is prepared with more than 40 ingredients.

MOLE DE OLLA. A country dish based on beef and corn, with plenty of broth. Served like soup. *Epazote* (an aromatic herb) predominates in the flavor.

CHILMOLE. A seasoning based on toasted chilis and other spices, used in the Southeast of Mexico.

MANCHAMANTELES. A dish prepared with several kinds of meat, chili, fruits and various spices.

From *Cocina Mexicana* (Mexican Cuisine).

the "Corn Civilization," it is also worth remembering that the use of chilis as a basic ingredient for native nourishment is unquestionable.

It is fitting to point out the existence of a native "gourmet" cuisine, as proved by the detailed testimony of several historians regarding emperor Moctezuma's table. This fact is mentioned because, since *mole* was one of the dishes prepared for the imperial table, its preparation was refined and included the basic characteristics which have been preserved by later *moles*, that is, it is a selective and careful combination of various chilis to which cocoa or chocolate, amaranth and several native spices are added in order to refine the flavor, until a fine and different flavor is achieved. The wild turkey plays a basic role in this combination.

Mole has a long historical career, and the people's destiny follows this career: if the native people were to mingle with the Spaniards, the dishes served at their table would do the same. It can be affirmed that *mole*, this gastronomical monument, is not the product of an imaginative nun, but of history's evolution.

In effect, *mole*, with its different regional versions, is being enriched with ingredients brought from the Old Continent, and with the spices from the Oriental Indies.

It is not surprising that investigators and connoisseurs of mole from Puebla make a humorous comparison between the Puebla baroque and *mole's* gastronomical structure; rather it could be said that this excellent dish is Mexicanly "churrigueresque" (Mexicanly Baroque).

It is said that Viceroy Don Tomás Antonio de la Cerda y Aragón, Count of Paredes and Marquis of Laguna arrived in Mexico in 1680, and among his virtues, he was the admirer and patron of another famous nun, who excelled in literature: Sister Juana Inés de la Cruz. The archbishop of Puebla, who wanted to receive this Viceroy with pomp and splendor, requested the Convent of Santa Rosa to prepare a native dish having special quality.

The task was designated to Sister Andrea de la Asunción, who selected *mole* to create her *mestizo* (half Spanish and half Indian) recipe, undoubtedly to adapt the dish to the flavor and preference of the newly arrived viceroy and his wife.

Others attribute the recipe to Friar Pascual, who, they say, created it for another viceroy, Bishop Palafox.

We prefer to believe that the recipe of the *mestizo mole* was created by the angelical hands of a woman, as this is more in keeping with Mexican culinary tradition, as we must remember that ever since pre-Hispanic times, the woman, and only the woman, has been the great heroine in Mexico's gastronomical tradition.

No one doubts that *mole* is the national dish *par excellence*, the leader in every Mexican table, whether rich or poor, whether select or popular; from gourmet cuisine to daily cuisine. This explains the reason why there are as many *moles* as there are regions in the country. But we must emphasize that all the varieties conserve certain fundamental characteristics. As expressed in a common phrase, "every *mole* is *mole*."

In the Valley of Mexico, the *mole* made in San Pedro Actopan is famous, to the degree that the prepared product is distributed throughout the country. The kitchens in San Pedro Actopan have substituted in modern Mexico, the function performed in viceregal Mexico in the famous convents in Puebla, who received orders from all over the country to prepare the famous *mole* made in Puebla.

There are all the imaginable varieties of *mole* in colors and flavors: red *mole*, black *mole*, green *mole*, yellow *mole*, *pipianes* (made with pumpkin seeds) and *manchamanteles* (with chili and fruits); recipes from the last century include up to one hundred different recipes.

Long live *mole*!

HUEXOLOTL.[1] THE TURKEY[2]

Before the Conquest, the Aztecs Ate Turkey

The traditional turkey (a gallinaceous bird) adorns Christmas tables in many countries throughout the world. In pre-Hispanic Mexico, it was known by the name of *guajolote* or rooster with a double chin, and it was found in the pine or evergreen forests, in the plateaus in the western and eastern parts of the country, and in the coastal region of what is now known as Tamaulipas and Veracruz. The turkey was widely used by the inhabitants, who tamed the bird.

---

1) GUAXOLOTE (*HUEXOLOTL*) This bird, called gallipavo by the Spaniards, is the rooster of these regions and the female, known by the name of *pípila* is the Mexican hen. The meat is tasty and even delicious when the turkeys have been carefully fed, in clean corrals, with abundant grains and water. Fifteen days before the turkeys are killed, they are given small nuts in the beak, beginning with one the first day; the second day, two, and so on, until the eve of their slaughter, without omitting the corn they may voluntarily eat during this time. (Continued on the next page).

Most experts coincide in affirming that the turkey originated in America and was then extended throughout the world.

The natives appreciated the bird due to its size and quality of the meat, and it formed part of their food during the festive celebrations, using it in different ways —usually with *moles*.

The turkey undoubtedly formed part of Moctezuma II's imperial table, because various historians mention that this species existed in the monarch's famous breeding pens.

It is present in the wide repertoire of merchandise in the famous market of Tlatelolco, which was so amazing to Cortés and to Bernal Díaz del Castillo.

Furthermore, it is present in the various *codices*, under the name of *huexolotl*, which, deformed and in Spanish produced the name of *guajolote* (turkey). Bernal Díaz del Castillo and other historians referred to the turkey; in 1525, this bird's excellence is mentioned, and they speak of how much the Spaniards appreciated this meat.

The Anglo-Saxon custom of preparing the turkey traditionally on *Thanksgiving Day* contributed to the bird's popularity as a select and festive dish for celebrations, which imposed its propagation in Europe. Certainly, the species of turkeys existing nowadays are greatly varied. There are turkeys of every color and size, due to its high degree of use and commercialization. But, undoubtedly, the turkey conserves the fundamental characteristics of its Mexican ancestors.

The turkey is a significant contribution of Mexico's traditional cuisine to the world.

They are cooked in numberless ways, both in the foreign and in the Mexican style, and they are delicious in all the forms, and easily digested.

Their own way of cooking the turkeys, learned from the natives of the country, is in *mole*. However, *mole* is made in such a variety of ways, that it would not be exaggerated to say that they are cooked in each house in a different way, although chilis are included in all of them, combining in a greater or lesser degree, the *ancho* chili with the *pasilla*, including more or less seeds of this type and of other kinds in orden to thicken the sauce, and spices in different proportions, adding tomatoes and green tomatoes, or omitting these.

From *Nuevo cocinero mexicano en forma de diccionario, 1888*
(New Mexican Cookbook in the Form of a Dictionary, 1888).

2) *GUAJOLOTE.* The turkey, bird originating in Mexico. The female is called *pípila.*
From *Cocina Mexicana* (Mexican Cuisine).

The *NOPAL* (PRICKLY PEAR)

Nopalli

The *nopal* (prickly pear), belonging to the cactus group, is abundant in extensive areas within our territory, mainly in the center and northern part of our country, and in Milpa Alta, where most of this vegetable is grown for use in Mexico City. The producers in this region are well-organized, and each year they celebrate the "*Nopal* Fair," where many different dishes are presented, from combined *nopalitos* to *nopal* jams, including soups and an infinite variety of dishes.

The *nopal* has a pre-Hispanic origin and is present in the cosmic symbol "eagle-serpent."

Friar Bernardino de Sahagún reports the following in his *Historia general de las cosas de la Nueva España* (General History of Things of New Spain):

"There are some trees in this land called *nopalli*, which means *tunal* [prickly pear grove] or tree bearing *tunas* [prickly pears]. This tree is monstruous; the trunk is made of leaves and the branches are made up of the same leaves. The leaves are wide and thick; they have a lot of juice and they are sticky. The leaves have thorns, and the tasty fruit grown on these trees is called *tuna*. It is a highly appreciated fruit. The leaves of this tree are eaten raw or cooked."

This plant or tree provides a fruit having a delicious sweet and juicy taste, known as *tuna*, of which there are different species: white, yellow and red.

The delicious flavor of the *tunas* can be enjoyed while eating the fruit in its natural condition, although it can also be prepared in water, jam and, crystallized candy. There is also a fruit known by the name of *xoconoxtli* or sour *tuna*, used in some sauces and in *mole de olla* (a soup-like mole, with corn).

The *tuna* also has medicinal uses: if it is eaten without the rind, but with the seeds, it cures gastrointestinal disturbances; its juice, taken regularly, normalizes the temperature of the digestive system and the kidneys and cures bilious diseases.

An insect known as *cochinilla* grows on the *nopal*. It is a worm that produces a certain coloring used to dye fabrics and to manufacture cosmetics. In pre-Hispanic Mexico, women used it to draw adornments on their bodies.

157

Among the tastiest candies made with *tuna* is the famous "*tuna* cheese" in San Luis Potosí, a product representative of this place.

AMARANTH

Huautli, amaranto, bledo, tzoalli or *alegría*

The use of amaranth dates back to the pre-Hispanic era. Friar Bernardino de Sahagún says that images of the gods were made with this paste and "after the festivity, the images were divided among the people, who ate them."

Amaranth was consumed in the daily diet like a vegetable when it was tender, and *atole, tortillas* and *tamales* people believed that this was a pagan custom. However, the plant survived. Nowadays, it is grown in different regions, mainly in Tláhuac, Milpa Alta, and Xochimilco. Furthermore, the Fair of *Alegría* is celebrated in Tulyehualco and Xochimilco, where Mr. Mateo Mendoza, its principal national and international promoter is found.

Due to present information, it is known that a combination of food based on corn, beans and amaranth produces sufficient amino acids to achieve good nutrition. It seems that in the United States there is a project to produce amaranth at an industrial level, since its high content of proteins has been recognized, and it is accepted as one of the most important foods for the future. Dietician specialists at NASA have given their approval, and this product was included in Mexican astronaut Rodolfo Neri's diet.

Like chili, amaranth is planted first in seedbeds or nurseries at the beginning of May, and eight weeks later it is transplanted on firm soil. Rains favor its growth, and it is harvested in October. When mature, this plant reaches a growth of an average of two meters, and presents different tones: deep red, green, yellow, orange, purple, and magenta.

Chemical analysis indicates that *huautli* contains 63% carbohydrates, 15.8% proteins, 7.12% fats, besides calcium and phosphorus. Amaranth helps to conserve the balance of calcium, phosphorus, and magnesium, and these minerals nourish the central nervous system.

With this plant's seeds, two types of *alegría* bread are made: fine and normal bread.

Fine bread is prepared with the well-cleaned seeds, roasted on a *comal* (a thin sheet made of clay used to bake tortillas). An equal amount of honey is boiled and then removed from the fire. The seeds are added and mixed thoroughly The mixture is then returned to the fire, stirring the mixture constantly to avoid burning or sticking to the bottom of the pan. When the mixture thickens, it is emptied on wooden molds, two centimeters thick sprinkled with starch. It is pressed with a rolling pin, so that the mixture may be well pressed and will not break when removed from the molds. The mixture is cut in strips, which are placed in boxes covered with wafers. (During the pre-Hispanic era, they were prepared with honey made by honey-ants.)

Present-day *alegría* bread is made with syrup made of *piloncillo* (brown sugar). The seeds are soaked during six hours, then they are allowed to dry and are roasted until they break open. The brown-sugar syrup is added, and they are emptied in molds which may be round, then they are sliced.

Amaranth Products

AMARANTH CEREAL. This cereal can be eaten directly, or with milk.

AMARANTH FLOUR. A ground granulated flour, used to prepare *tortillas*, cookies and *atole*. Emits a pleasant aroma, as it is 100% natural.

ALEGRÍA. (a sweet). Typical Mexican candy made with amaranth, honey or brown-sugar syrup, and decorated with nuts, pine nuts, peanuts, and raisins.

CORN, MARVEL OF MEXICO'S SOIL

Corn has one of the most prolific descendants that have nourished the Mexican people during centuries. Some of the offspring of corn are: the indispensable *tortilla*, toasted *tortillas*, *gordas*, *garnachas*, *memelas*, *martajadas*, *picadas* (small thick tortillas with a brim to avoid spillage of the combination of beans, sausage, cheese, onion, lettuce, lard, and salt that is placed on top the *tortillas*), and *pellizcadas* (the borders of the tortillas are pinched, hence the name), *tlayudas* (very big corn *tortillas*, originating in Oaxaca), *enfrijoladas* (corn *tortillas* submerged in the pot where the beans are cooked, with its broth), *enchiladas* (corn tortillas stuffed with shredded chicken or pork, covered with *mole* or chili sauce, cheese and cream), *chalupas* (flattened corn meal, then fried and covered with different kinds of chili sauce, shredded chicken or pork meat and minced onions), *quesadillas* (thin tortillas folded like turnovers, and stuffed with different dishes; originally, they were merely stuffed with cheese), *peneques* (closed *chalupas* in the form of turnovers); *papadzules* from Yucatán, *totopos*, *sopes*, *molotes*, *esquites*, *chilemole*, *panuchos, tacos, tlacoyos, chilaquiles.* As sweets, *pinoles*, sugar or brown-sugar *gorditas*, and as drinks, a rich variety of *atoles.**

---

* *Atole.* Popular drink originating in Mexico. It is prepared by dissolving corn flour in milk or water; the liquid is boiled and then strained. Later, it is sweetened, or cinnamon is added. There are different flavored *atoles.*

Chalupas. These consist of a flattened and fried dough, on which sauces are served, as well as shredded pork or chicken meat and chopped onions.

Chilaquiles. Dry, fried pieces of corn tortilla, dressed with tomato sauce, spices, and cheese.

Chilmole. Seasoning based on burned chilis and various spices. Originated in the Mexican southeast.

Elotes. From the Nahuatl *elotl* "ear of corn."

Enfrijoladas. Corn *tortillas* submerged in the pot of beans, with the corresponding broth.

Esquites. Grains of tender corn in its own juice.

Garnachas. Cone-shaped, stuffed with chopped meat and fried beans.

Gorditas. Thick corn *tortillas*, where different meat dishes are placed. Sprinkled with cheese and chili sauce.

Martajadas. Thick *tortillas* which, after being cooked in the *comal* are cut in the upper part, and pork lard or salted butter is added.

Memelas. Thick *tortillas*, usually eaten with beans, cheese, and a hot sauce.

Molotes. Rolls of dough, stuffed and fried.

Panuchos. Fried corn *tortillas*, dressed with beans, *pibil* piglet and pickled onions.

Pellizcadas. If the edges of the *garnachas* are pinched, these are called *pellizcadas.*

Picadas. Small, thick *tortillas*, with an edge so that the combination of beans, pork sausage, cheese, onion, lettuce, lard, and salt which are placed over the *tortillas* will not spill over.

Pinole. Toasted and sweetened corn flour. Eaten as a dessert.

Quesadillas. Thin, folded *tortillas* (turnovers), stuffed with various dishes. Originally, only those stuffed with cheese were called by this name.

Sopes. Small, somewhat thick *tortillas* with brim. These can be fried. They are prepared with beans, shredded meat, lettuce, crumbled cheese, and a hot chili sauce.

Tacos. Middle-sized and small *quesadillas.*

Tlacoyos. Corn turnovers stuffed with fresh lima beans or pork rind. Served hot from the comal.

Tlayudas. Big corn *tortillas*, originating in Oaxaca.

Tostadas. Leftover *tortillas*, fried and spread with fried beans. Also covered with various dishes.

Totopos. Pieces of flattened corn flour, toasted and crisp, used like spoons to eat with fried beans.

His Majesty: the Chili.

(Right) The super hot, spicy *habanero* chili from Yucatán.

Ingredients for a spicy sauce.

The divine Red Sauce.

Mole: the king of Mexican cuisine.

(Below) Pozole: sacred corn-based soup and offering for the gods.

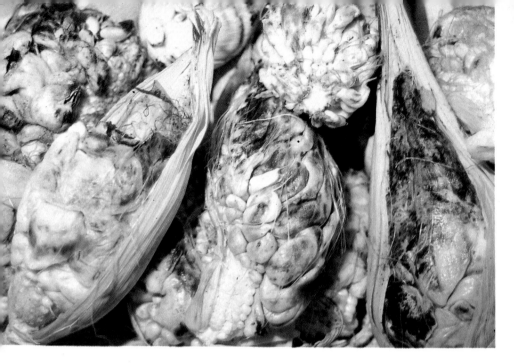

Huitlacoche: corn fungus, the favorite dish of pre-Hispanic nobles.

Distinctive national dishes. Mexican appetizers. *Sopes* (corn-based cakes filled with beans).

Handicrafted figures from the Mexican Revolution.

Other delicious corn products. The world famous Nachos.

Tamales, exquisite, delicately flavored appetizers. The kings of family gatherings. Here, the *tamal oaxaqueño*, wrapped in banana leaves.

And here, *tamal de mole*, wrapped in corn husks.

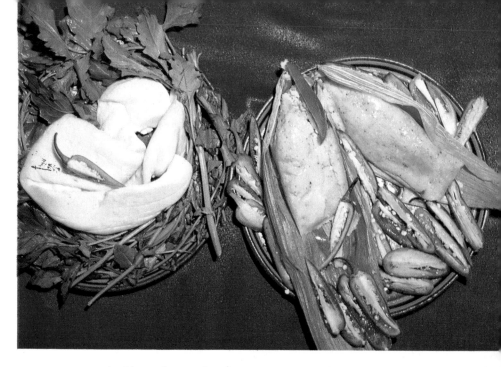

And here, the *tamal verde*, wrapped in corn husks and filled with green chili.

Amaranth, protein rich, divine seed of the gods.

The magnificence of the Amaranth plant, and some of its products.

Multi-colored mosaic of typical crafts.

Modelled clay fruit painted by hand.

Diabolical crafts.

Among Mexico's most famous crafts are the elegant, highly burnished, black clay ceramics.

A multi-colored array of the Mexican dolls.

The *china poblana*, a Mexican beauty, a *charro* couple.

Ingredients for *Chiles en Nogada*, typical patriotic dish from Puebla.

A view of the Plaza of the Constitution (the *Zócalo*). September, the patriotic month, is the month for buying a tiny Mexican flag.

The red, white, and green of the patriotic month of September.

Mexican Doll.

Magical *buñuelos* (deep fried dough covered with sugar).

A symphony of colors. The *wafer*.

MEXICO'S NATURAL GIFTS TO THE WORLD

CORN

BEANS

CHILI

AVOCADO

VANILLA

COCOA

CHOCOLATE

TOMATOES

SQUASH

CHAYOTE

ZAPOTE

MAMEY

PAPAYA

GUAVA APPLE

NOPAL

MAGUEY

RUBBER

SPIRULA ALGA

TOBACCO

AMARANTH

POINSETTIA

TURKEY

ACHIOTE

CHILACAYOTE

CHÍA

CAPULÍN

COPAL (RESIN)

EPAZOTE (AROMATIC HERB)

HUAUZONTLE

HUITLACOCHE (CORN FUNGUS)

MUSHROOMS

JÍCAMA

SWEET POTATO (YAM)

DEER

WILD BOAR

COYAMETL OR PIG

TEPEZCUINTLE

ARMADILLO

QUETZAL

HISTORICAL
MEXICO

THE MAGNIFICENT LEGEND OF THE MERCHANT CHINESE SHIP (*LA NAO DE CHINA*)

The presence of this ship in Mexico's traditions has left its trace in home decorations and in the Mexicans' way of dressing.

Undoubtedly, the fundamental significance of the legendary Chinese Ship, Philippine or Acapulco Galleon (since it was known by the three names) appears in the international trade sphere during the sixteenth and seventeenth centuries, as well as part of the eighteenth.

Aside from its outstanding historical importance in the trade of New Spain with other Spanish colonies and with Spain herself, to Mexico the Chinese Ship meant cultural exchange with other Oriental countries, an interchange which has left a considerable mark on our artistic and cultural expressions.

Among other influences that were left, new ways of dressing, furniture, utensils and the home decorations should be mentioned, as well as the culinary tradition, pictorial art, etc., all of which are enveloped in the atmosphere of adventure, legend and mystery that has always surrounded Oriental countries.

We should also mention that the merit of establishing a navigation route to the Philippine Islands belongs to the inhabitants of New Spain. As a matter of fact, the so-called "return trip" is considered the first record of Mexican maritime tradition, as the New Spaniards opened the route and kept it against all odds, fighting with pirates and privateers who ravaged the Pacific Ocean.

The Chinese Ship is our very own heritage. But let us return to the thread of our thoughts about the trading influences mentioned above. For this purpose, it suffices to read the memoirs of Manila's District Attorney, in which he lists some of the merchandise that the galleon carried to the port of Acapulco:

> *Balsam and ivory from Abada and Cambodia*
> *Camphor from Borneo*
> *Nutgall from Lequiois*
> *Diamonds from Goia*
> *Rubies, sapphires and topaz from Thailand*

From India: rugs, carpets, cotton (from the Mongolian Empire of India, which included Bengal), fine draperies, bedspreads, and quilts from Bengal; pearls and precious stones.

From China: all kinds of silks —raw and woven— in velvet and damask (the latter with brocades embroidered with fantastic designs in gold and silver), delicate Cantonese gauzes and crepes, the flowery Cantonese silk called "spring," taffetas, handkerchiefs, linen, napkins, and tablecoths, jars, porcelain, furniture, festoons, gold-plated objects, adornments, paper, and other greatly valued, beautiful objects.

From Japan: amber, pearls, colored silks, writing material, chests and tables made of precious lacquered wood with odd decorations, fine silverware.

Magnificent shawls from Manila, ladies' silk dresses (and dresses made of other precious fabrics). Thousands of pairs of silk stockings were sold —more than 50 thousand by one galleon— velvet skirts and bodices, capes, gowns and kimonos, silk beadspreads and tapestries.

In the eighteenth century the clergy came to own the trade. The Church absorbed most of the Asiatic wonders, since religious ornaments came from China: dalmatic gowns for archbishops and bishops, surplices, laces, vestments kept in mahogany and ebony chests of drawers, rich full-length gowns for friars and clergymen.

Gold bars, jewels (diamond rings, bracelets, pendants, earrings, necklaces), religious objects such as crucifixes, rosaries and lockets.

Hilts and sheaths for swords with inlaid precious stones, and sometimes alligator teeth mounted in gold.

The famous, coveted spices should be added to the above: cinnamon from Ceylon and Malabar, pepper from Sumatra and nutmeg from Java, cloves (and other spices) from the Mollusk Islands and Bunda.

It can readily be seen that most of this merchandise was not produced in Manila nor Philippine Islands; it was bought from Chinese, Japanese, and Indian merchants and from other Oriental countries.

This was how the Chinese Ship came to enrich Mexico's daily habits, cupboards and our recipes, as well as our taste and appreciation for Oriental decorations.

The Philippine galleon favored the birth of the famous commercial fairs held by different cities in New Spain. The arrival of the Chinese Ship constituted a national event. Everybody, men and women, anxiously waited for it.

The traditional *tianguis* (popular markets) of the pre-Hispanic era received a new aspect, originating new activities and crafts. In Puebla, a textile zone *par excellence*, the people began to manufacture velvets and silks which competed with those brought from Spain and from the East and which were later exported from New Spain to Cuba and Peru.

Mexican crafts were also enriched by lacquering techniques. It can be seen that the Chinese Ship had a powerful influence on our traditions and customs. It became so deeply rooted that we have always considered it our own, adopting and adapting it to our life-style.

And rightly so, because the Chinese Ship originated in our territory and was maintained through our effort.

Unfortunately, the success achieved by this commercial route caused resentment among the Spanish traders who were bringing merchandise from the Spanish Empire. They therefore placed numberless restrictions on this service, which lasted from 1571 to 1734. The route was able to continue during 163 years, until it was finally terminated.

The Chinese Ship never again returned with its splendid cargo. However, its magnificent legend has survived.

The attempts of the people in Acapulco to rescue the Chinese Ship from oblivion deserve to be congratulated. As it revives grand memories of the Port of Acapulco's past glories, already famous throughout the world in the sixteenth century.

The *China Poblana*

Of all the traditions, the one most deeply-rooted among Mexicans is that of the *china poblana*, the beautiful partner of the Mexican *charro*. Both are symbols of Mexican identity, perhaps because they were born together during the period when the Mexican Republic was reaffirmed after the French invasion.

Thus, it is not surprising that the history, origin, and the influence of this couple are enveloped in legend and mystery, due to the lack of a precise historical source.

In order to become acquainted with the profile of the couple, nothing can be better than the description which Carlos Rincón Gallardo, Marquis of Guadalupe and guardian without equal of the *charra* traditions of our country, made of the beautiful Mexican figure.

"The *china's* hair is combed parted in the middle, with two braids hanging down the sides, each with three-colored ribbons knotted into big butterfly bows holding the braids and adorning them at the ends.

"Around her neck she wears strings of corals; from her ears hang lovely earrings, and her bare arms are adorned with colorful bracelets.

"The pretty blouse, discreetly worn with a low-cut neckline, is embroidered wih gayly colored glass beads and the sleeves barely cover the shoulders.

"The bodice is made of green silk, in the same tone as the first color of our beloved national flag.

"The skirt is red —the color of blood— artistically spattered with bright sequins; it reaches her ankles, and when the little china girl rises discreetly to heel-and-toe the different Mexican dance steps, the rustling, starched underskirts peep through, decorated with a lovely circle of beautiful embroidery and lace.

"Around her waist there is a green, white, and red sash, whose silky ends hang down the left.

"The stockings are flesh-colored and the satin slippers are green, like the bodice.

"The speckled shawl, so fine that it could pass through a ring, or the famous Santa María shawls —usually brightly colored— are called *palomino coyote*.

"When she does not wrap the shawl around herself, but places it diagonally across her body to dance, it surrounds her waist from the back to the front, where the shawl crosses. As she dances she throws it across her shoulders, where it hangs down her back, displaying its beautiful fringes.

"This is the legitimate costume of the china *poblana*, as explained to me by famous experts, and nothing in it must be modified since the traditional clothes must remain unchanged."

Whence did this legendary figure come from, which even now, in our times, amazes us, charms us, and fills us with love for all that is ours? Most of the existing bibliography on the subject does not convince us with respect to either of the following two versions.

The first account which is the oldest and perhaps the most beautiful, legendary and romantic, states that the first *china poblana* who existed in Mexico was linked with the history of a woman of Asian origin who died in Puebla as a saint. She was Princess Mirrah, a descendant of the great Mongol Humayum, founder of a powerful Mongolian dynasty. By chance, one evening the beautiful princess was walking quietly with her younger brother on the coast of Delhi when she was seized from her father by the pirate Sir Towly, who immediately removed her royal clothes and sent her to the place where he kept the slaves who he would sell.

The legend also says that the Viceroy of New Spain, the Count of Gálvez, had requested the governor of Manila to buy "beautiful and graceful slaves to serve at his palace."

At the same time, a Portuguese merchant had received an assignment from Captain Miguel de Sosa —a trader from Puebla— and his wife, Margarita de Chávez, to buy a little Chinese girl to serve at his house. By chance, the pirate vessel that carried the princess, after travelling all over in search of more slaves, sailed to Manila to sell them, a hateful custom that had by then reached the dimensions of an overseas trade similar to that of other wares.

This happened during the first half of the seventeenth century. The governor of Manila attempted to buy the beautiful Princess Mirrah —whose name, like an omen, meant bitterness— for Viceroy Gálvez. However, his attempts were fruitless. The Portuguese merchant won the game, perhaps because he was shrewder. In any event, the Portuguese trader stealthily hid the princess in the galleon that was sailing to Acapulco. Some historians say that the governor of Manila bought the princess for Viceroy Gálvez and that in Acapulco, upon the galleon's arrival, she was bought by the merchant from Puebla (Captain Sosa), since the Count of Gálvez had been forced to travel to Spain due to problems with Archbishop Juan Pérez de la Serna.

Anyway, for whatever the reason, the fact is that Princess Mirrah arrived at Puebla with Captain Sosa. Because of her gentleness and pleasing manner, the latter's wife received her gladly. Father Aguilera, a fervent admirer of our "Chinese" princess, describes her as follows:

"She was one of the gentlest and most perfect beauties I have ever known. Her color was white, rather than olive, her hair was blond, she had a wide forehead, lively eyes, a well-balanced nose, and all her other facial features measured up to the graceful charm of her whole body...and all this added to her effective desire to maintain her chastity."

Miguel de Sosa and Margarita Chávez gave her a Christian education, baptized her with the name of Catarina de San Juan and finally married her off to a Chinese slave called Domingo Suárez and nicknamed *El Chino*. Historians say that the princess accepted the marriage submissively, but she never allowed *Chino* to enter her bed; forced by her husband's natural desire, she even asked God to take him away to heaven. Soon her prayers were answered and *Chino* mercifully died.

That was how an intensely religious life began for the *china poblana* Catarina de San Juan. It has made her famous throughout the region of Puebla, where the affectionate nickname of *china poblana* originated.

Little has been said about her garments, except that because of the great love that she felt towards the people of Puebla she adopted some of their clothes, which she combined with mementos of the garments worn in her native country. Because of the great admiration that the women who worked as servants felt for her, they also tried to imitate her gowns, which they proudly wore.

The second version is less romantic and exact. It parts from the fact that the word *china* relates to *quichua*, which originated in Peru and means "female." In the course of time, the word came to designate the servants familiarly and affectionately in Peru. It passed from Peru to all the countries of colonial America, until it reached New Spain. Thus it became the custom to call them *chinas*.

As for the garments, the explanation consists in the fact that they combine gowns which may have originated in the clothes worn by *salmantinas* which were also made with bright colors and embroidered with sequins and beads.

The fact is that by the beginning of the nineteenth century, the *chinas* were famous for their garments, for cleanliness, and elegance and grace. They were known as common people devoted to tasks such as selling flavored water, and providing services for small restaurants, laundries or other domestic activities.

The above background and other information closer to our present history will allow us to outline the tradition of the *china poblana*.

During the war against Maximilian's and Carlota's Empire, Mexican ranchers, known as the *chinacos* of Juárez played an important role. Due to the clothes they wore, they are the nearest ancestors to the present Mexican *charro*. They are known for the important battles they waged against the French, especially around Puebla.

Juárez' *chinacos* were aided by the *chinas* (the women of Juárez' heroic and brave followers) from Puebla, consequently, *chinas poblanas*. Now then, due to the Mexicans' gay and boisterous nature, even during the uproar of battles and the nights of truce and respite, guitars were heard, with *sones*, *jarabes* and *huapangos* from all the regions in the country, and the *chinacos* danced those gay and musical Mexican tunes —usually known as *jarabes*— with the *chinas*. This was how the symbolic couple of the *china* and the *charro* originated. Its fame grew with the victory of the Republic, giving birth to the well-known *jarabe tapatío* (a combination of typical dances from different regions in the country, within a spontaneous and natural choreographic unit), which owes its name to the *tapatíos'* (people from Jalisco) great ability in dancing and music.

The legendary or historical account of Catarina de San Juan constitutes a tradition accepted by Mexico's people which, in the event that it should merely be a beautiful legend, explains some of the fundamental characteristics of the *china poblana* in a certain way more in tune with the Mexican spirit and with the historical reality of the customs from the East, and the garments sold by the Philippine Galleon.

The *china poblana's* magnificent garments, and the demeanor and poise that her dress demands, deserve a legend of princely origin. In fair return, the Mexican *charros* have paid this historical debt, granting Catarina de San Juan the title of queen and patroness of Mexican *charrería*.

Be that as it may, it is an unshakable truth that the *china poblana* —as described— has reaffirmed her presence in the national sphere, arm in arm with the Mexican *charro* —after defeating the invaders— by taking part in that Mexican epic. The Republic owes its victory over the Empire to the *china* and the *chinaco*.

171

Puebla

Historical Nobility

The great Mexican cuisine is an open book with many fascinating and attractive chapters. Regional cooking —which preserves certain general characteristics to identify it as Mexican— has a strong character. Such is the case of Puebla's culinary tradition.

To speak of Puebla's cuisine is to talk about a legendary baroque art, a marvelous and faithful reflection of its own history. Undoubtedly one of the most varied and refined cuisines in Mexico, it has been able to link its most famous dishes with historical events and fascinating legends.

Due to its geographical position, Puebla became the crossroads of the merchandise brought from ancient Europe and from the mysterious East. Soon after the arrival of Hernán Cortés, pack animals passed through Puebla, carrying on their backs wares from Spain which were to become the Spanish cauldron's contribution to the native pot. It was a happy encounter, revealing the present lineage of Mexican cooking. After a time, the Chinese Ship, which in fact was the Manila Galleon, the ship that in colonial times made the voyage between Mexico and the Philippine Islands, brought to New Spain new ingredients for food as well as other goods: fabrics, perfumes, ivory carvings, furniture, Manila shawls...just to mention a few.

As previously mentioned, the Manila Galleon was at that time the ship in charge of making the annual maritime voyage established by the Spaniards between the ports of Acapulco and Manila, a service it performed from 1571 to 1734.

In addition to its economic importance, it constituted a cultural link transmitting Oriental characteristics —Orientalism — to Mexican colonial art. Among its culinary contributions are the spices: cloves from China, pepper, ginger and saffron from India, and cinnamon from Ceylon. Oregano had originated in the Mediterranean countries (Greece and Italy) and then passed on to France and Spain; cumin and coriander are European herbs which became acclimatized in Mexico. Considering the background of its native cuisine plus the contributions from Spain and from the East, it is not surprising that the cuisine in Puebla should have become one of the first strong *mestizo* (white and Indian) cuisines, finely prepared and in tune with Puebla de los Angeles' baroque spirit.

Since Puebla had been one of the most important ceremonial centers of the pre-Hispanic peoples, the evangelizers found fertile soil for the Christian doctrine. Thus Puebla appeared to be an ideal city for the founding of convents which, aside from carrying out their spiritual function, were to become the birthplace of an imaginative cuisine. The angelical hands of the nuns gave shape to the delicious dishes which were to make the Puebla cuisine famous and privileged as the prototype of the great Mexican cuisine.

DISHES FROM PUEBLA

The *chalupas* from the San Francisco district of Puebla are delicious, as well as numerous dishes based on *huitlacoche*, a fungus formed by humidity on the grains of corn, with which delicious *quesadillas* are also prepared.

Semitas are pieces of bread made with white flour, that originated in Puebla, and are favorites for snacks and *tortas* (Mexican sandwiches) covered with sesame seeds. Incidentally, the traditional *tortas* of Puebla began with the *semitas*.

The traditional dishes from Puebla are:

chileatole
*pipian** made with dark corn
green *pipian*
mole from Puebla in different versions and forms.

---

* *Pipian*. The country's own dish made with red or green chili and pumpkin seeds, almonds or any oily seed, such as pumpkin seeds, sweet almonds, sesame seeds, peanuts and even cotton seeds. The amount of ingredients vary in numberless ways from home to home.

Pumpkin seed pipián. The necessary amount of pumpkin seeds is roasted and then well ground, until it looks like chocolate; a ball is formed and placed to boil vigorously in water. In the meantime, the necessary *ancho* chilis are prepared by removing their seeds and veins and then fried in lard. Part of the chili seeds are also added, which must be fried and well ground with the chili. When the ball of pumpkin seeds is well cooked, the water is removed, the ground chili dissolved and fried in lard, adding the pumpkin seed mass. Water is added and the desired ingredients such as fruits and vegetables, to make the *pipian* but no salt until the dish is ready to be removed from the heat for otherwise the mixture will separate. *Pipian* can be prepared with any seeds that have an oily substance, but they must always be roasted and refried without adding salt until the last minute. Any kind of meat, especially pork, can be cooked in this sauce, and the fried fruits are added after covering them with a beaten egg mixture, though this is optimal. *Chayotes*, radishes, potatoes, *chilacayotitos, romeritos, nopales*, and all kinds of vegetables can be added, as well as meat, fish or shrimp.

From: *Nuevo cocinero mexicano en forma de diccionario, 1888* (New Mexican Cookbook in the Form of a Dictionary, 1888.)

173

The *mole* from Puebla, a baroque dish *par excellence* and a masterpiece of Mexican cuisine, exists in as many versions as there are homes in Puebla. The most famous recipes are those from the nuns' convents; they are inexact and omit certain details and ingredients well known to cooks of the time but they are indispensable for today's less experienced cooks.

According to the results of the investigations carried out by Artemio del Valle Arizpe, Mexico City's historian, we recall that Sister Andrea de la Asunción from the Dominican Convent of Santa Rosa one day prepared this dish in honor of Bishop Manuel Fernández de Santa Cruz and his guest —none less than the Viceroy of New Spain, Antonio de la Cerda y Aragón— in March 1681. Thus, the beautiful legend of the *mole* was born.

As part of this culinary legacy, the *moles* made by the Santa Mónica, Santa Teresa and Santa Clara nuns are outstanding.

Among Puebla's wonderful desserts we have: figures made of almond marzipan paste, with infinite possibilities for sculptors. To begin with, the easiest thing to do is to form small fruits, then works of art, religious images, pictures, utensils, animals, miniature buildings and many other figures. Other desserts are: almond kisses, lemons stuffed with pineapple and coconut, the Santa Clara *rompopes* (a kind of eggnog), the popular sweet potatoes in little cardboard boxes, aristocratic sweet potatoes —when they are crystallized and decorated with little roses— and pumpkin seed and pineapple *jamoncillos* (candy made of milk).

It is easy to see that one of the most fascinating and attractive chapters in the great open book that is Mexico's gastronomic tradition is the one written by the angelical hands and the creativity of the women of Puebla, whether they dress in a nun's habit or their sacred mission consists of being a mother, housewife or lady of the house. The Mexican woman's talent is infinite, as infinite as the gentle look in her eyes, as her love and tenderness, her devotion and dedication.

We can therefore understand that there will be wonderful new contributions from Puebla's cuisine to Mexico's cookbook.

CIVIC HOLIDAYS
IN THE MEXICAN REPUBLIC

ivic holidays in Mexico are celebrated in every city and in every town. The most important dates are:

February 5 - Commemoration of the proclamation of the 1917 Constitution.

March 21 - Birthday of Benito Juárez, "the native of Gueletao," "the Worthiest Man in all the Americas."

May 5 - Anniversary of the 1862 Battle of Puebla, when General Ignacio Zaragoza defeated the French invaders.

September 15 and 16 - Anniversary of the beginning of the War of Independence (1810).

November 20 - The beginning of the Revolution of 1910 is celebrated with a grand sports parade.

A SYMPHONY IN THREE COLORS

THREE-COLORED SEPTEMBER

National Traditions

Every year, during the month of September our great capital, usually so rushed, turns into a symphony, in three colors.

September, the month *par excellence* of national celebrations, announces its arrival with the appearance of thousands of vendors throughout the city districts, who sell Mexican flags in all sizes, harmoniously embedded in big flagpoles made of reed or wood, that affix a three-colored smile of joy and festivity on the capital's appearance. At the same time, shop windows begin to be adorned with the national symbols.

This tradition is almost two centuries old, since the custom of decorating houses and shops with the national colors was established in 1825 to commemorate the celebration and consummation of our Independence. September 16 was celebrated with splendor; later, the celebration of the President's annual report was added on September 1, as well as of the Cry of Independence on the night of September 15, the heroic feat of the youths of Chapultepec on September 13, and Morelos' birthday on September 30. Consequently, September has been called the Month of the Nation.

Strangely enough, the tradition of placing little Mexican flags, crosswise one over the other, on the doors of houses, on cars and buses, to exalt the patriotic morale of their occupants, depended for a long time on their manufacture in large quantities in Japan, since there were no companies in Mexico capable of producing the required amounts. However, when Mexico ceased to have a diplomatic and commercial relation with the Axis countries —including Japan— during the '40s, the Mexican companies had the opportunity of manufacturing these flags.

Every year millions of Mexican flags, shuttlecocks and festoons are made, bedecking the streets of our country with the three-colored decorations.

The Reason for "the outcry of Independence"

The tradition of celebrating the glorious anniversary of our Independence, "the Mexican's cry of liberty," in September is older than the flag itself. It dates back to 1812, when in the midst of bloody battle, General Ignacio Rayón celebrated our liberty in Huichapan. Thus it is written in *El diario de operaciones militares* (the log of militar operations): "The 16th day: today, at dawn, the glorious memory of the cry of liberty uttered two years ago before the Congregation of Dolores by the illustrious heroes and serene clergymen Hidalgo and Allende was commemorated with a volley of the artillery and ringing of bells..."

That year, Andrés Quintana Roo wrote a beautiful proclamation entitled, *La junta suprema de la nación de los americanos en el aniversario del 16 de septiembre* (The Supreme Meeting of the Americans' Nation on the Anniversary of September 16), which he signed together with Ignacio Rayón as president and José Ignacio Oyarzábal as secretary.

The following year, José María Morelos y Pavón included proposal number 23 in his *Sentimientos de la nación* (The Nation's Feelings), which to the letter says the following: "The 16th of September shall also be celebrated every year as the anniversary date of the day when the voice of Independence was raised and our blessed liberty began, for on that day the lips of the Nation were opened to claim her rights, and the sword was taken up to make herself heard, always recalling the merits of our great hero, Don Miguel Hidalgo and his companion, Don Ignacio Allende..."

Since that day the 16th of September has been celebrated without fail as the national holiday *par excellence*, with the exception of the year 1847, due to the invasion of the United States.

The outcry of Independence in a natural way came to be celebrated on the night of September 15, since it was customary to begin the celebration of the 16th with an evening soiree attended by the current president and the authorities. This was how the ceremony of the Cry of Independence originated, in the mid-nineteenth century, the shouting of "hoorays" and "long lives..." for Hidalgo, and Allende (as proposed by Morelos), to whom other heroes of our Independence were gradually added.

Obviously this is one of the most deeply-rooted and significant traditions, celebrated by the people joyfully and with conviction. It is therefore not surprising that this patriotic spirit has been embodied in popular traditions which are expressed throughout the month of September, with a true explosion of the nation's colors. Today, as in 1810, the country's will is expressed in a single cry, over and over again:

Long live Mexico!
Long live our Independence!
Long live the heroes who gave us a homeland!

That is why September is and will forever be the month of our national traditions.

CHILIS (PEPPERS) IN WALNUT SAUCE

The Key Expression of the Spirit which Stimulates the Great Mexican Cuisine

The appearance of the famous chilis (peppers) in walnut sauce coincides with our nation's Independence and the reassertion of our sovereignty.

In 1821, when our Independence was consummated, the Mexicans' spirit reached a climax due to the many historical events which proved to be decisive for our country. We could call it "Mexico's tricolor year," since for the first time the month of September wore the three colors of the flag which had been created that same year.

Agustín de Iturbide, author of the Iguala Plan of the Cordoba Treaty with the last viceroy, Juan de O'Donoju, was the main character in these events. Iturbide was the principal signer of our Independence decree. For these, and other reasons he was acclaimed in 1821.

Upon his return from the village of Córdoba, where he signed the Treaty, he decided to visit Puebla, whose inhabitants were loyal to him because he had been able to achieve Puebla de los Angeles' surrender. Perhaps for this reason Iturbide decided to celebrate his saint's day in this beautiful city. His followers offered him a splendid banquet on August 28, 1821, the Day of Saint Augustine, to celebrate his saint's day. With great splendor the three colors of the newly-born national flag (green for independence, white for religion, and red for unity), were displayed as well as a careful selection of Puebla's special dishes prepared by the angelical hands of the contemplative Augustinian nuns from the Convent of Santa Mónica, who had been so involved in our culinary tradition.

The nuns, full of the patriotic spirit and zeal that prevailed in those days, decided to prepare a dish in the three colors that represented the three guarantees. So this was how the skillful and gentle hands of the nuns created the peppers in walnut sauce, originating in the purest patriotic and national spirit.

178

To this purpose they used seasonal ingredients, for any cuisine is a child of the soil and the palate. Tender walnuts and the vermilion crown pomegranate covered two of the flag's colors white and red, with their sauce and the grains from the pomegranate. According to the recipe, when the pepper is covered by a beaten egg mixture, the green color is furnished by parsley leaves.

And so that historical year also left us an important event for Mexican cuisine.

September, the month of the Nation, origin and historical background for the tradition of sweets in Mexico: an identity along the routes of our country and in the whole world. Mexico: its candies, sweets and ambrosia.

To speak of Mexican sweets is to penetrate in the country's history and technology, to go back to the origins of Mesoamerican man, who later merged into the mosaic of races, people and languages that formed the splendid Anahuac.

Sweets —like technology, art, and culture of these ethnic groups— have made diverse contributions in the course of time; some of which have been significant and valuable. The most outstanding is the sugar cane, brought to these lands after the Spanish and Western conquest.

But that is no reason to forget the old liking for native ambrosia. Specifically, chocolate became Mexico's gift to the world.

Ancient Mexico's ambrosia. Native ambrosia. Ambrosia is a term originating in the Greek *ambrosia*, which in turn is derived from *ambrotos*, meaning "immortal, divine."

The tasty dishes or food of the gods were called ambrosia in Greek mythology. Tasty, delicious dishes that please the spirit, symbolically speaking. A drink of delicate flavor.

The pre-Hispanic people of Mesoamerica did not know the sugar cane, but they did know the honey produced by bees, and reaped from maguey, prickly pears, and corn cane. In combination with seeds, they have survived to our days, as proven by the *alegría*.

The pre-Hispanic people of Mesoamerica cooked the grains of corn to prepare the traditional *tortilla*, but it was very thin; by covering it with different kinds of honey, they produced a delicious dessert from the grains of corn: *pinole*. Both soldiers and the missionaries admired the refinement achieved by confectionery in the Mexican cuisine, due to the great variety, the exquisite seasoning, and appearance of the tasty dishes presented on clay tableware from Cholula (polished, burnished and polychromed), as well as all kinds of heating utensils to keep the food at an adequate temperature.

The desserts were outstanding in this refined cuisine, as well as numberless types of *atoles* (hot beverage basically made with corn flour) sweetened with honey and fruit.

When speaking of the pre-Hispanic people of Mesoamerica we particularly refer to the Olmec culture, cradle of all Mesoamerican civilizations, from which the Aztecs, Chichimecs, Tarascos, Mayas and Toltecs were derived.

Mexico's gift to the world is chocolate.[1] Undoubtedly, among the food of its type, the most significant is chocolate, a delicious beverage, due to the different essences mixed into the ground cacao, and to the aromatic vanilla from the region of Papantla. Pre-Hispanic chocolate was prepared with a corn meal beverage, ground cacao, vanilla,[2] and bee honey. It was served after beating it vigorously, in coconut and *huaje* mugs, or in baked clay mugs.

Friar Bernardino de Sahagún, refers to chocolate —after praising the pleasant flavor of this wonderfully stimulating drink of the Mexicans of old— as a beverage that provided energy and was therapeutically useful for curing numerous diseases and physical weaknesses.

PRE-HISPANIC DESSERTS

Xocolatl and Other Sweets

The *Nahuatl* term *xocolatl* comes from *atl* (water) and *xocotl* (choco), a reproduction of the sound of boiling water, and of beating the cacao with a wooden beater. The cacao grain was greatly valued as proven by its use as money in commercial transactions and in payment of taxes to the emperor.

One of the best-known versions regarding the etymology of the term chocolate is provided by Dr. Cecilio Robelo: chocolate: *xococ* (sour) and *atl* (water): sour water, because cacao with water and without a sweet is quite sour.

---

1) *Chocolate*. This is the country's own beverage, preferred to tea and coffee for breakfast by Mexicans, be they rich, middle-class or poor. Each individual drinks a more or less high-quality chocolate, according to his taste or resources. Such a large variety of ingredients are usually mixed into the cacao and in different amounts that if we tried to gather all the recipes and manufacturing methods for chocolate, these would form a volume that is too big and a bit useless. Since the methods described on these pages suffice to make excellent chocolate, each person can add or reduce the amounts according to his or her taste; adding the ingredients or aromas he likes best.

2) *Vanilla*. An aromatic fruit in the form of a pod. In Nahuatl it is called *tlixochitl*, which means black flower.

Francisco Javier Clavijero, a Jesuit priest, made interesting comments on chocolate.

This is the origin of the famous beverage, which together with its Nahuatl name, *xocolatl*, was adopted by European countries, who altered its name and improved it in accordance with each country's taste.

Not only chocolate multiplied and was used lavishly after the conquest, but also *aguamiel*. *Aguamiel* is a sweet, unfermented liquid that becomes *octli* or *pulque* —widely consumed by the natives of Anahuac— in particularly the people in the high plateau.

Aguamiel, a sweet, refreshing, therapeutic and spiritual Mexican drink, was indispensable at the banquets of the great *tlatoani* and the grand Moctezuma II, where more than three hundred different dishes were prepared, and most of them accompanied by *aguamiel*. According to the illustrious gentleman from Veracruz, Don Francisco Javier Clavijero, chocolate and *aguamiel* were recommended by witch doctors and medicine men for various diseases, especially those of a gastrointestinal nature.

Corn also constituted a delicious cooked dessert, sweetened with different honeys. *Pulque* was made with the juice of the *metl* or *maguey*. A delightfully juicy, sweet fruit called *quiote* was obtained from its thickest leaves —cooked underground— and mezcal was extracted from its flowers.

Hernán Cortés, in the *Cartas de Relación* (Letters of Record), he wrote to emperor Charles V, said: "There are many kinds of fruit here among which the *capulín* (a small fruit similar to the Spanish cherry or plum) is found. The people know and sell honey and beeswax and honey made from corn cane, which is not as syrupy or sweet as sugar."

It is impossible to forget our heraldic symbol in the history of sweets, the *nopal* (prickly pear cactus).

The *nopal*, and its decorative fruit, the tuna or prickly pear were generously lavished on these inhospitable, dry, and arid regions, but more than a fruit, the *tuna* is a delicious dessert with abundant carbohydrates.

Nopales and *tunas* form the heraldic coat-of-arms deeply rooted in Mexico City.

The *tuna's* honey was and is a pleasing ambrosia, which the peasants in Mexico's arid valleys still enjoy with brown *tortillas*.

MEXICAN SWEETS DURING THE COLONIAL PERIOD

In addition to this sober but vigorous background in the history of sweets, the sixteenth-century Mexican received two splendid and magnificent contributions from the Spanish conqueror: sugar cane and cow's milk.

Hernán Cortés introduced the cultivation of sugar cane to Mexico. He planted sugar cane in his estates at Tlaltengo and Los Tuxtlas in Veracruz. From then, it extended to Morelos, Guerrero, and the Valley of Mexico. The sugar cane achieved a definite change in the Mexican people's nutrition. The product obtained from it was called *piloncillo*, the result of a concentration of the *guarapo* or cane juice in the pans on the fire of rudimentary sugar mills. It changed native recipes and extended the horizons of Mexican sweets.

The output of sweets in Mexico increased gloriously with the advent of sugar, milk, and the fruits native to Mexico and Spain. Thus a geography of regional candy began to be formed.

Confitures (sweets)

The word confitures is derived from the term *confection*: to prepare, to make, to fix sweets with fruit such as *mamey*, black *zapote*, white *zapote*, *chicozapote*, pineapple, *chirimoya*, *pitaya*, *tejocotl* or *tejocote*. Pears, apples, figs, grapes, quinces, pomegranates, and other European fruits were thus pleasingly substituted.

The friars Pedro de Gante and Bernardino de Sahagún revealed magic formulas and secrets to prepare confitures.

In their convents the nuns created and invented delicacies that were sins of gluttony, with imaginative names such as *picones* (tipsy), macaroons (coconut candy), *jamoncillos* (candy made from milk), almond cheeses, kisses-sighs, angels' gifts, *cabujones* (stones) with big heads of almonds and raisins, and wonderful marmalades, royal sweets made of bishop's milk, *cafiroleta* and *cafirolonga*, candied sweet potatoes and pineapple, *alfeñiques* (sweetened almond paste) from San Lorenzo, paste and jellies from the Bernardine nuns, *buñuelos* (fritters) from San José de Gracia, milk, pecan and coconut delicacies with bright *canelones* (cinnamon candy) and little apples.

Sublime fruits made of almonds, little pocket eggs, *susamieles*, illustrious macaroons, glazed candy from pumpkin, *chilacayotes*, translucent *acitrones* (made of maguey leaves), candied almonds, and thousands of other delicacies were prepared in Mexico's convents.

183

CANDY AND BONBONS IN THE ROMANTIC NINETEENTH CENTURY

These delicacies were also prepared outside the convents, in distinguished French-style candy shops, pastry shops, and cafés.

We recall the great Veroly Café of 1838 in Mexico, a carefree refuge for country folk, travelers and traders, after the turmoil of their work. What did the travelers drink at the Veroly? They drank triple chocolate drinks (three equal parts of cacao, sugar and cinnamon), accompanied by small rolls.

Pastry, illustrious toast, sweet rolls, *atole* (a hot drink made with corn meal) and little *tamales*, coffee and cream with a vanilla flavor, sweet bread, chocolate from the Clarisa nuns, and little *huesitos* (bone-shaped pieces of sweet rolls) from the Convent of the Holy Spirit, honey perfumed with orange rind, and pastries. Among the public promenades the famous "Stroll of the Chains" was a popular amusement. It consisted of joining hands in chains to form waves; the largest chain was formed in the Cathedral's courtyard around 1850. It was a happy occasion for everyone, drowned in the street vendors' shouts and cries.

Sweets in Mexico have been a means of identification along the wide roads of our country and throughout the world. Sweets, candy and ambrosia from our times, from our Mexico. Mexican candy, fantasies of color, appearance and power, a sculptural art in talented hands.

Cajeta. Candy made of goat's milk and sugar, a specialty of Celaya, Guanajuato.

Cocada. A candy based on coconut meat. A specialty of the convents with many delicious variations.

Chocolate. Before Europe became an enthusiastic consumer, chocolate was the Mayan and Aztec drink. The cocoa seed is used as a monetary unit in some regions of the state of Oaxaca.

Nance (or *nanche*). A tree that grows in the states of Veracruz and Tabasco, with a fruit similar to the cherry which is eaten raw, in jams, or pastes, etc., and also is conserved in alcohol.

Nopal. The cactus that produces *tunas*. After removing the thorns, the leaves are used in salads, sauces and sweets.

Piloncillo. Unrefined sugar from the sugar cane.

Tuna. The fruit of the *nopal*.

From: *Cocina mexicana* (Mexican Cuisine).

THE
RANCHER'S
MEXICO

RURAL MEXICO'S FOLKLORE

HE MARIACHI AND HIS ORIGIN

A Symbol of Mexico

The versions regarding the origin of the word *mariachi* are many and quite varied, a fact which sometimes makes its meaning more of a legend than a reality.

One of the best-known and most accurate versions dates back to the years 1864-1866, when French festive music was played at gatherings and weddings denominated *mariage*, a word which in time became *mariachi*.

Another version was proposed by a few scholars from Cocula, who state that in 1839 a kind of *mariachi* was already known, although in some towns (like Cocula, Jalisco) they were known as "violins or guitars from the hills."

Others believe that in 1840 Plácido Revollado's *mariachi* group was already firmly established; its members played the harp, the guitar and two violins.

Another variation states that *mariachi* was the name of a small dais approximately half a meter high, 1.60 meters long and 85 centimeters wide. *Jarabe* dancers or musicians who played the harp, the violin or the guitar, as well as quartets made up of drums, cymbals, and violins performed on this dais.

There is a tree called *mariachi* both in southern Jalisco and in Michoacán, whose white porous wood is used to manufacture guitars. From it stems, supposedly, the meaning of a musical group.

It is equally difficult to determine when, where, and how this kind of musical group, so closely linked to popular tradition, was born. But we *can* affirm that native music, interpreted with drums, timbrels, (rattles), and whistles, constitutes a significant antecedent.

In Jalisco —formerly New Galicia— as string instruments such as the harp, the violin, and the guitar, were introduced, new styles appeared, both religious and profane. As to the former, litanies were heard, and among the latter a type of tune deriving from Spanish rhythms such as *seguidillas*, *tiranas* and *sevillanas*, stood out. In this fashion, the region created its own style.

We should point out that these tunes —as well as the *jarabes*, *sonecitos* and *valones*— quickly became popular in Nayarit, Colima, southern Jalisco and in part of Michoacán, regardless of the fact that they were unacceptable in the high social spheres. On the contrary, they were greatly accepted among the farmers, who made these tunes into the region's heritage.

Unlike other states, where groups playing string instruments remained limited to their original sphere, lyrical musicians multiplied throughout Jalisco's territory, combining their art with activities pertaining to the rural sectors.

As mentioned above, these groups were not accepted by everyone, since they were considered to be an amusement of poor people and drunks. Due to the lack of stimulation and proper treatment by the landowners, the *mariachis* enlivened serenades, cockfights, and bars.

The *Mariachis's* Instruments

Undoubtedly the people who spread the custom of the *mariachis* were the muleteers, who on their way through haciendas, inns, and barns or store-rooms popularized tunes such as: *El tecolote* (The Owl) from San Gabriel; *El burro pardo* (The Brown Donkey) from Tecalitlán, and many more.

The *mariachi* played string instruments: the violin, the regular guitar, and a larger one. The latter were usually manufactured by the people who played them. As for their garments, they were not very different from the clothes used for daily work: a big straw hat, *huaraches* (sandals) and coarse cotton trousers and shirt.

The native violins were made of *guasima* wood, a very flexible material; however, most of the violins were manufactured abroad. The guitar was made of cedar and *rebelero* for the cover and acoustic box, although some-times armadillo shells were used, which did not produce good sounds. The harp was manufactured with the best kinds of woods, cedar, *pinabete* and *guasima*, which grew abundantly in the region; the strings were made of skunk guts.

The large guitar is a Mexican instrument which is not usually found in any other type of musical group except the *mariachi*. According to word-of-mouth tradition this string instrument was invented in Cocula, and it is larger than the normal guitar. The box is made of cedar and mahogany and the segments of the cover are made of *tacota*, a white wood only found in some regions of the state of Jalisco.

In the beginning the flutes were made of clay, wood, and reeds. They had a scale of five sounds, like the clarinet, the piston, and the drum, but were used irregularly and tended to disappear.

188

This is how the *mariachi's* music was created, in accordance with the traditional ways of using the voice and the instruments. Its themes revolve around the relationship between men and women or, between a man and animals, or discuss social cooperation, the land, luck, pride, and masculinity.

During the decade of the twenties and the Revolution, the *mariachi* had problems finding a definite place within the social structure, mainly due to the high cost of living. A larger number of groups began to appear in the state of Jalisco, particularly in San Pedro Tlaquepaque, where they were called *mariacheros.* They were also found in the bars and saloons in Guadalajara, seeking to better their luck. Still others came to Mexico City.

The most famous *mariachi* groups were undoubtedly those from Cocula and Tecalitlán. The Pulidos and the Marmolejos were two authentic groups. The latter was outstanding, and one of the first to record in a foreign country, during the Chicago Municipal Fair of 1932.

The Charro's Costume and the *Mariachi*

The connection between the *charro's* costume and the *mariachi* was apparently established in 1901, when Miguel Lerdo de Tejada, a composer and pianist, dressed the musicians of his typical orchestra as *charros,* in order to Mexicanize their image. However, it was not until the beginning of the thirties that the groups from Jalisco began to wear uniforms. Silvestre Vargas —of the famous *mariachi* from Tecalitlán— recalls the first time he was able to dress his men in simple suits made of drill and cheap brass decorations, a wide-brimmed hat, bow tie, and boots.

Although the *mariachi* has passed through different stages, its general characteristics have been accepted by the people, as one of Mexico's most meaningful symbols.

THE *JARABE*[1] *TAPATÍO* (THE MEXICAN HAT DANCE)

A Hymn to Women's Grace and to Men's Ability

Blood catches fire with its chords and the flame of enthusiasm begins to shine in the hearts of all the people of Jalisco. The couple is made up of a *charro* and a *china* both wearing colorful costumes. We could say that the types they represent embody the spirit of our people, for whom the *charro* and the *china* are the national couple.

189

The Mexican *china* wears a silk castor,[2] that is green around the waist and the rest red. Luminous designs made with golden sequins decorate this skirt, under which shapely calves wearing fine stockings peek out; on their feet —Mexican women usually have tiny feet— they wear green satin slippers, thus completing the graceful figure of the national dancer.

The shirt,[3] embroidered with lovely silk emblems in different colors, leaves the most beautiful part of the shoulders, back, and breast unscrupulously bare; over her arms, the rich silk of the Santa María shawl twists and turns with iridescent effects. The dark eyes of the *tapatías* (women from Jalisco) and their thick braids, that interlaced with ribbons, reach down to their waists, complete the beauty of this national type of Mexican woman.

The *charro* is a manly type, in whose costume the splendor and perhaps vanity of ranchers can be divined. The short jacket, made of yellow suede or dark woolen material is decorated with silver embroidery; the tight pants are also studded with beautiful *alamares*;[4] the *jarano*,[5] with the wonderfully renowned embroidery, can hardly bear the weight of the gold and silver embroidery that brightly covers the entire hat, in spite of its extremely wide brim.

The *jarabe* is of Spanish origin, although it can still hold reminiscences of the beautiful primitive native dances. Perhaps it descends from the first native dances, the Spanish heel-tapping dance or from the *seguidillas* that originated in the sixteenth century.

Musically the *jarabe* is a melodic phrase, with simply harmonies. The tempo is frequently six by eight, sometimes three by four or two by four; and the tune is always lively.

Jarabes have been composed by the people themselves. There are some that are truly interesting, due to their rhythm. We shall mention one of these.

In every two tempos of three beats, one tempo of two beats is interpo-

---

1) *Jarabe.* A collection of popular tunes and dances.

2) *Zagalejo.* Name given to the castor or skirt worn by the *china poblana*.

3) *Camisa.* (Shirt) In the traditional language used by *charros*, this is how the *china poblana's* blouse is called.

4) *Alamares.* Clip and button or fringes usually sewed on the edge of the gown or cape, used to button it up or merely as a decoration. The border is usually fringed.

5) *Jarano.* A hat made with the *jara* (rockrose) stem; however, in time its use was generalized and now felt hats are also called *jaranos* because they have the same shape.

lated, leaving the melodic phrase unfinished. This anomaly is precisely what constitutes the originality and beauty of this dance.

It is usually believed that these amalgamated tempos are of Basque origin, but in fact, they have been found in popular Serbian* and Russian tunes, and especially in Finnish melodies.

THE CHARRERÍA

Symbol Par Excellence of Mexican Nationality

Jalisco has been the birthplace of Mexican nationality, through the *tequila*, the *jarabe tapatio*, the *mariachi*, and naturally the *charrería*. To speak of "the national sport *par excellence*" is to recall numberless men who with their tenacity and dedication have made it a reality.

Thus, the native, the *mestizo* (half-breed) who had not been allowed to ride a horse during the Conquest set an example and created a new sport, when the use of the horse in the colonized territories began to spread due to increasing agricultural requirements.

Charrería, as a show, has been improving radically with respect to its origins: formerly, carried out in the fields as part of obligatory country duties and for the wholesome entertainment of the inhabitants of the *haciendas*; it is now a professional *charro* competition made up of ten basic skillful maneuvers, of which some present certain variations leading to greater elegance in their performance.**

The first of these *charro* exercises is the Horse's Test, which can be summarized as the rider taming the beast; the second maneuver consists of the *piales en el lienzo* (trapping in the arena), where the rider twirls his rope, aims it at the back legs of the mare as she runs towards the corrals, in the closed arena, excited by the rustler. The third maneuver is the *coleadero* (throwing a young bull) and consists of the *charro* chasing the young bull and knocking the beast down by twisting the bull's tail.

Riding a young bull is one of the maneuvers usually entrusted to young people who, mounted on the bull's back, have to tame him. This taming is

---

* *Serbian*: A Slavic people which forms the main nucleus of the ancient kingdom of Serbia, now Yugoslavia.

** The author would like to thank Licenciada María Elena Franco Quiroz, Director of the Museum of *Charrería*, for her technical assistance.

performed inside the arena, with the ring closed. Later, the *trabajo de la terna* (the work of a team of three) is carried out in the arena, and it is divided in two parts: lassoing the head and trapping the bull until the rider can knock him down and clean him.

Taming the mare is one of the most exciting and beautiful exercises, due to the animal's impressive resistance. The *manganas* (lassoing) on foot and on horseback are next, and they are considered the most important of the *charro's* maneuvers. The *charro* must concentrate on the pace of the mare, which has been excited by the "rustlers," throw the rope at the exact moment and succeed at making it fall between the animal's legs in order to knock her down. Finally, the competition culminates with the *paso de la muerte* (death's step) in which the horseman, riding bareback and risking his life, springs from his horse onto a wild mare.

In 1920 a group of men began to practice these maneuvers every day in the fields. These few visionaries from Jalisco then decided to officially found their "charro" groups and established the oldest association existing in the Mexican Republic, the *Charros* de Jalisco (the Jalisco *charros*). This group began to grow, develop, and generate new associations.

In 1932, Pascual Ortiz Rubio declared September 14 to be *Charros* Day.

This artistic and expressive sport, which shows the *charros* not only as fair men, but also as brave and expert in the mastery of the horse and the rope, was considered the only completely Mexican sport in 1933, in accordance with a decree enacted by the President of the Republic of the time, Abelardo L. Rodríguez, a true fan of *charrería*.

Charros undoubtedly represent an important tradition in the folkloric mosaic of Mexico. And no less can be said about their feminine counterpart, the Adelita, a renowned celebrity from the Revolution whom today we can admire in the spectacular *escaramuzas* (skirmishes), a colorful and rhythmic expression of women's ability to tame the horse.

Currently numerous *charro* associations throughout the country compete in a friendly way all year round, in various national and state championships, as well as fairs and important celebrations. Considering all these different *charreadas* and *jaripeos* (a kind of rodeo), it would be unfair not to enjoy them, as one of the most beautiful expressions of the Mexican soul.

At present, *charrería* is united by a single light, by one hope: to turn this decidedly Mexican sport into our country's letter of identification forever.

Mexican desserts (peanut cookies).

Molasses-coated Mexican sweet (*muéganos*).

Mexican desserts (*polvorones* or sugar cookies).

Mexican candy popularly called angel hair (*cabellitos de angel*).

A colorful and tasteful table. A delightful assortment of the Mexican sweets.

Silk *rebozo* or shawl.

Paliacate, the multi-colored Mexican handkerchief.

Charrería, symbol *par excellence* of Mexican national pride.

The Margarita. The most delicious cocktail made with Tequila. Adults only!

The *Mariachi* originated in Cocula, Jalisco, and the *Charro*, symbol of virility, gallantry, and bravery.

Elegantly colorful typical clothing of native women.

Bark paper.

The Dance of the Old Men, source of humor and entertainment.

The Mexican party. Broiled meat Tampico style (*carne asada a la tampiqueña*).

Traditional folk dances.

Tarahumara folk dances on the Day of the Virgin of Guadalupe.

A Tarahumara family from northern Mexico.

Tarahumara mother and child.

Tarahumara doll set against the rugged terrain of the Sierra Tarahumara.

A handcrafted puppet.

The tragic and hair-raising vigil for the return of the Dead.

Carnival celebrations in the state of Puebla.

A colorfull pre-Hispanic dance.

From the Day of Dead, sugar-coated, delicately flavored Bread for the Dead.

The *Jarabe Tapatío.*

TO DIE AT THE FEET OF MY VOLCANOES

I want to die at the feet of my volcanoes,
sheltered by the twilight
as the moon rises over the valley,
the ancient valley of my ancestors.
Thus I wish to fulfill the ritual
of anticipating my death,
of being dust and returning to dust.
For I was made of lava,
and Anahuac's luminous air
was the eternal gust which formed my breath.
I want to die at the feet of my volcanoes,
contemplating forever the imperial plains and
my valley! My ancient valley,
eternally guarded by volcanoes
and the blazing history of my fellow men!
By anticipating death in this way
on my two white mountains,
my wish is stubbornly renewed,
my desire of death...yes!
But at the feet of my volcanoes!

Sebastián Verti

TEQUILA

Tequila is a typically Mexican liquor obtained by fermenting and distilling the *aguamiel* (agave juice) from the *maguey*.

During the pre-Hispanic period, the *maguey* was the plant from which *octli*, an intoxicating drink, was obtained, called *pulque* after the arrival of the Spaniards.

The historians of the era say that when Hernán Cortés arrived in Tenochtitlan on November 7, 1519, he was received in a friendly manner by Moctezuma II, ruler of the Mexicas. Among the gifts presented to Cortés, was a *Tonalamatl*,* a book of rituals inscribing the tribes' historical and religious traditions.

No exact information exists about distilled drinks until after the first period of colonization. It has been said that the Tiquila tribe prepared this drink in Amatitlán, Jalisco, as soon as it learned to cook the heart of the *maguey* and to ferment and distill its juice.

It is told that on a certain occasion, lightning struck a dozen *agaves*. The effect of the lightning revealed the heart of the plant, and the intense heat made it burn for a few moments. This caused the *agave* juice to turn into a drink which proved to be very pleasant to the taste of the men who had witnessed the event. Later, they brought about the phenomenon themselves in order to obtain the drink from the *agave*.

The Spanish doctor, Jerónimo Hernández, points out that in 1651 tequila was used by the people to heal diseases of the joints by rubbing in the liquor.

Tequila has given its name to the liquor, just as Cognac bears the name of French spirits.

The name *tequila* is protected in Mexico by the Law of Industrial Protection (presently of Inventions and Brands), in accordance with the rulings issued by the Ministry of Industry and Commerce on November 22, 1974. The name may only be applied to the liquor obtained from the distillation of the *agave* grown in the municipality of Tequila in the state of Jalisco, as well as some neighboring municipalities.

Bernal Díaz del Castillo, in his *Historia verdadera de la conquista de la Nueva España* (True History of the Conquest of New Spain), relates that the

---

* *Tonalamatl.* A ritual calendar covering 260 days (20 months of 13 days each).

natives of Jalisco learned to burn the *agave* leaves from the Huicholes. This is the process that comes before making the liquor called *mezcal*. Since the Tiquila tribe learned to prepare it, the drink was named *tequila*.

The Medical Society of London, in a report dated in 1875, expressed the following opinion: "...Mexican tequila, when consumed moderately, is a powerful auxiliary in purifying the blood, and stimulating the functions of the digestive system, and it is recommended in some cases of lack of appetite..."

In the eighteenth century Juan Sánchez de Tagle founded the first modern tequila distillery. The noble gentleman made use of the best methods he had seen for preparing the drink and began to export tequila to the Philippine Islands in exchange for silks and Oriental brocades.

The *maguey's gima,*[1] like the sugar cane harvest, or like cotton-picking, is the traditional beginning of tequila production.

The *agave* reaches maturity between eight and ten years of age, the ideal time to carry out the *gima* and obtain a top-quality juice.

The presence of sugar in fruits, grains, and vegetables is essential to producing an alcoholic drink. It is found in the maguey's "pineapple," as a starch which is transformed into sugar by means of a cooking process. Immediately thereafter, the juices obtained (*mosto*) are fermented, and the sugar from the agave turns into alcohol. This liquid goes through several distillations and is eventually diluted until it reaches the "full" line, but it is submitted to quality-control tests (the most reliable method of analyzing the product is by chromatography, due to its accuracy and speed).

Our tequila is consumed in a *caballito*, a tequila glass scarched with salt and lemon, or in a typical small Mexican mug, also with lemon and salt of course.

Let us make a toast: to health, money and love!

THE MEXICAN *REBOZO* (SHAWL)

The origin of the Mexican shawl is lost in the mist of daily customs. It is therefore difficult to determine the original source of this garment.

Some people express the opinion that the shawl was inspired in pre-Hispanic garments, basically the so-called "sun shawls"or "humeral veils" mentioned by various historians. It is said that the Malinche was famous for

---

1) *Gima.* From the Nahuatl *xima*, to cultivate, to scrape.

her attire, because she had intentionally increased the proportions of her sun shawls in order to distinguish herself among other women.

On the other hand, there are those who believe that the *rebozo* was derived from the so-called "rebociño andaluz" (the little Andalusian shawl), which in turn originated from Arab garments, or from the Hindu sari that arrived in Mexico via the Chinese ship.

But whatever the origin of the Mexican *rebozo* may be, it is not to be denied that this garment acquired its singular characteristics during the seventeenth and eighteenth centuries and reached its point of maximum popularity during the latter century. Since the middle of the eighteenth century, the shawl has evidently been considered to be typically Mexican both by natives and by foreigners. During the nineteenth century, the use of the *rebozo* continued, as shown by the fact that Empress Carlota wore it for the first time at one of her receptions in the Borda gardens of Cuernavaca, in order to win the Mexican ladies over. Maximilian also attended, dressed like a *charro*, instead of in formal attire.

The tradition of the *rebozo*, has survived with some ups and downs, although it is the garment that the common women, particularly peasants, wear. It is the garment that adorns the graceful bodies of girls on picnics; and that distinguishes the attire of common, everyday women in Mexico.

The *rebozo* is not only used to cover the head, or to cross over the chest like a simple decoration. It is also the provisional cradle of poor children and the handkerchief with which women wipe their tears. It is an improvised basket with which native women carry their vegetables to the marketplace; and a baby's blanket as he quietly sleeps near his working mother. The *rebozo's* end, when twisted and placed over a woman's head, is used as a base for baskets full of fruit. When extended, it can cover a pot of *tamales* on a neighborhood street.

Disregarding its Spanish or pre-Hispanic origin, it can be said that the natives' requirements and taste transformed the original garment, until it became a typically national article.

The *rebozo* is woven in a texure similar to that of a shawl. It is longer than it is wide, and is sometimes worked with fringes or with complicated designs on the ends. The most common type is grayish-blue or blue-black, usually in soft tones, and with a strange monotonous design, similar to the feathers of a wood pigeon. These *rebozos* are worn by all common women. Women in the Bajío, Tepic, and of Sinaloa prefer light gray or light blue *rebozos*; natives of the Valley of Mexico, the states of Morelos or Hidalgo prefer dark blue *rebozos*; and those from the states of Puebla and Oaxaca use *rebozos* with wide blue and white stripes.

The brightly colored silk *rebozos* are generally used for parties. Some of them look like snakeskin and others are vaguely similar to Oriental fabrics.

Altogether, this feminine garment is produced in a variety of colors and qualities of raw material. However, the weaving is practically identical; that is, it follows a single principle with only slight variations.

The most common type of *rebozo* is made of ordinary thread. There are rebozos made of very fine thread, called *rebozos de bolita*, and others of the finest silk.

Rebozos of excellent quality are made in Michoacán, the state of Mexico, San Luis Potosí, Puebla, Oaxaca...almost all the country's regions. But the *rebozos* from Santa María del Río, San Luis Potosí and Tenancingo (in the state of Mexico) are the best known and have the largest demand.

The *Paliacate* Is Not Just an Ordinary Handkerchief

A *paliacate* in its purest meaning, is a large, and brightly colored, flashy handkerchief.

It began to be used during the seventeenth century. At that time, it was tied around the head so that the hat would not hurt the skull, since the hats had small crowns. Furthermore, the hat's felt was protected against perspiration in this way.

At first, it was called *paño de hierbas* (herbal cloth). Later the *paliacate* came to be so big, that it fell down the back. People began to use it like the brim of a hat, to protect themselves against the sun, and the name was changed to *paño de sol* (sun cloth). The material used for the *paliacate* varied, from the simplest fabric used by the common man to silk.

The *paliacate* at first was tied on the head, later the forehead, and finally around the neck. In Maximilian's and Carlota's time, it became a bow tie, and many a wealthy gentleman used it this way.

The *paliacate* was always enhanced in some way, embroidered with women's hair, it was given as a gift to the fiancé with his initials. It also derived into a fine neckerchief.

For a time leather was used around the neck, but it proved to be too uncomfortable.

The *paliacate* is used in the Mexican provinces especially by farmers, since its size absorbs abundant perspiration, and its bright colors enhance the necks of their users.

To the young people of our times it may seem ridiculous, but the *paliacate* became fashionable years ago. *Paliacates* were "in" among boys who wore them tied around their foreheads, in different colors, to match their clothing, or knotted around their wrists and legs. The young have adopted this adornment bequeathed by our ancestors as they please. The genuinely Mexican garment is also worn in some Latin American countries.

The *paliacate*, despite its changes, seems to be disappearing, but it is proudly used in some states of the Republic, and is a well-defended beautiful and original Mexican tradition. Tied around the neck, the head, or the forehead, it is a distinguishing mark of the working class.

We recognize José María Morelos y Pavón, "The Nation's Servant," as the man wearing a *paliacate* around his head. Like him, many other of our heroes have worn it throughout history.

It is said that Don José María Morelos used it in order to hide the "potato plasters" he used to mitigate the migraines he suffered from.

MISCELLANEOUS

THE PRE-HISPANIC NEW YEAR'S TRADITION

Although one of the most beautiful and poetic customs of our Aztec ancestors has disappeared, the historian Friar Diego Durán relates that on New Year's Day — March 1— the people used to go out to the country, to the sown fields and to the orchards in order to touch the reborn plants, flowers, and fruits with their hands. Men, women, and children thus strolled through the flowery *chinampas* in order to fill their hearts with colors and fragrances. The most devout made bouquets that they took to their temples.

What a lovely tradition with which our forefathers expressed their love and communion with nature!

Perhaps the only trace of this custom can be found in the Mexican's sensitivity to the joy of colors and the rhythm he imprints on his country dances.

AMATE PAPER

EXICO'S TRADITIONAL HANDICRAFT

Amate paper is made the same way as during pre-Hispanic times, but it is different from that invented in China more than two thousand years ago.

The ancient Chinese method consisted of grinding and sifting the fibers. On the contrary, the Otomi method preserved the long fibers, making *amate* paper more durable despite its porosity. Its thickness and texture are pleasing to the touch. The fanciful forms and tones of the fibers make it a material of enormous aesthetic possibilities. Painters from Guerrero especially prefer this paper.

THE *AMATE* TREE

Amate paper is made with the bark of the tree bearing the same name, which grows as a semi-parasite, i.e feeding off the moss from the rocks or off the sap from other trees. It takes more than 30 years to attain maturity sufficient to produce enough fruit that will in turn produce seeds.

The bark is normally extracted from young trees with a diameter of 25 to 30 centimeters. An incision is made around the lower part of the trunk, which allows the bark to be pulled off in a single layer from the bottom towards the top. Before the bark can be used as raw material for paper, it must be dried in the sun.

The manufacturing process is simple. The load of *amate* —around 50 to 100 kilos— is placed in a pot full of water. Once it is boiling, ashes and a sack of approximately 60 kilos of lime are added.

It is boiled for at least five to six hours, until the fibers are soft. Later, on a table previously covered with soap suds, the strips of bark are placed in a square and one by one, beaten with a flat, smooth stone called *muinto,* the same size as a *tejolote*, in order to join the pieces.

The strokes must be even in order to give the paper the same thickness all over. Once the task is completed, the bark is left to dry in the sun, and is then ready to be exhibited and sold.

202

In Puebla's Northern Mountain Ranges

The *amate* plant grows on the slopes of a hill called Del Brujo in Puebla's northern mountain range. The place is quite inaccessible, and therefore the inhabitants of San Pablito Pahuatlán were able to manufacture *amate* paper during more than five centuries.

The witch doctors of the place called it *huarachito* and used it to make sacred images or gods, which they cut out from folded paper, and used in healing ceremonies.

Amate paper was used by Mesoamerican tribes to make the codices (manuscripts), on which they recorded their history or the knowledge they wished to preserve or communicate.

Its Prohibition during the Period of Colonization

During the period of colonization, the manufacture of *amate* paper was forbidden in order to avoid its use for religious rites. Nevertheless, the inhabitants sustained its production.

The artisans of the state of Guerrero needed to extend their painting activities when they rediscovered the characteristics of *amate* paper. The figures and images they had formerly painted on pieces of clay were then transferred to the native paper, which could also be transported without breaking.

Hundreds of pieces of *amate* paper have travelled throughout the world with scenes from the inhabitants of Guerrero's daily life. Birds, flowers, and animals, among other designs, are hand-painted on them.

The fame these pictures have achieved has allowed them to be considered as one of Mexico's traditional arts.

At present they embody the meeting of two Mexican regions: the San Pablito Pahuatlán region of Puebla, where the sheets of paper are made, and the middle Balsas region of Guerrero, where they are masterfully painted.

MICHOACÁN'S DANCE OF THE OLD MEN

SOURCE OF JOY

The Dance of the Old Men originated in Michoacán and it has spread throughout the country as a colorful symbol of this state. However, a historical study has revealed several surprises.

Several authors sustain that this dance is of pre-Hispanic origin. They base their statements on a phrase found in Friar Diego Durán's *Historia de las Indias de la Nueva España* (History of the Indies of New Spain): "Another dance of the old men was performed. The dancers wore hunchbacked old men's masks and their dances were graceful, talented, and caused much mirth..."

According to the information obtained from various bibliographic sources, the Dance of the Old Men as we now know it, was created during the present century. Cucuchuco, Jarácuaro, and Santa Fe de la Laguna are the towns where the oldest history of groups of "old men" can be found. The dance was interpreted spontaneously for many decades, i.e., without a definite choreography. The dancers went out into the streets, jumped and danced about, and held humorous dialogues with the people.

The first group of "old men" was formed in Jarácuaro in 1927. Two decades later another group appeared. Accompanied by two violins and a *jarana* (small guitar), it interpreted the dance in two parallel lines of about fifty people who danced to fulfill a promise made to some religious figure in return for a favor.

Although it is difficult to trace the origins of this dance, it seems to have begun in several towns during religious festivities.

In 1937, the dance was presented at the *Palacio de Bellas Artes* (Palace of Fine Arts) as part of an exhibition of traditional dances promoted by the Ministry of Public Education.

Another fact that has contributed to the modification of the dance was its presentation in contests such as those carried out eighteen years ago on the island of Janitzio, during the celebration of the "Day of the Dead." It was also used to enliven shows in the hotels in Pátzcuaro and in other cities. During the administration of president Luis Echeverría, and sometimes at his own personal invitation, groups of "Old Men" travelled to Rumania, Spain, and France.

In some cases, in exchange for their performance of the dances created in their towns, the groups of "Old Men" received resources similar to those obtained from the handicrafts they usually manufactured in their struggle against unemployment. In other instances, the earnings are collected by hotels or merchants, while the dancers only receive a minimum payment for their nightly performance of the dances that in the past were known as a source of joy.

A GASTRONOMICAL VIEW OF THE STATE OF MEXICO

The state of Mexico's territory has always surrounded the great capital, formerly of the Aztec Empire and today of the Mexican nation. Its culinary tradition partakes of the general characteristics of Mexican highland cuisine, although it possesses its own accents and traits. This is a tradition deeply rooted in the Pre-Columbian culinary tradition, the colonial period, and the Mexican tradition itself.

On the other hand, the highlands have always been a privileged place for the concentration of products and goods. In view of the enormous variety of gastronomical elements and ingredients proceeding from all over the country and even from abroad, the only possible response can be the creativity and talent of the makers of the *Mexiquense* (state of Mexico) cuisine.

If we were to stroll through the famous market of Toluca, particularly on a Friday, we would be able to prove everything we say and would realize that the state's culinary wealth is not limited to its famous sausages and preserves, but goes beyond the imagination of any famous gourmet. Even he would find many elements worth enjoying, including exotic foods such as the large variety of mushrooms and *colorín* flowers.

It can therefore be no surprise that the *Mexiquenses'* gastronomical tradition is made up of an extensive and varied number of snacks and entrées, soups and bouillons, salads, and many main dishes, such as trout, rabbit, chicken, lamb, pork, and numerous splendid desserts.

We have we said that the Mexiquense cuisine has its own characteristics. Perhaps it is not usually identified as an original cuisine, but this is only because the state of Mexico has and still is contributing many of its dishes to the highlands' cuisine. There are its sausages, cheeses, dried meat, recipes for *escamoles* (a kind of grasshopper) and *maguey* worms, *colorín* flower soup, a variety of dishes made of mushrooms and lima beans, a special way of preparing trout, and particularly *mixiotes,* barbecues, pork in *pulque* sauce, and many other dishes that the people living in the capital have enjoyed as their very own since remote times.

Any effort to come to the rescue of *Mexiquense* cuisine is therefore to be admired. The Loredo Organization has taken up the task of preparing

206

menus with the traditional recipes of the blue ribbon *Mexiquense* cuisine.

Many of these delicious dishes are familiar to Mexico City's gourmets. Their only novelty would be, perhaps, to know that they are dishes originating the state of Mexico's typical culinary art.

To justify the above it suffices to rapidly mention some of the delicious dishes that as a whole deserve the titles given to *Mexiquense* cuisine by some of yesterday's and today's foremost experts: "The cuisine which is a theatre of wonders," or "the imaginative cuisine," due to its delicious flavors, variety of ingredients, and balance in preparation, which all delight even the most discriminating tastes.

SOME TASTY MEXIQUENSE DISHES

Among the *botanas* (snacks)* or entrées, the following can be mentioned: a large variety of red and green sausages seasoned with all kinds of spices or dry meats, splendid fresh cheeses, creams, and cottage cheeses.

Pickled pigs' feet *à la Acambay*, which are served with vegetables and fruit in a vinaigrette sauce.

Mushroom and squash flower turnovers, as well as roasted *tortillas* stuffed with mushrooms and chicken (in Texcoco).

Maguey worms and *escamoles* in exotic sauces made of *chipotle* chili or seasoned with *pulque*.

Tortas de chorizo with potatoes (Mexican-style sandwiches made with a type of French bread and stuffed with sausage and potatoes) that are eaten as a snack.

As to bouillons or soups, we have: green bouillon, a unique Malinalco style, *colorín* flower soup with pork, a unique mushroom soup, or the better known *nopales* and egg soup from Santiago Tianguistenco, bone marrow soups from Toluca, and especially the gastronomical contribution of the mallow soup.

Among the salads, we have: lima bean salad (from La Marquesa), *nopales* salad, and of course infallible marinated mushroom salad from Valle de Bravo.

And as far as the main dishes go: fresh trout in wine and almond sauce, orange sauce or fine herbs, wrapped in paper or simply broiled with a slight garlic seasoning.

The typical cheeses, barbecues, and rabbit, chicken or lamb *mixiotes** according to the *Mexiquenses*, "are eaten a lot because they are delicious," and together with the leg of pork in *pulque* sauce, are some of the best recipes from Naucalpan.

Seasonal dishes are the delicious *colorín* flower cakes, made with blue *tortilla* corn meal to emphasize their exoticism, *enchiladas* (folded tortillas) stuffed with *charales* (tiny dry fish), as a contribution from Zumpango lake. We must not forget chicken, pigeons, *huilotitas en pipian* (birds cooked in a sauce with pumpkin seeds), *mole de olla* (a kind of soup made with pork, beef or chicken, and various vegetables), and mushroom *mole*.

To round off the meal, home-made desserts, *biznagas* (candy made from a certain kind of cactus), *chirimoyas*, coconut desserts made with milk and pine nuts, a candy made of *capulín* glazed *xoconoxtles* (the fruit of the *nopal*), and many other delights transform the Mexican families' tables into authentic multi-colored still-life paintings.

---

* *Botana*: Snack served with drinks. The snacks served in bars are varied and very tasty. Similar to the Spanish *tapa*.

Cecina: Dry salted meat, sometimes served with a chili sauce.

Gusanos de Maguey: Maguey worms, which are delicious when fried. The white worms (*meocuil*) are more highly valued than the red ones (*chilocuil*).

Mixiote: Maguey leaf used to wrap food and steam-cook it.

Moscos: Alcoholic drinks prepared with liquor and different fruit juices. A speciality of the State of Mexico.

Tortillas: A round and flat bread made of corn meal.

DIFFERENT TYPES OF *TORTILLAS*

Chilaquiles: Cooked in a sauce, with cheese and cream.

Enchiladas: Folded in two and submerged in sauce, they are eaten with chicken, cheese, and cream.

Quesadillas: Stuffed and folded in half.

Tacos: Rolled *tortillas* with any kind of stuffing.

Tostadas: Fried *tortillas*.

Totopos: Tortillas cut in four parts, and then folded to form triangles. Fried and toasted, they are called *totopos*.

Caesar's salad

aesar's salad was created in 1925 in the city of Tijuana, Baja California, when, upon the petition of an important group of clients of Caesar's Restaurant, Mr. Caesar Cardini included in his menu a salad basically prepared with olive oil, wine, vinegar, mustard, salt, anchovies, egg, Parmesan cheese, fried bread, and, of course, lettuce.

Tamaulipas and its Broiled Meat

The habit of eating broiled meat is principally found in the border region, in central and southern Tamaulipas.

One of the most famous dishes originating from the port of Tampico is broiled meat *a la Tampiqueña*. This typical recipe is of recent gastronomical tradition and was created at the beginning of this century.

Tamaulipas' culinary history was difficult. Our forefathers of the Huasteca region used to hunt wild animals. Several tribes would assemble on a remote ranch and prepare a succulent banquet for their guests. They lit fires and placed previously prepared pieces of meat, obtained by hunting, around the heat.

At that time settlers and travelers did not easily venture into the northern regions, since someone had spread the rumor that the Indians took the soldiers as prisoners.

The Comanches' vindictive behavior —with good reason— sowed fear among the members of the Border Committee, who visited Northern lands around 1827.

Despite all these obstacles, they carried out a census which had interesting results regarding the annual consumption of meat. In Laredo alone, 365 heads of beef, sheep, and goats were consumed.

This remarkable growth of the cattle-raising industry leads us to assume that our ancestors lived quietly, without economic crises, eating meat, corn and beans *charra* style. It is only fair to add that the Indians in the south were peaceful, compared with those in Texas.

On the other hand, Hermenegildo Sánchez García, in his *Crónica del Nuevo Santander* (History of New Santander) written in 1803, states that the natives ate deer meat, while in Real de Borbón now Villagrán, the natives had the habit of eating the broiled meat of wild or domestic animals.

At the border and in centeral Tamaulipas, broiling meat is quite an event, perhaps a gathering among friends. The families get together around a metal broiler and cook their *fajitas americanas* (steaks cut in strips) or *costillas al carbón* (charbroiled ribs) in an improvised way. The broiled meat is served with beer, *charra* beans, *guacamole*, and *totopos*.

However, the residents of Tampico are more inclined toward fish and seafood, which they call *mariscada*, instead of broiled meat.

210

Tampico is located in southern Tamaulipas. Several rivers and lakes adorn its landscape: the Panuco and Tamesí Rivers, and the Chairel and Carpintero Lakes.

The city is an important trading center for the Huasteca region. For one the meat market for Huasteco heifers converges here. Cattle-raising is mainly carried out in the municipalities of Aldama, Soto la Marina, Altamira and González. The broiled meat from Tampico is a result of José Inés Loredo's inspiration. During the 1930's, he was the chef of the Hotel Bristol restaurant. For a year, in 1933 this unique personage was also the mayor of Tampico.

Mexican cuisine has contributed two dishes during the twentieth century, as a proof of its quality and strength: Caesar's salad and broiled meat, Tampico style. Caesar Cardini and José Inés Loredo are immortal names in Mexican gastronomy.

THE NAMES OF THE STATES IN THE MEXICAN REPUBLIC

AGUASCALIENTES
The abundant springs of thermal water existing here have given their name to this state and its capital.

BAJA CALIFORNIA
There is insufficient information to interpret the meaning of the roots of the word California, but it is believed that it comes from an Indian language. It is also assumed that it is derived from the Latin terms *calida* (warm) and *fornax* (oven), i.e. "warm oven," a name with which Hernán Cortés seemingly baptized this region during his 1536 expedition due to its intense heat. It is also believed that the name proceeds from the sixteenth century novel *Las sergas de Esplandián* (Esplandian's Feats) by García Ordóñez de Montalvo, which describes a peninsula called California and its queen Calafia.

CAMPECHE
Cam-Pech or *Ah-Kim-Pech* is the region's original name, since Pre-Columbian times. In Maya it means "land of serpents and ticks."

COAHUILA
The word Coahuila is derived from the Nahuatl terms *coa* (snake) and *huila* (that creeps along) or "creeping snake."

COLIMA
The name Colima comes from the Nahuatl words *coliman*, *colli* (hill, volcano or grandfather) and *maitli* (hand or dominance). Together, they mean "place conquered by our grandparents or ancestors," or "where the Ancient God rules."

CHIAPAS
The word Chiapas has a Nahuatl origin and is formed by two terms: *chía* (name of a seed used to prepare a refreshing drink in the region) and *apan* (in the river). Therefore its meaning is "in the river of *chía*."

212

CHIHUAHUA

The word Chihuahua comes from the Tarahumara term *chihuahuara* which means "place where sacks are made."

FEDERAL DISTRICT (MEXICO CITY)

This is its name because it is the seat of the federal powers.

DURANGO

The word Durango has a Basque origin and means "fertile lowland covered with rivers and surrounded by high plateaus or mountains."

STATE OF MEXICO

The word Mexico is derived from the Nahuatl terms *mextli* (moon, or moon goddess) and *xictli* (navel or center). The word is therefore interpreted as "he who is in the center of the moon," "in the center of Mextli Lagoon." According to other versions, it means "place of the god Mexitli."

GUANAJUATO

The word Guanajuato comes from the Tarascan terms *quianax* (frog) and *huasta* (hill), i.e., "hill of frogs."

GUERRERO

This state bears the name of Guerrero in honor of General Vicente Guerrero, a hero of our Independence.

HIDALGO

The State of Hidalgo bears the name of Miguel Hidalgo y Costilla, in honor of the Father of our Country.

JALISCO

Jalisco comes from the Nahuatl term *xalisco* which means "sandy place." It was taken from one of the principal kingdoms that formed the Chimalhuacan Confederation.

MICHOACÁN

Michoacán comes from the Nahuatl terms *michin* (fish) and *can* (place), i.e. "place or region of the fish." Another version proposes that it is derived from *michmacuan*, a Tarascan term meaning "to be near the water."

MORELOS

This state bears its name in honor of José María Morelos y Pavón, a hero of our Independence.

NAYARIT

Nayarit is formed by the Cora word *Nayar* (god of battles) and the suffix *it* (adverb of place). Together, it means "region where the god of battles is worshipped."

NUEVO LEÓN

Its original name was *Nuevo Reino de León* (New Kingdom of León), a title granted by King Philip II after the Conquest with reference to the Iberian kingdom of León.

OAXACA

Oaxaca comes from the Nahuatl terms *huaxin* (jugs) and *yactl* (hill or nose, point or cliff), i.e. "hill of jugs."

QUERÉTARO

Querétaro is derived from the Tarascan term *qertaro* (place of sorrows) and from the Otomí *damarel* (the biggest ball game).

QUINTANA ROO

This state owes its name to Andrés Quintana Roo, an outstanding figure within the movement for Mexico's Independence, and the establishment of the Republic.

SAN LUIS POTOSÍ

Named in honor of Louis, King of France, and Potosí, as a comparison of the wealth found in the Cerro de San Pedro mines with the Potosí mines of Bolivia. Another version about its origin is that the name was given to the state in honor of the man who was viceroy at the time, of its creation Luis de Velasco.

SINALOA

Sinaloa is a word belonging to the Cahita dialect, formed by the terms *sina* (a kind of *pitaya*, a Mexican fruit) and *lobata* (round house). The name *sinalobata* turned into *sinaloba* and finally to Sinaloa, which means "round pitaya."

SONORA
The name comes from the term *ópata zunutle* which means "place of corn."

TABASCO
Tabasco comes from the Nahuatl term meaning "flooded land," although the definition "place with an owner" has also been given to the name.

TAMAULIPAS
Tamaulipas means "place of many prayers" or, according to other sources, "place of high mountains."

TLAXCALA
The word Tlaxcala comes from the Nahuatl term meaning "land of corn" or "place of tortillas" (place of corn bread).

VERACRUZ
The word Veracruz comes from the latin term *vera* (true) and *cruz* (cross), i.e. "the true cross."

YUCATÁN
When the Spaniards arrived at the peninsula, and they heard the natives speak, these were saying *uh u uthaan* which means, "hear how they speak." It is believed that the name of Yucatán originated in this way.

ZACATECAS
The name of this state and its capital comes from the Nahuatl terms *zacatl* (grass) and *tecatl* (people), i.e. "grass people."

SOME
MEXICAN
MAIN DISHES

MEXICAN CUISINE'S MAIN DISHES

I n order to present some of the most representative recipes of Mexican cuisine's main dishes we have selected fourteen that can be easily prepared in virtually any part of the world.

The ingredients are easy to find and, in some cases, they may be substituted by others with excellent results.

From us to you, we would like to wish you luck when you prepare these delicious dishes. They are very easy to do, just follow the instructions and enter the world of Mexican cuisine.

Taste some of our most celebrated culinary traditions that come from the heart of our most beloved **MEXICAN TRADITIONS**.

Again, good luck and *buen apetito*!

NOPALITO AND SHRIMP SALAD
(makes 8 servings)

Ingredients
> 1 jar (28 oz.) *Nopalitos*, rinsed and drained
> 1 can (medium size) shrimp, shelled, cleaned and cooked
> 1/4 lb. olives
> 4 tablespoons of chopped coriander *(cilantro)*
> 1 large onion, finely chopped
> 3 tomatoes, peeled and diced
> 1 avocado, sliced
> 2 lemons, squeezed for juice
> 1/4 cup olive oil
> 1/2 orange juice
> Dash salt, pepper and oregano

Preparation
Combine all ingredients except for the avocado in a large mixing bowl. Refrigerate for about 3 hours. Just before serving, pour into serving dish, garnish with sliced avocado and serve with *tortillas* or *tostadas*.

Preparation time: 15 minutes.

Vegetarian *Panchitos*
(Makes 6 servings)

Ingredients
10 *tortillas*, cut in large triangles
1 cup fried kidney beans
1/4 kg. grated Manchego or fresh cheese
1 large avocado
1 can (7 oz.) Nachos

Preparation
Fry the cut *tortillas* in a pan with enough oil until crisp. Fry and mash the beans, mash the avocado and first spread the fried *tortilla* with beans, then the mashed avocado and the grated cheese. Finally add slices of *nachos* on top of each *Panchito*.

Chicken *Tostadas*
(makes 8 servings)

Ingredients
2 chicken breasts, boiled and shredded
1 sausage (*chorizo*) crumbled and fried
1 small sliced onion
6 chopped *Chipotle* chilis
5 leaves of thinly sliced romaine lettuce
1 cup fried beans
4 tablespoons fresh cream
100 grs. crumbled aged cheese
16 medium *tortillas*, fried and drained

Preparation
Heat oil in a deep frying pan, fry the onion and crumbled sausage and add the shredded chicken, and let sauté for 10 minutes. Meanwhile, spread the fried *tortillas* with a very thin layer of beans, then add the sausage with the chicken, the sliced onion, the *chipotle* chilis in small portions, the cream and the crumbled aged cheese. Serve warm.

Preparation time: 20 minutes.

NOPALITOS WITH TOMATO
(makes 8 servings)

Ingredients
28 oz. jar of *Nopalitos*
2 tomatoes, peeled and diced
1/4 cup chopped coriander (*cilantro*)
1 small chopped onion
2 tablespoons oil
1 garlic clove
1/2 tablespoon powdered chicken bouillon

Preparation
Rinse and drain the *nopalitos*. In a saucepan, heat oil and fry onion, garlic, tomato and *cilantro*. Add powdered chicken bouillon, cover and cook for 3 minutes. Add *nopalitos*. Serve with *tortillas*.
Preparation time: 20 minutes.

CHICKEN ENCHILADAS WITH *MOLE**
(makes 5 servings)

Ingredients
9 1/4 oz. jar of *Mole*
2 chicken breasts
10 corn *tortillas*
1 cup of grated white cheese
1 sliced onion
salt to taste

Preparation
Boil the chicken breasts in 4 cups of water with salt. When cooked, put the boneless and shredded chicken on a separate dish. Warm up the oil and fry the *tortillas* slightly one by one. Add the shredded chicken to each *tortilla* and roll it up like a *taco*. Put them on a heat-resistant plate and coat them with the contents of the jar of *mole*, which has already been dissolved in 2 cups of hot chicken broth (where the chicken was cooked). Sprinkle with white cheese and put the sliced onion on top.
  * Corn pancake or *tortilla* filled with chicken and chili sauce.

Meat filled potatoes with Home Style Mexican hot sauce
(makes 8 servings)

Ingredients
6 large, long boiled yellow potatoes
200 grs. ground beef and pork
1/2 onion, chopped fine and fried
1 bunch of parsley, finely chopped
1 garlic clove, chopped and fried
1 tablespoon consommé
100 grs. chopped, fried bacon
1 can Home Style Mexican hot sauce
100 grs. cottage (*cotija*) cheese
Salt and pepper to taste

Preparation
Peel the potatoes and carefully make a hole by removing the potato flesh. While the chopped bacon is being fried with the meat, simmer with the consommé, add the onion, garlic, Home Style Mexican hot sauce and finally the parsley. Mix well and season and remove from the heat. Fill the hot potatoes with these ingredients. Serve with cottage (*cotija*) cheese.
Preparation time: 15 minutes.

Whole stuffed *JALAPEÑO* peppers
(makes 8 servings)

Ingredients
1 can whole *Jalapeño* peppers
1 medium onion
1 can tuna fish
4 chopped parsley
5 tablespoons mayonnaise
3 tomato slices
Salt and pepper to taste
1/2 lemon (juice)

Preparation
Devein the peppers. Boil in water with vinegar for 10 minutes. Leave

them in the vinegar-water for several hours if you want to make them less hot. Meanwhile, mix the mayonnaise with the chopped onion, the chopped parsley and the tuna fish to form a paste type mixture. Lastly, add the juice of 1/2 lemon. Mix all together and immediately stuff the peppers. Serve on a big plate with tomato slices.

Preparation time: 15 minutes.

Mexican style Pork and beans
(makes 8 servings)

Ingredients
1/2 kg cooked black beans
1 kg cooked pork meat in small pieces
4 tablespoons oil
1 tablespoon salt
1/2 can red sliced peppers
1 cup prepared white rice
1 medium onion in slices
3 sprigs chopped coriander (*cilantro*)
4 lettuce leaves

Preparation
Cook the beans with the onion, salt and oil. When the beans are half cooked, add the small pieces of pork meat and let it boil until the meat is soft. When the hot rice is ready, serve this dish, gently mixing the rice with the beans in their juice with the pork. Adorn with lettuce leaves, the red peppers, the sliced onion and the chopped coriander.

Preparation time: 15 minutes.

Mole de olla in Chipotle sauce
(makes 8 servings)

Ingredients
1/2 kg well cooked stewing beef
1/2 kg diced cooked beef shank
3 marrow bones
2 garlic cloves
2 corn cobs in pieces

3 chopped *zucchini*
1 sprig of *epazote*
2 tablespoons consommé
1 onion
2 tablespoons *Chipotle* sauce
1 *pasilla* chili

Preparation

Cook the stewing beef and shank in the water. Singe the *pasilla* chili and devein. Place in hot water and blend the garlic, onion, chili and *chipotle* sauce. When the meat is well cooked, the sauce is poured over it and the corn cob pieces, the *zucchini*, the *epazote* and the marrow bones are added. Let it boil for 15 minutes more. Add the consommé and serve hot.

Preparation time: 15 minutes.

CHICKEN WITH *MOLE**
(makes 6 servings)

Ingredients

9 1/4 oz. jar of *Mole*
6 chicken legs with thighs
2 garlic cloves
1 small onion
salt to taste

Preparation

Boil the chicken in a pot with enough water and add the salt, the garlic and the onion. When the chicken is cooked, take it out and let it drain. In a saucepan, mix the contents of the jar of *Mole* with 3 cups of hot chicken broth and cook for a few minutes until it thickens. Do not stop stirring. Serve with *tortillas* and sesame seeds.

* Stew prepared with chili sauce.

SEA BASS WITH *JALAPEÑO* PEPPERS
(makes 8 servings)

Ingredients

8 fried sea bass fillets

1 can tomato purée
1 can Mexican Home Style sauce
1 large chopped tomato
1 medium chopped onion
2 chopped garlic cloves
10 olives
slices of green *jalapeño* peppers
1 tablespoon capers
1 tablespoon consommé
2 sprigs parsley
5 bay leaves
Salt and pepper to taste

Preparation

Fry the garlic, onion, chopped tomato and the slices of green *jalapeño* peppers into strips in a frying pan with oil. Brown all this and immediately add the chopped tomato, the Mexican Home Style sauce, sprinkle consommé, salt and pepper to taste and let simmer 5 minutes. Add the sea bass fillets and the capers for 5 more minutes. Remove from heat and let rest. Arrange on a plate and garnish with parsley.
Preparation time: 20 minutes.

CHICKEN BREASTS IN MEXICAN GREEN SAUCE
(makes 8 servings)

Ingredients

3 flattened chicken breasts cut in half
1 cup cooked, finely chopped spinach
1 can Mexican Green sauce
1 chopped hard boiled egg
3 tablespoons chopped, fried onion
1 tablespoon consommé
1 fried, chopped garlic clove
4 tablespoons cream
Salt and pepper to taste

Preparation

Fry the chicken breasts in oil seasoned with consommé and pepper. In a pot, mix the finely chopped spinach with the onion, the lightly fried garlic and the chopped egg. Heat the Mexican green sauce. Once everything is hot, place the chicken breasts on a plate and part of the mixture on top of each breast. Adorn with cream and the Mexican green sauce to taste.

Preparation time: 20 minutes.

VERACRUZ STYLE FISH
(makes 6 servings)

Ingredients
- 6 medium fresh sea bass fillets
- 1 lemon (juice)
- 3 tablespoons oil
- 1/4 sliced onion
- 1 garlic clove, chopped fine
- 2 green bell peppers, cut in strips
- 5 tomatoes, peeled, seeded and chopped
- 6 olives
- 5 capers, cut in half
- 1 tablespoon granulated chicken broth concentrate
- 8 *Serrano* peppers

Preparation
Wash the fish with cold water and add some lemon juice drops. Let it rest for 5 minutes. Warm the oil and fry the onion, the garlic cloves and the bell peppers in a ceramic casserole. When the onion is transparent, add the tomatoes, the olives, the capers and the granulated chicken broth. Cover the casserole, bring the mixture to a boil over low heat, stirring from time to time. Add the sea bass fillets, watching that they remain completely covered by the sauce. Cover again and let the fish cook slowly for 15 minutes. Serve on a plain dish and top with *Serrano* peppers.

PUEBLAN CHILIS IN WALNUT SAUCE (*CHILES EN NOGADA*)
(makes 9 servings)

Utensils: Wet cloth, pot, saucepan, container, blender and big plate

226

Ingredients

17 Pueblan chilis (*chiles poblanos* or green peppers)
3 tablespoons oil or lard
1 minced garlic clove
2 tablespoons minced onion
500 grams (1 lb) ground pork loin with 50 gr (2 oz) of jam
500 grams (1 lb) broiled tomatoes, peeled, minced and without seeds
2 cup broth
2 pinches saffron
1 pinch ground clove
2 pinches ground cumin
1/8 teaspoon ground cinnamon
1 apple
1 pear
2 peaches
30 soaked raisins
30 almonds
3 tablespoons minced candied *biznaga* (bisnaga)
1 teaspoon sugar
salt and pepper to taste
1 glass dry sherry
100 fresh walnuts
250 grams (1/2 lb) of fresh cheese
1 1/2 slices of bread soaked in milk
cinnamon and sugar to taste
2 red pomegranates
1 cup milk

Preparation

Roast the chilis until they get black and wrap them with the wet cloth to later remove the skin. Open them and take out the seeds and the veins. (Soak them in hot water with salt if not desired to be hot).

Heat the oil or lard, fry first the garlic and the onion, afterwards the meat and finally the tomatoes. Add the broth and let it fry until the meat is soft.

When everything is well fried, add the spices, the fruits cut in little pieces, the raisins and candied bisnaga. Add sugar and salt to taste, and half glass of dry sherry. Let it thicken, remove it from the fire until it is luke-warm. Then stuff the chilis with the meat mixture.

227

Walnut sauce (*Nogada*)

Clean the nuts one day before, soak them and remove the skin. Let them stand in milk.

One hour before serving the peppers, grind the nuts with the cheese and soaked bread, add sugar, cinnamon and 1/2 glass of dry sherry. If the sauce is very thick, add cream or milk.

There are two ways of serving the chilis, the classical, Puebla style which means to cover them with beaten eggs (beat egg whites until soft peaks form, then beat in the yolks and a little flour). Cover the peppers with this and fry them in very hot oil or lard. When they are cold put them in a big plate, cover them with the walnut sauce and garnish them with just the pomegranate seeds.

The other way is to cover the chilis with just the walnut sauce and the pomegranate seeds.

MEXICO

THE SUN PEOPLE

There are two ways of interpreting the word Mexico, originating from the Aztec Nahuatl tongue as a pure word created by a sublime people.

Mexikko

me, from *metl* = *maguey*

xik, from *xiktli* = navel

ko, from place or location

"Place of the maguey's navel"

Metzxikko

metz, from *metztli* = moon

xik, from *xiktli* = navel

ko, from place or location

"Place of the moon's navel"

IN MEXICAYOYELIZTLI AIC IXPOLIUIZ
"Mexicanism will never perish"

THE MODERN MEXICO OF
THE YEAR
2000 MUST BE BUILT
UPON OUR ANCESTRAL
ROOTS

THIS IS THE HISTORICAL
CHALLENGE
FACING FUTURE
GENERATIONS

MEXICO'S TRADITIONS ON THE THRESHOLD OF THE YEAR 2000

Mexico is more than the name of a country within the context of universal history.

Above all, Mexico is a completely creative, vigorous, sensitive, and tremendously vital country. It is melancholic and euphoric, resourceful and indolent, epic and lyrical, dramatic and sarcastic, sublime and wild, loving and jealous, unselfish and rebellious, tender and bitter; mystical, transcendent, solemn, iconoclastic, childish, primitively spontaneous, devout, reverent, docile, silent, uninhibited, disrespectful, indomitable and full of praise, an exalter of leaders and canonizer of saints.

It is a paradoxical country, true, but always loyal to its race, proud of its past, transfigured in its aspirations, and full of hope about its future fate.

This paradox may seem confusing and disconcerting to strangers, albeit always attractive and charismatic. But in their contrasting and bold, vital game —exactly like this country's geography— Mexicans give their existential style free and torrential flow, expressing and filtering it freely and spontaneously into traditions and customs, despite changing times and suffocating modern ways.

Undoubtedly these traditions and customs are the root and sap of everything Mexican. It is amazing that they have remained alive at present, not only under the protection of peasant and farmer communities, but on the urban level as well, in the great metropolitan mass that crowds with the asphalt and concrete what was once the wonderful valley of Anahuac. Even there the traditions are still kept alive, like wild flowers, set in the arrogant city environment. Very few national capitals of our world can boast of maintaining alive as many varied community traditions as those that underlie life in the urban perimeters of the Mexican capital, and that are reborn every new day of every year. It is the victory of humanity in the face of the big city's arrogant stance.

Some of these truly popular expressions have been gathered in this book, as the *vox populli*, as a vibrant, and perpetual testimony of all Mexico's resonant vitality, as if precisely drawn lines in a profile of Mexico's historical identity.

To contemplate these traditions alive and well —as they were and still are— on the threshold of the year 2000 is comforting and makes us proud. It is the rebirth of the certainty that for Mexico the future will always be a gateway to hope, against all odds, as long as it is based on our ancestral heritage of transcendent values.

About the Cover

The Aztec Calendar

Since the appearance of man on earth, the development of human activities has demonstrated the importance of measuring time, which is why different methods have been created to do so. Many calendars have been based on observation of the elements and natural phenomena, such as the movements of the Sun and Moon.

The Aztec Calendar comes down to us from the Olmec civilization (the origin of all Mesoamerican cultures). The Aztecs were highly knowledgeable in astronomy; they observed what happened in the skies of their universe. They adopted and perfected the calendar by correlating the movements of the Sun with those of the planet Venus and the constellation of the Pleiades. Profound knowledge of the Aztec Calendar was reserved for the wise, who transmitted its basic principles to the youths in the compulsory school or calmecac.

Sculpted from a huge, single block of basalt, this monument is marvelously carved in bas-relief. It has a diameter of 3.60 meters and weighs 25 tons. In the main plaza of the great, ancient city of Tenochtitlan, it occupied a very important place, located over one of the temples called Quauhxicalco.

The temple was demolished at the time of the Spanish conquest, so the monument remained buried for 270 years, until it was discovered on December 17, 1790, at the southeast side of what is now the Plaza of the Constitution in Mexico City.

It is now on permanent exhibit in the Mexica Hall of the National Anthropology Museum near Chapultepec Park, Mexico City.

Chiles en Nogada

A patriotic red-white-and-green dish combining green chiles filled with a meat, nut and raisin mixture, bathed in a delicious, white, walnut-based sauce, and garnished with pomegranate seeds.

Black clay ceramic from Oaxaca

Among Mexico's most famous crafts are the elegant, highly burnished, black clay ceramics from the state of Oaxaca, which has one of the richest folk art traditions today.

Day of the Dead's ornate skulls

Ornate, brightly colored skulls, such as the ones made by the Linares family, play an important role in Day of the Dead celebrations, when the living confront death with both humor and respect.

Trajineras from Xochimilco

The riotous colors of the traditional *trajineras* fill the floating gardens of Xochimilco, especially on weekends when entire families crowd onto these little boats for a picnic and a serenade on the canals.

BIBLIOGRAPHY

Aguilar, Fray Francisco de. *Relación breve de la conquista de la Nueva España*. México, Instituto de Investigaciones Históricas, UNAM, 1980. (Serie: Historiadores y cronistas de Indias.)

Álvarez, José Rogelio. *Enciclopedia de México*; tomo III. México, Compañía de Enciclopedias de México,1987.

Álvarez, José Rogelio (Dir.) *Enciclopedia mexicana*. México, SEP, 1988.

Banco Nacional de Comercio Exterior. *Lo efímero y lo eterno del arte popular mexicano*. México, Fondo Editorial de la Plástica Mexicana, 1971.

Benavente, fray Toribio de (Motolinía). *Historia de los indios de la Nueva España*. México, Porrúa, 1969.

Castillo Lepón, Luis. *El chocolate*. México, Dirección General de Bellas Artes, 1917.

Clavijero, Francisco Javier. *Historia antigua de México*. (Facsímil de la edición de 1853.) México, Editorial del Valle de México, 1981.

Cocinero mexicano. México, Imprenta Cumplido, 1845.

Cruces Carvajal, Ramón. *Lo que México aportó al mundo*. México, Panorama, 1986.

Dávalos Hurtado, Eusebio. *Alimentos básicos e inventiva culinaria del mexicano*. México, SEP, 1966. (Serie: Peculiaridad mexicana.)

Díaz del Castillo, Bernal. *Historia verdadera de la conquista de la Nueva España*. México, Porrúa. 1976.

Dirección General del Museo de Culturas Populares. *Yo soy como el chile verde*. México, SEP, 1986.

Durán, fray Diego de. *Historia de las Indias de la Nueva España e islas de la tierra firme*. España, Banco de Santander, 1990.

Épica náhuatl. México, UNAM, 1945. (Biblioteca del Estudiante Universitario, núm. 51.)

237

"El Dulce en México." *Artes de México*, núm.121.

Farga, Armando. *Historia de la comida en México*. México, 1980.

Fiestas y ferias de México. México, Botas.

García Cubas, Antonio. *El libro de mis recuerdos*; 6 ed. México, Patria, 1969.

Girondella D'Angelli, Alicia y Jorge D'Angelli. *El gran libro de la cocina mexicana*. México, Larousse, 1987

González Obregón, Luis. *México viejo*. México, Joaquín Porrúa, 1982. (Edición especial para Roberto Hoffman.)

Guerrero Guerrero, Raúl. *Los otomíes del Valle del Mezquital. Modos de vida, etnografía y folklore*. México, SEP, 1983.

Guinness. "Mayor Tamal. Nuevo récord para México." *Libro de los récords*, 1991.

"La cocina mexicana." *Artes de México*, núm. 46.

"La cocina mexicana." *Artes de México*, núm. 107.

"La cocina mexicana." *Artes de México*, núm. 108.

Larousse Universal Ilustrado. Diccionario enciclopédico en seis volúmenes. Francia, Larousse, 1969.

León Portilla, Miguel. *La filosofía náhuatl estudiada en sus fuentes*; 2 ed. México, UNAM, 1959.

León Portilla, Miguel. *Los antiguos mexicanos a través de sus crónicas y cantares*. México, FCE, 1988.

Lomelí, Xavier, Xochimilco. *En las horas de los siglos*. México, Delegación Política de Xochimilco, 1987.

Los indios de México y Nueva España. México, Porrúa, 1966.

Majo Framis, Ricardo. *Conquistadores españoles del siglo XVI*; 4 ed. Madrid, Aguilar, 1963.

Miguel i Verges, José María. *Diccionario de insurgentes*. México, Porrúa, 1969.

Novo, Salvador. *Historia gastronómica de la Ciudad de México*. México, Porrúa, 1972.

Nuevo cocinero mexicano en forma de diccionario. México, Miguel Ángel Porrúa (ed.), 1888. 993 pp. (Reproducción facsimilar, 1989.)

Pérez, Enriqueta (comp. & ed.). *Recipies of the Philippines*. 19th Edition, 1973.

Prescott, W.H. *Historia de la conquista de México*; tomo I. París, Librería-Editorial Ch. Bouret, 1878.

Rincón Gallardo y Romero de Terreros, Carlos. *El libro del charro mexicano*. México, Porrúa, 1945.

Ríos, Eduardo Enrique. *Imagen de Tenochtitlan 1519-1521*. México, Banco Nacional de México, 1971.

Riva Palacio, Vicente (dir.). *México a través de los siglos*. México, Cumbre, 1963.

Rivera Cambas, Manuel. *Los gobernantres de México*. México, Joaquín Porrúa, 1983. (Biblioteca de Historia Manuel Porrúa.)

Sahagún, fray Bernardino de. *Relación de la conquista de esta Nueva España como la contaron los soldados indios que se hallaron presentes*. (Facsímil de la edición mexicana de 1840.) México, Arda, 1989. (Biblioteca Mexicana de la Fundación Miguel Alemán, A. C.)

Secretaría de Desarrollo Social. *Milpa Alta*. México, Hersa, 1988. (Colección: Delegaciones políticas.)

Secretaría de Turismo. *Directorio nacional gastronómico*. México, 1986.

Torquemada, fray Juan de. *Monarquía indiana*. México, UNAM, 1983.

Vázquez Santa Ana, Higinio. *Fiestas y costumbres mexicanas*. México, Botas, 1953.

W.H. Inc. (eds.) *Léxico hispano. Enciclopedia ilustrada en lengua española*; tomo II. México.

Zavala, Bertha. *La cocina mexicana*. México, Bertycel, 1990.

This edition of 5,000 copies
was printed in Impresora
Publimex on june 29, 1993
Calzada San Lorenzo 279, Local 32
09900, Mexico, D.F.